I0518017

WORDS ARE SNAKES
WITH ARMS

A YEAR IN POEMS

ALEX BROWN

No part of this book may be reproduced in any form or by any electronic or mechanical means, including information storage and retrieval systems, without written permission from the author, except for the use of brief quotations in a book review.

Open Kimono Publishing, LLC

12740 York St, STE 64

Thornton, Co 80241

Copyright © 2024 by Alex Brown

All rights reserved.

Printed in the United States of America

Published in 2024 by Open Kimono Publishing, LLC

The Library of Congress has cataloged the hardcover edition

Names: Brown, Alex, 1994- author.

Title: Words are Snakes with arms: A Year in Poems

Description: First edition. |

Identifiers: | Hardcover ISBN 978-1-961763-08-1

Paperback ISBN: 978-1-961763-09-8

E-book ISBN: 978-1-961763-10-4

Subjects: LCGFT: Poetry.

Classification: PS3602.R6965 A6 2024

DDC: 811.6

IC record available at https:// Iccn.loc.gov/

Designed by Alex Brown

Title-page and part-opener photograph copyright & by Alex Brown

Our books may be purchased in bulk for promotional, educational, or business use. Please contact your local bookseller or Open Kimono Publishing at info@openkmedia.com

www.openkimonopublishing.com

www.x.com/openkimonopub

www.facebook.com/openkimonopublishing

To my wife Lupita,

Before I met you, I thought I understood much about life and what love was. I had no idea. The more I learn, the more I realize how little I truly know. You have shown me not only what true love is but how true love feels. Your love has transformed my understanding of the world and opened my heart in ways I never thought possible.

Through your poise and resilience in the face of adversity, I learn from you every day. Your strength is a beacon that guides me through my darkest hours. In my life, I had never truly looked up to anyone; of course, there are many I respect and am lucky to have in my life- but you have opened my eyes to another reality. A reality where unconditional love not only exists but thrives. Your unwavering support and steadfast love have been my anchor in turbulent times.

You are more than my wife, more than my companion, and my best friend. You are my biggest ally, my greatest fan, and my inspiration. I look up to you not only for your courage, resilience, and unflinching honesty but as the epitome of the kind of person we should all strive to be. Your grace under pressure, your kindness in moments of hardship, and your unwavering commitment to those you love are nothing short of remarkable.

Every day with you is a lesson in what it means to live a life of purpose and love. You have taught me the true meaning of dedication and sacrifice. Your love has been a sanctuary, a place where I find peace and solace. In your eyes, I see the reflection of the best version of myself, someone who is capable of loving deeply and living fully.

You have shown me that true love is not just about grand gestures but about the quiet, everyday acts of kindness and understanding. It's in the way you listen, the way you care, and the way you stand with me, no matter what. Your love is a constant reminder of what is possible when two people commit to each other with their whole hearts.

Thank you for being my rock, my confidante, and my everything. Your love has added so much meaning and direction to my life. I am endlessly grateful for your presence and everything you do for us. I look forward to every moment we share, knowing that with you by my side, I am truly blessed.

Wordsaresnakeswitharms
[words-are-snakes-with-arms]
noun

1. A metaphorical concept representing the dynamic, flexible, and sometimes dangerous nature of language and self-expression.

2. The embodiment of words as creatures with the potential to grip, to hold, to ensnare, but also to caress, to comfort, and to soothe; reflecting their duality in communication.

3. An encapsulation of the inherent power of language, acknowledging its capacity to charm like a sinuous serpent or grasp like an armed being; an image portraying the skill and subtlety required to effectively wield it.

4. A reflection of the author's unique perspective of language's function as both a mirror and shaper of human emotion, thoughts, and experiences, much like a snake with arms, poised with a paradox of lethality and tenderness.

— ALEX BROWN

INTRODUCTION

Before you set foot into the labyrinth of verses that lie ahead, let's take a pause, a moment of stillness in which to acquaint ourselves with the narrative behind this extraordinary expedition. "Words Are Snakes With Arms" is not merely a collection of poetry; it is a chronicle, an audacious endeavor of work written with courage and candor, piecing together a year in my life.

The genesis of this remarkable anthology is rooted in the intimacy of day-to-day existence. Each poem is a microcosm of a single day, encapsulating the emotions and thoughts that stirred within me that day, in that exact moment. The ebb and flow of joy and despair, passion and indifference, clarity and confusion - all find a place in this narrative. Each piece is like a small window thrown open to offer glimpses into my private world, now made public for you to delve into.

As you navigate through this collection, expect rawness. Anticipate grit. These words, akin to serpents with arms, coil and uncoil, grasp and release, in an unending cadence of expression. They can be striking in their sudden lunge, soothing in their sinuous flow, or startling in their dormant potential.

To embark upon this journey is to be prepared for an intimate confrontation with reality in all its varied hues. These are not just verses, but vestiges of my authentic lived days, teeming with love, loss, longing, revelation, and everything in between. Reading this anthology is akin to traversing through the four seasons of a year - each day, each poem, brings with it a distinct flavor, a unique experience that mirrors the fluidity of life itself.

In "Words Are Snakes With Arms," you'll find no pretenses, no false fronts. This is a stark, unfiltered exploration of human existence, cloaked in the beauty of poetic expression. So, brace yourself to be moved, to be provoked, to be enthralled and at times, to be jolted into self-reflection. This journey of a year of my life, unraveled in poetry, awaits you.

Prepare to meet the snakes with arms.

They have stories to tell.

1. Frayed Symphony of Existence - Sunday July, 23 2023 20:38 MST

In a husk of existence, haunted, forlorn, outgrown,
    discarded aside, existing, though vitality overthrown.
    Lost within the labyrinth, fear becomes my own,
    ripped and terror-stricken, through yesteryears,
    today, and unknown.

With dread of the morrow, today, and the past's gray,
    through a spectrum of torment, in agony, I sway.
    So overwhelming, the pain, like a ceaseless ballet,
    in a glass display of monotony,
    I've become the unwelcome play.

The relentless drone has claimed its prey,
    chiseling my soul, into nothingness, into fray.
    Jaded and outdated, in this disarray,
    I yearn for escape, I long to break away.

2. Quest for the Elusive 'Why' - Monday July, 24 2023 18:43 MST

In the realm of yesteryears, frayed yet entrapped,
    restlessly seeking when this moment will elapse.
    The 'how' ascends now, under 'why's' steely grasp,
    rendering every 'how' in the present's clasp.

What force shall till the days in its sashay,
    the morrow? Or the yester sun's chalet?
    A purpose I seek, a beacon in the gray,
    my reason, my compass, to guide my way.

My reason, my 'why,' that elusive spy,
    how may I seek, where does it lie?
    In what hidden corner does my purpose sigh,
    as I quest to discern, how to find my 'why?'

3. Infinity's Void: A Human Tapestry - Tuesday July, 25 2023 21:03 MST

In the grandiose disaster of existence, where agony holds infinite reign,
    one must bow to destiny, surrender to its chain.
    Boundless is the torment, like an incessant rain,
    a truth as hard as granite, a reality we ascertain.

Hunger stirs within me, a yearning unfed,
    beyond the remnants on my plate, a deeper need has bled.
    A banquet of the intangible, where my spirit must be led,
    for sustenance I crave, much more than daily bread.

An itch lies beneath my skin, elusive to my grasp,
    a relentless phantom seducing me in sin, within my clenching clasp.
    A pain that clings like vinyl, an unsolicited asp,
    latched onto my soul, within its venomous rasp.

A void expands within me, devouring light and joy,
    a hollow echo resonating, life's vibrant hues destroy.

I become an empty vessel, reality's mere toy,
devoid, I stand, a specter, existence can't alloy.
In this intricate web of suffering and quest-
lie the strings of our humanity, in pain and hunger dressed.
Within this sprawling space, by fate and void oppressed,
we seek, we yearn, we strive - in this lies our true test.

4. Life's Echo: A Personal Inquiry - Wednesday July, 26 2023 21:33 MST

In a bleak existence, my toil I despise,
　　it leeches my spirit, into the abyss it flies.
　　An infinite black chasm, where my essence complies,
　　a relentless oblivion, under indifferent skies.

The quest for meaning, a demoralizing trail,
　　through a piercing veil and entrails, where all compasses fail.
　　Demeaning it feels, as I wander frail,
　　in the vast emptiness, like a ship without sail.

Striving but inevitability stagnant, in this paradox I nest,
　　with progress elusive, I find no rest.
　　A relentless examination, life's perpetual jest,
　　a conundrum spun in time's unending fest.

Life's meaning universal, is not my quest,
　　for that answer is impersonal, at its best.

Rather, what seeks life from my humble behest,
what purpose does it hold, in my empty individual chest?

Is it in the false fruits of my labor, or the traces of my strife,
does it lie in my journey, or the core of my life?
The question resounds, cutting sharp as a knife,
what, oh what, does life seek from my life?

5. Perception's Crucible - Thursday July, 27 2023 MST - 21:46

Entangled in the weave of truth and fabrication's twine,
  time alone falters, in this existential design.
  Tales, they rise and wane, beneath the
  conscious sign,
  where real and unreal, in strange harmony, align.

My triumphs stand apparent, through the lens
  of perspective's eye,
  just as my shortcomings, in memory's halls, lie.
  Replayed in vivid detail, under the mind's watchful sky,
  in this lack of consciousness, where my ethos shall testify.

The choices I make, are mine and mine alone,
  my destiny hangs in balance, on decisions' throne.
  In the hands of fate, my life is sown,
  by the seeds of tomorrow, by my hand are grown.

. . .

I elect my perception, shape reality's mold,
in the canvas of my mind, my world unfolds.
A world I cannot win.
I choose my suffering, let this truth be told,
in the crucible of pain, strength finds its hold.

Life, a grand narrative, of victories and strife,
a paradoxical symphony, a finely-tuned fife.
In the facade of truth and illusion, amidst the trials rife,
I find my purpose, I craft my life.

6. Destiny Unstrung - Friday July, 28 2023 MST - 21:13

A point bereft its pole is but a twig,
    regardless of its stature, be it small or big.
    Devoid of shock, of peril it is free,
    even to the unfamiliar, clear it would be.

The Rod of Fate, it's merely an instrument, you see,
    held by the ignorant, it loses its decree.
    Its power, its terror, its lethal design,
    all seem to wither in a fool's confine.

In capable hands, it sings a fearsome song,
    in a fool's grasp, its melody goes wrong.
    Without wisdom's guide, its potential is lost,
    a tale of caution, that comes at great cost.

Just as a songbird needs its song,
    as a bell longs for its gong,

so too does destiny's spear,
cry out for a hand that can steer.

A weapon, a tool, an extension of might,
in the hands of the wise, it shines bright.
But left to the fool, its song is unsung,
destiny's spear, by the foolish, is unstrung.

7. Echoes of Silent Dread - Saturday July 29, 2023 03:33 MST

Nestled among identical edifices in the heart of suburbia stands an unassuming house. Within its modern shell of concrete and glass, beneath the stark glow of LED lights, a tempest of anxiety churns. Its lone inhabitant, a man of no particular mention, is embroiled in the ceaseless tumult of his own thoughts, in a constant parade of fear and dread.

For him, isolation is not dictated by physical walls, but by the stormy landscape of his own psyche. He is pursued by an intangible specter, a terror void of form but as real as the air he breathes. It is an incapacitating fear of the unknown, a dread of an unfulfilled life, an existential dread of the infinite void.

Everyday objects within his home transform under the weight of his anxieties. The innocuous toaster becomes a symbol of life's monotony, each pop a sobering echo of passing time. The persistent hum of the refrigerator, a chilling reminder of relentless despair. His once welcoming living room, now a personal prison.

As the sun rises, his sense of doom amplifies, his own consciousness pounding a haunting rhythm akin to a hidden, guilty heartbeat. His reality, consumed by this relentless dread, tints each passing day with shades of gray, rendering every moment a somber echo of the last.

Caught in his self-induced nightmare, he watches his days dissolve into a gnawing abyss of worry. His life, overshadowed by the relentless fear of living, has morphed into an eternal test of endurance.

The ticking of the clock slices through the sterile silence, each tick echoing his impending oblivion. Each chime, a haunting reminder of the relentless march towards the end, gnawing at the edges of his sanity. His dread of existence, of not living life fully, is gradually consuming him, his existence a testament to a constant struggle.

8. Odyssey of the Astray - Sunday July 30, 2023 11:48 MST

In a vast expanse where horizons blend,
  where paths entwine and compasses bend,
  a traveler wandered, alone and astray,
  seeking the light, the break of day.

Forests deep, where shadows creep,
  mysteries kept in silence steep.
  Mountains high, with peaks of snow,
  hid truths untold, from long ago.

Lost in thought, lost in space,
  the wanderer sought a familiar face.
  Each step taken, in trepidation,
  led further away from the destination.

The moon cast shadows, cryptic and long,
  spilling tales of an ancient song.

Of travelers past, who'd lost their way,
in the confusion of night, ensnared by gray.

Within this void, a spark did gleam,
a glimmering hope, a fleeting dream.
For even when lost, one truth remains,
endless paths lead to open plains.

With every stumble, lesson learned,
with every turn, a new page earned.
the journey itself, the truest prize,
discovery dawned in the wanderer's eyes.

And as stars above began to sing,
direction bestowed by the night's own wing,
the traveler found, in being lost,
a self reborn, a soul un-crossed.

So, in life's maze, when paths do twist,
remember the magic, the shimmering mist.
For being lost is not the end,
but a new beginning, a chance to mend.

9. Lost in the Frost - Monday July 31, 2023 21:48 MST

In the land where winter's grip was tightest,
    where shimmering snow made days the brightest,
    there ventured forth a soul, bold and lone,
    seeking warmth in a world of cold stone.

Lost in the frost, each step a mystery,
    the wanderer moved, rewriting history.
    Frozen lakes guarding tales of yore,
    of ancient kings, and battles galore.

The northern lights, a call of desire,
    ignited the sky, a spectral fire.
    Beneath their glow, the cold did bite,
    challenging the heart, dimming the light.

Wolves howled in chorus with the wind's keen song,
    in this icy realm, where nights grew long.

The traveler's spirit, unbowed and clear,
pressed onward, letting go of fear.

Glistening forests, with trees like spires,
hid secrets deep, and old campfires.
Embers of laughter, of days gone past,
urged the wanderer, to make memories last.

But amidst the chill, a hope did smile,
a hearth's warm glow, a distant dream to beguile.
For in the heart of the winter's embrace,
lies the promise of spring, a tender grace.

Lost in the frost, begrudgingly finding the way,
the journey itself, the light of day.
And as dawn broke, ending the night's long cost,
the wanderer found, what once was lost.

For in the heart of the coldest frost,
are lessons learned, and fears oft tossed.
In the embrace of winter's might,
there lies the strength, the will to fight.

Named it shall be, for all to recall,
the tale of resilience, standing tall:
"Lost in the Frost, Found in the Dawn",
a testament to hope, forever drawn.

10. ANTIDECITED - TUESDAY AUGUST 1, 2023 03:47 MST

In the forgotten soul where feelings intertwine,
   where thoughts surge, and worlds combine,
   there lies a state, neither black nor white,
   the 'antidecited', a gray twilight.

Neither decided nor cast aside,
   floating adrift on life's vast tide.
   Overwhelmed by choices vast,
   deleted from decisions past.

A limbo state, a pause in time,
   a silent, haunting, muted chime.
   For in this space, the soul feels trapped,
   by indecision, its wings are wrapped.

Within this realm, a hope does grow,
   a beacon's light, a subtle glow.

For every soul that's antidecited,
holds the power, to be reignited.

To rise above, to find a way,
to seize the moment, come what may.
For in the heart of uncertainty's sea,
lies the strength, to simply be.

Overwhelmed no more, decisions clear,
the antidecited finds what's dear.
Embracing life, with all its tide,
finding purpose, no longer to hide.

So, when you feel lost, overcast,
remember the antidecited, and moments vast.
For in the perpetuity of doubt and delight,
lies the path, to set things right.

11. Between Shadows and Dawn - Wednesday August 2, 2023 21:32 MST

In mirrors cast by doubts so deep,
    where silent fears their vigils keep,
    there lingers a soul, both lost and bound,
    living a lie, with truths unfound.

Afraid to live, for pain might stay,
    fearing death, keeps life at bay.
    In twilight's grasp, the heart does sigh,
    caught in the limbo, of earth and sky.

Each fleeting moment, a masquerade,
    behind masked smiles, the truth does fade.
    Yearning for freedom, but permanently chained by fright,
    a candle's flame, dimmed in the night.

But within this gloom, a longing persists,
    a glimmer of hope, in the darkest mists.

For even in lies, the truth does weave,
a tale of strength, for those who believe.

Though living may hurt, and death may allure,
    the heart's true journey is ever-pure.
    To find one's truth, amidst the guise,
    is to understand life's grandest prize.

So to the soul, living that lie,
    know that the dawn always follows the night.
    Embrace the pain, let tears purify,
    for in true living, we learn to fly.

12. Chains and Dizzying Heights - Thursday August 3, 2023 23:29 MST

In chains of habit, I'm held so tight,
    from dizzying heights, I view the night.
    Addicted, bound, my vision's sharp,
    within, there lurks a burlap tarp.

From mountaintops, I see the fray,
    of life's vast connection, in disarray.
    Bound by desires, by cravings strong,
    I wonder where my heart belongs.

I'm not ailing what wellness eludes,
    in this unflinching sanity, reality demurs- where truth deludes.
    Twisted narratives, tales that swell,
    painting scenes of a self-made hell.

Deep inside, a nothingness remains,
    a fleeting hope, amidst the chains.

For even in descent, lessons are learned,
and with each dawn, a new page is turned.

Such is my life, a teeter-totter on the edge,
balancing desires, promises a plague, pledged.
In this crafted world, where realities meld,
I search for peace, a story yet untold.

13. Guiding Conscience - Friday August 4, 2023 22:00 MST

Time eludes, a wisp in the breeze,
    moments fleeting, like finger nails scrapping pleas.

Freight exudes, a weight so profound,
    bleeding silence, the world's only sound.

Amidst the rush, and chaos that intrudes,
    only my conscience firmly concludes.

Guiding me through the dim and the light,
    a beacon of truth in the darkest of night.

In the river of memories that cascade,
    it's my conscience that lays the spade.

. . .

For in its wisdom, clarity is found,
a timeless song, an eternal resound.

In the midst of all that's amiss,
my conscience seals, with a silent deadly kiss.

The knowledge that, come what may,
it remains steadfast, leading the way.

14. Desire - Saturday August 5, 2023 19:46 MST

In the still of night, the Reaper takes his claim,
  a recurring nightmare, always the same.

All seems aligned, but I'm adrift at sea,
  caught in a current, struggling to be free.

My wants, like pulsing desires, grow louder than shouts,
  eclipsing the quiet needs, casting out doubts.

I'm drawn to these desires, in their glowing spree,
  the essentials tug, pleading his plea.

This burning within, so fierce and so raw,
  feels like a hunger, without any flaw.

.   .   .

It's grasp is tight, won't let me break free,
  a cycle unending, a chained decree.

Each twilight's descent brings the dream once more,
  a death of wants and needs, an internal war.

In this restless slumber, where passions decree,
  I seek a dawn where balance lets me be.

15. Quest for Veritas - Sunday August 6, 2023 10:29 MST

In a world where obsession takes its toll,
  where perfection's quest consumes the soul,
  no indiscretions, not a single flaw,
  amidst the pristine, a void we saw.

Veritas, once bright, now fades from view,
  lost in the maze of what's deemed true.
  Blinded by ideals, so sharp, so keen,
  the essence of truth remains unseen.

The river of reality, once clear and deep,
  now stirs with illusions, in its steady sweep.
  Chasing shadows, ignoring the day,

Veritas slips, quietly away.

. . .

In the sandpaper wretched silent corners, where hearts still yearn,
the ember of truth continues to burn.
For beyond obsession, past the façade's cost,
lies the path, where veritas isn't lost.

Seek not in perfection, but in the raw and real,
in the tangled tales of how we truly feel.
For amidst the chaos, the noise, the din,

Veritas awaits, for those who look within.

16. Journey Beyond Frailty - Monday August 7, 2023 18:34 MST

On a journey for health, seeking the grail,
  windswept paths, through storm and hail.
  It isn't a quest just for the weak

- but for every soul, something unique.

The stalwart heart, too, feels the strain,
  muscles that tire, thoughts that wane.
  Strength may ebb, memories blur,
  within, a resilient spirit does stir.

Every stumble, each faltering step,
  brings lessons learned, promises kept.
  For even in weakness, in the fading light,
  there lies a will, a reason to fight.

. . .

What is the point, one might ask,
    in this Herculean, unending task?
    It's not about conquest, nor tales to regale

- but the journey itself, the wind in the sail.

For in seeking health, in braving the trail,
    we find inner truths, beyond the frail.
    Though moments may come when hope seems to pale,
    the quest is not in vain, nor destined to fail.

17. Shadows of Reality - Tuesday August 8, 2023 19:12 MST

In the darkest depths of mind, a battle unfolds,
 where sanity's grip both tightens and holds.
 Reality blurs, distinctions wane,
 a knife of duality, pleasure and pain.

Fake wears the mask of the genuine, true,
 while the real hides, lost in the hue.
 Confusion reigns, perceptions shake,
 uncertainty lingers in every wake.

In this topsy-turvy, inverted realm,
 conjectures rise, take the helm.
 A witch-hunt ensues, driven by lore,
 seeking truths that exist no more.

A story spun, a fable retold,
 where innocence is traded, and trust is sold.

Amidst the chaos, the deafening gale,
a resilient spirit strives not to fail.

For in the grapple with sanity's test,
   lies the heart's quest, a journey to best.
   Seeking clarity, a beacon, a trail,
   to navigate the storm and set sail.

18. Crystal Steps and Verdant Dreams - Wednesday August 9, 2023 21:54 MST

Upon a fragile path I tread,
  each step weighed, by fear and dread.
  Glass beneath, so sharp, so thin,
  sharp shards cut to the bone, the fragility of the world within.

No longer do my feet know the touch,
  of grassy knolls, the earth's gentle clutch.
  They've forgotten the pungent odor of daisies white,
  the cool embrace of dew at night.

My world's reduced to this delicate plane,
  balancing joy with shards of pain.
  The verdant fields, once vast and wide,
  now feel distant, pushed aside.

Deep within, a memory stirs,
  of wind-swept hair and nature's purrs.

A longing grows, a yearning so vast,
to once again feel the past.

For while the glass may hold its sway,
dreams of green won't fade away.
In time, I'll break this crystal snare,
and find my way back, to the open air.

19. Echoes of Another Self - Thursday August 10, 2023 06:32 MST

In a realm of sleep, deep and surreal,
   the lines blur, a matrix feel.
   I see myself, subtly not quite the same,
   a doppelgänger, without a name.

This other me, so free and wild,
   untamed spirit, nature's child.
   For a fleeting moment, he takes the stage,
   unburdened heart, free of cage.

I, the watcher, bound and worn,
   witness joy while feeling torn.
   Envy stings, as emptiness brings play,
   in this twilight, between night and day.

In the quiet, a truth is born,
   a silent wish, both hopeful and forlorn.

For the reality that feels so fake,
is the one I yearn, wish to partake.

Though nightmares may come, with tales they weave,
it's in their world I sometimes believe.
For within their grasp, in dreams we stake,
the chances we missed, the paths we didn't take.

20. Temporal Tether - Friday August 11, 2023 03:33 MST

At 333, a moment stands still,
    a timepiece's hands scratching abrasively, against my will.

Triple hands, though only one for me,
    in this temporal turbulence, a sight to see.

Vision falters, the world becomes haze,
    voices drift, in a muffled maze.

Words stumble, no longer clear,
    time's grip feels ever near.

As moments meld, slip and slide,
    my timeline anchors, by my side.

. . .

It screeches cries of now, of the present day,
    even when time seems to fray.

In this swirl of seconds, minutes, hours,
    where past and future interlace, empower,
    I find my grounding, my tethered stay,
    for my heart knows, it's still today.

21. MASQUERADE OF THE MIND - SATURDAY AUGUST 12, 2023 16:37 MST

In a ballroom, dim and grand,
    gather faces from every land.
    A party designed for joy and cheer,
    within, I'm gripped by a gnawing fear.

Not the individuals, not a single face,
    but the crowd itself, an overwhelming space.
    A sea of voices, laughter, and cheer,
    but all I hear is the rush in my ear.

The glittering gowns, the sparkling wine,
    in the midst of it all, I wish to decline.
    The clinking glasses, the rhythm, the beat,
    my heart races, skips a beat.

Each step I take, feels heavy and slow,
    in this whirlwind of faces, I barely know.

The chatter grows louder, the room starts to spin,
a cacophony outside, a silence within.

The allure of the party, the promise it holds,
My stomach churns, my courage folds.
The taste of fear, so bitter, so clear,
each passing moment feels like a year.

Behind masked smiles, beneath the veneer,
is a trembling soul, grappling with fear.
For in the heart of the festivity and cheer,
lies the haunting thought that the end is near.

Amidst the chaos, a realization grows,
that fear is but a shadow, an illusion that shows.
For while the masses may seem daunting and vast,
it's in finding one's center, that peace is amassed.

In the end, it's not the party, the crowd, or the sphere,
but our inner battles, that we truly must clear.
For when we confront, understand, and steer,
the dread dissipates, and courage draws near.

22. Yearning Beyond the Facade- Sunday August 13, 2023 10:48 MST

In the midst of the crowd, I stand alone,
  overwhelmed, defeated, my spirit's tone.
  Day after day, the same song plays,
  tomorrow's but a mirror of today's forays.

The sun rises and sets, in a repeated sideways glance,
  in this routine, I seek a chance.
  For a touch of new, a break from the old,
  a story that's mine, waiting to be told.

I dream of a seat, a place of my own,
  where choices are mine, where seeds are sown.
  Not just a face in the vast sea,
  but a soul with a voice, yearning to be free.

Here I stand, tied by invisible threads,
  to norms, to judgments, to societal threats.

A facade all around, a masquerade so vast,
where true selves are buried, shelved in the past.

In this world that prides its sober veneer,
I'm but a pawn, a silent seer.
Deep within, a flame does burn,
for a turn of the tide, for the tables to turn.

To break free from these chains that bind,
to seek, to explore, to truly find.
An opportunity, a moment that's just mine,
to shine or falter, to cross that line.

For amidst the monotony, the repetitious days,
lies a heart that yearns, in countless ways.
To be its own, to rise or to fall,
to seize the moment, to answer the call.

23. Transient Echoes - Monday August 14, 2023 21:00 MST

In a world where rocks throw themselves-
    and light extinguishes its own beam,
    where dreams may shatter, hope does dream,
    in every twist, turn, ascent, or fall,
    embrace the rhythm, embrace it all.

Temptations allure, moments of dread,
    paths unknown, where souls may tread,
    push forth, journey on, through rise and through wane,
    for no sentiment, in the end, shall remain.

Glimpses of wonder, flashes of fright,
    guiding you through day and into the night,
    continue to stride, through clear skies and through mist,
    for no emotion, in time, will persist.

With the sirens call of dawn and the stillness of dusk,

in moments of silence or in life's bustling husk,
march ahead, through tranquility or uproar,
for no sensation, forever, shall endure.

So, in the flow of existence, swift or slow,
with every high peak or deep shadowed low,
proceed with courage, be it sunshine or rain,
for no passion, at last, will sustain.

24. Significance - Tuesday August 15, 2023 18:09 MST

In the dimming silence of life's fleeting hour,
    I contemplate existence, its transient power.
    Amidst the vastness, with its radiant display,
    will my brief existence merely fade away?

Each note I've sung, each tear I've shed,
    are they but dust, lost to time's vast spread?
    In the infinite expanse, where galaxies swirl,
    will my tiny mark matter, in this vast spatial twirl?

The dreams I've chased, the hopes I've clung,
    to the melodies of life, have they gone unsung?
    When all is still, and the night draws near,
    will my essence vanish, consumed by Earth's fear?

Deep within, a somber truth does lie,
    perhaps our existence is but a sigh.

A fleeting wind in the grand, eternal night,
a brief glint, then lost to sight.

In this vastness, perhaps we're but a dream,
a momentary shimmer, a transient beam.
For in the grand nothingness of space and time,
our brief existence may never truly chime.

25. Desolation - Wednesday August 16, 2023 20:22 MST

In endless nights, cuts deepen and cling,
a ceaseless cycle of suffering they bring.
Each dawn, a mirage, cruelly the same,
in a world where despair is the only claim.

The clock's hands move, but joy stands still,
an endless descent, a bitter pill.
Days blur into gray, void of any hue,
where dreams once vibrant, have lost their due.

A deluge of tasks, like chains that strangle,
with every breath, more reasons to mangle.
Each one a torment, heavy and grave,
leading me further into the abyss they pave.

In the midst of chaos, a plea to be alone,
away from this world, its heart of stone.

For silence and darkness, my only reprieve,
from a world that takes more than it'll ever give.

But even in corners where one seeks escape,
desolation lingers, donning its cape.
For in this void, there's no way to flee,
from the relentless grasp of melancholy.

Solace is a myth, a tale untold,
for in this darkness, nothing takes hold.
Despair is the constant, the unending tide,
in a world where our destiny to die shall forever reside.

26. Drift - Thursday August 17, 2023 20:50 MST

In a place where evil hides,
    lost and drifting with the tides,
    unfamiliar roads underfoot,
    each turn uncertain, each step afoot.

Scared of what the future holds,
    torn between stories new and old,
    the night's embrace feels cold and stern,
    for the light of dawn, I yearn.

Amidst this fear, hope's song is sung,
    a melody for the lost and young,
    for even when torn, and paths unclear,
    the heart's compass will draw us near.

27. Whispers of the Sleepless City - Friday August 18, 2023 23:54 MST

A sorry that never sleeps but my money it keeps,
    a hustle, a riddle, wrapped in city beats.
    Neon signs, tall tales, hidden in deep alleyways,
    promises decay, debts to pay.

Lights and grandeur, illusions they cast,
    selling compelling thoughts, mournful and vast.
    Gleaming towers, mirrored in moon's silver light,
    hide darker truths, out of plain sight.

A moral man walks, with hesitation in his steps,
    amidst the lure, his conscience he keeps.
    For what can rattle, twist, and turn his core,
    but the city's secrets, the myths of yore.

One that leaves a moral man's stomach in knots,
    the glamour, the glitter, and clandestine plots.

But beneath the façade, beneath the concrete maze,
lie stories untold, in a ghostly haze.

A city that never sleeps, they boldly declare,
its silence speaks, if you dare to care.
For what is seen is not all that lies,
the unseen battles, the unheard cries.

"Come, be part of the dream!" the billboards cry,
though the dream's cost is often too high.
Beneath the shimmer, the allure, the spree,
is a game of shadows, a happenstance of glee.

It is nothing but a sly lie, the city's hymn,
with every corner holding a secret, grim.
What hisses beneath, and in plain sight too,
is an attempt to blind, to shade the true hue.

Amongst the chaos, hope does persist,
in blatantly cloaked tales, in moments kissed.
For even in a city, with its deceptive might,
there are those who seek, and find, the light.

28. Neon Faust - Saturday August 19, 2023 21:36 MST

In the heart of a neon desert, where dreams collide,
    I played my hand, my desires untried.
    The dice rolled, the cards did sway,
    fortune's favor seemed mine that day.

Bright lights beckoned, whispering of gold,
    promising power, fame, tales yet untold.
    The roulette wheel spun, my pulse did race,
    glimpses of black, red, and green,
    caught in the allure, the city's embrace.

For every win, the stakes grew high,
    till the chips in hand reached the sky.
    But with each bet, a darkness, a greed, grew near,
    a price to be paid, something dear.

In the mirrored halls, where reflections deceive,

I met a figure, a pact to conceive.
A soul's weight in riches, the deal was cast,
eternity's gamble, sins amassed.

As coins poured in, and celebrations rang,
a chilling silence, a serpent's fang.
For in the city where dreams can unfurl,
I'd won the world, but lost my soul's pearl.

In a desert of lights, where fortunes are told,
beware the cost of glittering gold.
For the highest stakes, beneath the neon glow,
are not always seen, in the show's underbelly throw.

29. Elixir - Sunday August 20, 2023 10:13 MST

I sought a glass, a potion to drink.
    To quell the thoughts, to silence the din,
    drown out today, let oblivion win.

Amidst the clamor, the rolling dice's call,
    a liquid solace, to cushion the fall.
    To forget the morrow, the weight of today,
    in golden elixirs, I wished to sway.

Coins jingle, victories freshly reaped,
    still a hollow feeling, inside it seeped.
    For all the glitter, the fortune's sweep,
    I found I could no longer earn my keep.

In a desert of dreams, where hopes might sink,
    all I yearned for was that missing link.

A momentary escape, a brief respite,
from the dazzling days and endless night.

30. Chains of Time - Monday August 21, 2023 15:45 MST

In a lofty chamber, against the city's vast glow,
   awaited a man, caught in memories' throes.
   Eyes trained below, anticipation's tight band,
   for a package bearing time's dark command.

This artifact aged, from an epoch so stark,
   stories of power, of a journey to embark.
   In dreams, its ticking rang, a siren's song clear,
   its pull irresistible, drawing him near.

Each vision more haunting, its presence defined,
   by dawn's first light, evil intertwined.
   Its grip on him grew, insidious and deep,
   promises of power, secrets it would keep.

Deep within, a growing dread took flight,
   for this very timepiece darkened the light.

To unlock doors better left closed, futures best unsaid,
its hands didn't guide, but dragged him instead.

A doorbell resounded, his fate drawing near,
in trembling hands, he held what he'd come to fear.
The watch, its face cold, its power unveiled,
its hands danced to rhythms, of storms and gales.

Its face bore glyphs, old and malign,
its hands moved, not by sun, but by some dark design.
Compelled to don it, its weight cold and stark,
it pulled him, controlled him, snuffing out his spark.

Through twisted landscapes, where nightmares reside,
with the watch as his shackle, no place to hide.
Its ominous pulse, a constant reminder of his fate,
drowning in his own bone's marrow, it was too late.

The saga of a man, once free, now confined,
by time on his wrist, his will undermined.
In the cruel drudgery of ages, where true costs intertwine,
he was lost, ensnared by time...

31. Escheated - Tuesday August 22, 2023 11:46 MST

Stuck in a windowless cave where light once gleamed,
defeated, my spirit's not as it seemed.
My soul feels escheated, lost in the fray,
every dawn merely mirrors the gray.

Screams of yesteryears taunt and jeer,
echoing regrets, amplifying my fear.
The joy once held, now starkly depleted,
in this abyss, all dreams are defeated.

No solace in sight, no comfort to clutch,
stuck in despair, in sorrow's cold touch.
The labyrinth of loss, so intricate, seated,
where once there was life, now all's been escheated.

32. Timeless Farewell - Wednesday August 23, 2023 12:06 MST

In the silent chambers of the night,
    a spectral shimmer broke the gloom,
    not of fright, but radiant light,
    an essence simmered within my room.

Eyes, once heavy, now lay wide,
    beholding wonder unseen,
    vivid colors did coincide,
    in a display of spectral sheen.

My hand did reach, to touch the gleam,
    I found no substance, only air,
    in that void, a heartfelt theme,
    a presence of deep love was there.

Though formless, still I understood,
    the spirit's message, pure and good.

. . .

By the dim light of time's display,
   the early hours were shown to me,
   but when I sought the glow's array,
   it vanished, leaving mystery.

Awakened by the sun's first ray,
   a ring, a call, a voice did tell,
   of a beloved, gone away,
   a heart in sorrow's depths did dwell.

Solace in the thought did lie,
   for in that spectral lingering so clear,
   a final, silent, loving goodbye,
   from one who was, in life, so dear.

Gathered 'round, a tale unfolds,
   of clocks that ceased their chime,
   at that very moment, the story holds,
   she departed, transcending time.

In synchrony, time did decree,
   a bond unbroken, a love set free.

33. Lost Memories - Thursday August 24, 2023 22:43 MST

A riddle that refuses to be unraveled,
    its segments have traveled, disappeared in the fray,
    I tread with heavy feet, reluctantly,
    navigating lives of yesteryears,
    endeavoring,
    to push aside,
    those painful echoes, the mournful tunes,
    that haunt my every step, casting looming dunes.

In the quiet corners of my mind, they lay,
    Spilling cans of gasoline, of regrets, mistakes of the day.
    The cherished fumes, tales that once brought delight,
    now obscured, lost to the night.

I search, amid the vast expanse,
    for fragments of joy, a fleeting glance,
    of memories that once sparkled, once shone,

before they drifted, before they were gone.

Hoping against hope, in this vast maze,
    that one day the path will clear, the fog will raise;
    and the pieces I've lost, the tales untold,
    will find their way back, their stories retold.

34. Wings of Hesitation - Friday August 25, 2023 20:14 MST

In the vast expanse,
    one lone bird, isolated by chance,
    hesitant
    to soar high,
    above the boundless sky.

The entire firmament
    is ripe with wonder,
    packed with mysteries
    aching to be unveiled.

One bird
    is anchored-
    fearful to ascend,
    to journey,
    to unearth the concealed.

. . .

Wind can ruffle,
  enough to make feathers quiver,
  But currents, updrafts, and breezes
  soothe the shiver.
  Floating amidst clouds,
  in a realm of doubt,
  beginning to feel chill,
  gliding in solitude,
  coasting air,
  all in a silenced, hovering thrill.

Bitterness-
  and tempests
  suppress
  the thirst for adventure,
  whom to confide in,
  without a double safeguard?
  To reshape his world,
  into one of serenity,
  one bird
  requires a magical decree,
  how can one bird
  truly be free,
  without embracing the entirety of the sky?

35. Halloween - Saturday August 26, 2023 22:16 MST

Amidst the midnight hour, lanterns aglow,
    ethereal mist weaves, dancing to and fro,
    majestic trees stand, silhouettes so stark,
    ghouls vomit secrets, beneath the cloak of the dark.

No telling, no guessing,
    whom their cold breaths might tease,
    for in their chilling embrace,
    silent pleas get lost in the breeze.

Specters in their ethereal form,
    moan with tales of the past, so forlorn,
    while the rain, not to be outdone,
    drips and drizzles, joining the nocturnal fun.

Owls, those watchers of the ancient night,
    hoot with a haunting delight,

their eyes piercing through the enigma,
that the night of Halloween does weave, a dilemma.

For within its intricate, sticky web,
lies tales of the old, the allure of the ebb,
entrapped, ensnared by its bewitching allure,
Halloween's mystery is a siren song, that's for sure.

To those daring to pierce its veil,
to navigate its maze, to unveil its tale,
it offers treasures, both eerie and pure,
only the adventurous, the brave can ensure.

36. My Constant - Sunday August 27, 2023 12:21 MST

At times you seemed distant, wrapped in your own thoughts,
and my emotions fluttered, tangled in endless knots.
Often, you wouldn't hear my desperate plea.
Leaving me grappling, longing to break free.

Through countless moments, adrift and unsure,
I silently hoped you'd be my secure moor.
We've navigated life's intricate confusion,
traversing its challenges, its foggy haze.

Each step, each stumble, each lesson learned,
ignited the flame, the passion that burned.
Just when clarity began to dawn, shining so clear,
and I believed I was free from every lingering fear,
I felt myself like a leaf, detached from its tree,
whirling, twirling in life's unpredictable spree.

· · ·

The roads I've taken, the paths I've tread,
 are they leading me forward, or in circles instead?
 I find myself pondering, in solitude's embrace,
 seeking the purpose, the rhythm, my life's pace.

With every heartbeat, every tear I've dispelled,
 I quest for answers, for tales to be retold.
 Where is the end, or the beginning anew?
 In this vast expanse, where do I find the true hue?

At moments, I stand still, my thoughts unbound.
 My feet never seem to be settled or strong;
 I find myself trembling no matter the ground.

37. Seekers of Solace - Monday August 28, 2023 09:40 MST

Both sad and forlorn,
    many souls, weary and worn.

Seeking solace, some trade their soul,
    for a fleeting taste, an ephemeral lore.

While others search, day and night,
    for phantoms, out of reach and sight.

These shadows, elusive and so sly,
    exist only in the mind's eye.

Numbness takes hold, our shield and defense,
    masking pain, in the present tense.

. . .

We dig our retreats, deep and vast,
  hoping to escape, the haunting past.

With eyes upturned to the vast blue sky,
  bloodstains blur, a tear, a sigh.

Questioning the worth of every endeavor,
  in hope's light, we may try forever.

38. In the Shadow of Paper Lies - Tuesday August 29, 2023 21:48 MST

We barter our essence, days, and nights,
    for paper deceptions, dimming our lights.
    Its value?

A mirage, cruel and sly,
    a haunting taut of a life gone awry.

Life, in its frailty, mirrors fiat's charade,
    a vaporous currency, decaying in the shade.
    bound by limits, we're given no more,
    than hushed secrets from a distant shore.

Above, cold stars, indifferent to our plight,
    gaze upon us with chilling, emotionless light.
    Time ticks, it drips, each moment a curse,
    leading us closer to the universe's hearse.

. . .

Death, the shadowed reaper, strikes without care,
   heeding not cries, nor pleads, nor prayer.
   No distinction of youth, or tales of old age,
   all meet the same fate- life's final page.

The toll is exacted, in silence and cold,
   a merciless transaction, our existence sold.
   The chill is relentless, hope's flame grows weak,
   in this somber chance, no solace we seek.

The present is a void, empty and vast,
   a fleeting mirage of a shadowy past.
   In the abyss of existence, so deep and wide,
   it's in the darkness where our truths subside.

39. The Almighty Dollar-
Wednesday August 30, 2023
08:13 MST

In empty pockets, my hopes reside,
  debt's hollow sickly green figure by my side.
  A perilous fret, it spins and weaves,
  endless bills, an incurable disease.

Circling like vultures, they await,
  each dollar earned seals my fate.
  For my soul, I pay the toll,
  still, the darkness takes its hold.

Drained and weary, I often wonder,
  is there an end, or just more thunder?
  But giving up, that's the key,
  for storms don't pass, and seas overflow with blood.
  Currency stained from the fingers of greed.

Life's worth is not in coins or gold,

but in life lived, and tales retold.
I have no life lived- mine's been sold.
I make the rich richer, trying to eke out an existence.
How I yearn to live,
bound free from the almighty dollar's chains.
shackled and cold,
penniless I scratch for a nickel.

Those nickels scratch at my soul.

My existence is a poor blackhole.

40. Stasis- Thursday August 31, 2023 19:59 MST

The sun's rays cease to cast,
    where hopes once bright now fade so fast,
    the heart grows numb, no longer stirred,
    by song of bird or a powerful word.

The weight of dread, a constant toll,
    siphons away the vibrant soul.
    Fear's grip, so tight, till paradoxically,
    it sets one free- from fear's decree.

In that void, emotions die,
    where colors merge to grayscale sky,
    every value, once held dear,
    disappears, as does the fear.

For what is fear when all is feared?
    What's left when tears have long been cleared?

A barren land, a silent maze,
where time stands still, and nights are days.

No sun to rise, no moon to wane,
no joy to cherish, no more pain.
Just a stillness, a silent crest,
an arrest that none can attest.

Deep within that hollow chest,
lies a flicker, a quiet quest,
for even in the numbness vast,
hopes of renewal might outlast.

In melancholy's icy grasp,
in silence, hands begin to clasp,
for even when emotions cease,
the heart seeks solace, yearns for peace.

May that ember, though dim and slight,
ignite the dark, and bring forth light.
For numbness too shall pass with time,
and the soul shall again, in rhythm, chime.

WORDS ARE SNAKES WITH ARMS

41. Reluctant Journey - Friday September 1, 2023 19:32 MST

In the still of the night, I ponder my plight,
    oh, the woe is the thought that I have to go,
    against the tide, against the flow,
    I dread the stay, the looming mass it might throw.

The days seem long, the nights even more,
    afraid of the duration, of what's in store,
    with every step, I feel the weight grow,
    a burden so heavy, a constant undertow.

Time and tide wait for none, it's said,
    in my heart, a hesitation is bred,
    I can't control it, the future unknown,
    the journey ahead, so alone, so overthrown.

The howling of the wind, the rustling leaves,
    tell tales of old, of heroes and thieves,

but my story's different, it's a song of despair,
a melody of reluctance, an unanswered prayer.

The world spins on, indifferent to my cry,
as I seek answers, to the how and the why,
the path is set, destiny's cruel show,
I don't want to go; I know I must attend this show.

Each footstep crashes with a heavy sigh,
every heartbeat asks the question, "why?".
But onward I march, into the abyss,
hoping for light, yearning for bliss.

For life is a journey, with its ups and downs,
a mixture of smiles, and occasional frowns,
though the road may be tough, and the way unclear,
I'll face it head-on, conquering every fear.

For in every woe, a lesson's concealed,
in every sorrow, strength is revealed,
so even as I go, with a heart full of woe,
I'll find the courage, and let the dread go.

WORDS ARE SNAKES WITH ARMS

42. Conquering Shadows - Saturday September 2, 2023 22:02 MST

In the shadow of night, a challenge takes flight,
for the soul that's entwined in an ageless fight.
The compass points north, but the path is unclear,
does the future bring hope, or just a draining fear?

The night may be long, with its cold, chilling sway,
but beyond the horizon, there's a promising day.
Though chemicals churn, and the mind may deceive,
in the heart of the storm, there's a strength to retrieve.

The present may blur, with the past intertwined,
a collision of the moments, in the calamity of the mind.
Through all the confusion, a beacon remains,
guiding through darkness, breaking the chains.

Demons may speak, casting dangers of doubt,
but the spirit's resilient, it won't be snuffed out.

For every fall, there's a rise to embrace,
a journey of healing, a redeeming grace.

Drown out the noise, listen closely within,
the courage to conquer, starts from deep skin.
Face every demon, let the battle commence,
for in the heart of the storm, lies resilience immense.

Stand tall and firm, as the night gives way,
to the warmth of dawn, and the promise of day.
For though challenges come, and may try to deceive,
with hope as your shield, in yourself, believe.

43. Calls of Liberation - Sunday September 3, 2023 10:39 MST

In shallow dirty waters unfamiliarly deep, I silently weep,
    each dawn's cruel light, my secrets keep.
    Awakened, burdened, my heart does ache,
    I summon strength, for the world I fake.

With faces familiar, feelings astray,
    the ones called family, seem miles away.
    Smiles are a mask, conversations rehearsed,
    seeking an oasis, in a desert I'm immersed.

Behind closed doors, in the still of the night,
    my soul yearns to soar, to take its true flight.
    Held by invisible chains, by expectations and roles,
    drowning in a sea, with no compass or poles.

Hummings of laughter, from memories now past,
    scratch out dreams, too fleeting to last.

In crowded rooms, I stand all alone,
seeking my place, a space of my own.

When will the time come, for me to break free?
To live for myself, to be who I wish to be?
The world may not understand, my quiet plea,
yearning for peace, for serenity, for me.

The road is long, winding, and unknown,
I must walk it, to find a home of my own.
A place where my heart, beats true and unfurled,
where I can finally, truly, live in this world.

For now, I'll find strength, in moments so small,
in days I stood tall, refused to fall.
I'll look to the stars, and in their vast might,
find hope for tomorrow, and the courage to fight.

For a life that's my own, where dreams intertwine,
a world where my soul, can brightly shine.
The journey is hard, the path may be steep,
but in pursuit of my peace, my promise I'll keep.

44. They're in the Attic - Monday September 4, 2023 22:03 MST

In the quiet corners of night,
  stabs a pain too sharp, too bright.
  Glass cries in a fragile tone,
  bending metal, a heart overthrown.

Against jagged stones, metal does yield,
  splinters against timber, no longer shielded.
  Hastening to gather, what's left behind,
  a sanctuary sought, a refuge to find.

Moments of fury, of shout and spite,
  awaken the dead, dim the light.
  A house resounds with a door's fierce slam,
  as one seeks escape, the other, a dam.

The engine roars, voicing its rage,
  fading footsteps, a sorrowed stage.

Tears like rain, continue to pour,
lost in the anguish, the heartache's raw core.

Dawn may break, but the scars remain,
of fists clenched tight, and emotional strain.
Though plastered walls may be patched in time,
the hidden chambers echo the rhyme.

In memories' loft, darkness may linger,
replaying the past, with each pointed finger.
Healing may come, but at a slow pace,
for the attic of memories, leaves a lasting trace.

45. Muted - Tuesday September 5, 2023 20:36 MST

Muted.
   amidst the cacophony that engulfs,
   always,
   Muted.
   As I stand untouched.
   Muted.
   Soul's pursuit of contentment,
   thoughts remain unrested,
   gaze ventures,
   seeking solace unknown,
   a balm for the pained.
   Muted.
   Listening to blog curdling screams,
   beyond the span of youthful days,
   an innocent visage hides much,
   the windows to my soul,
   betray the inner quake.
   Muted.
   Feigning the naivety of early years,
   the quiet unveils the reality,

playful days evaded capture,
I plummeted,
beyond tender years.
Muted.
speechless tales,
evident, unquestioned,
quiet tumult,
resounds loud and clear,
here I remain.
Muted.
my fortress,
my ultimate shield.
MUTED.

46. Patience - Wednesday September 6, 2023 19:57 MST

Silent musing,
    not in pursuit, nor in eager chasing.
    Dreams don't sprout from ardent wanting,
    they surface when patience is unrelenting.

Watch the world with a keen gaze,
    let inspiration come in gentle waves.

Not in hunger, nor in frantic race,
    but in the stillness, in quiet's embrace.

A creature on the wall, it stands upside-down so high,
    neither to chase nor to bid goodbye.

When it nears, in stillness you lie,

embrace or release, under the sky.

Seek not fame, or the world's delight,
    for true creation is an inward flight.

Let not ambition cloud the sight,
    in waiting, one finds the truest light.

47. Chronotale - Thursday September 7, 2023 20:28 MST

A fracture forms, time's tether unmasked;
    a rift, a break, an enigmatic line in glass,
    melding the worlds of time and wine.

Stories of epochs, both ancient and new,
    the last supper's end, for another's debut;
    mysteries fold and tales intertwine,
    where past meets the future in convoluted design.

Vindication, a force so pure and so clear,
    obscured by the vindictive, looming ever near;
    both sides of a coin, two faces of fate,
    each telling a story, each carrying weight.

We drink deeply from the chalice so grand,
    aware that our days are like grains of sand;
    in its inevitability, in fate's firm grasp,

we question, we ponder, to life we still clasp.

The hourglass tips, its sands swiftly fall,
  audaciously, defiantly, it wishes to stall;
  time might slip, it might twist and turn,
  but sands cling tight, their persistence we discern.

Every being, every glow, each ephemeral mite,
  partakes in this both day and of night;
  each breath, a story, each sigh, a tale,
  forever continues, without ever growing stale.

This ever-turning revolver's wheel,
  we bear witness, the bullet we feel,
  we steal and we deal;
  bound by destiny, by stories so vast,
  chosen by fate, for roles long since cast.

48. Time is Calling - Friday September 8, 2023 22:13 MST

In the vastness of time, so wide and deep,
    where life's patterns play and evil does creep,
    it's all chaos, a whirl so untamed,
    a gross misunderstanding, never fully named.

From the rivers that flow to the trees that stand,
    I often ponder, how does life expand?
    The rush of emotions, the struggles we face,
    the intricate pathways of the human race.

"I've no idea," uttered the wind to the tree,
    how amidst this chaos, we come to be.
    Standing tall, or swayed by life's demand,
    each finding a place in this vast land.

Today, with its urgency and its fervent chase,
    seems to anchor us, to a certain place.

As moments fade and new ones come to the fore,
tomorrow's significance will be no more.

Our disputes, our dramas, the tears that fall,
    in the expanse of time, might mean nothing at all.
    The tales we weave, though told with pride,
    may in time's river, simply subside.

For the challenges we face, the dreams we chase,
    in the grand narrative, might find little space.
    Amid this reality, so stark and raw,
    there's a beauty, a truth, without a flaw.

For while moments might seem fleeting and small,
    the bonds we forge, rise above all.
    So, in a hundred years, when our tales grow thin,
    the love we shared will be life's greatest win.

49. Silhouette - Saturday September 9, 2023 09:46 MST

Where hues fade and blur,
    the essence of hollow looming does occur.
    A silent midnight, deep and profound,
    where hushed echoes are the only sound.

Emeralds pale during the festive feast,
    against the shade which never ceased.
    The polished finish of a melody's seat,
    notes that fleet.

In the quiet when light does recede,
    a void of illumination, a blank slate indeed.
    Mysteries dark, where enchantresses tread,
    cloaked in mysteries, by moonlight led.

In corners obscure, an eight-legged grace,
    lies in waiting, in her silent space.

Where trees stand tall and secrets hide,
a fragrance burns, side by side.

Moments lost in the canvas vast,
of moonlit hours, and memories past.
The embrace of night, so tender and deep,
where dreams are spun, and secrets keep.
Of a hue, eternal, forever to last.

50. More Than Anything, I'm Tired - Sunday September 10, 2023 12:51 MST

More than anything, I'm tired.
    In a dim-lit room of fluorescent glow,
    my head aches, my psyche expires.
    Where keyboards clack and weary eyes do peer,
    a spirit dulled by repetition's blow,
    the crushing weight of life draws ever near.

More than anything, I'm tired, can't you see,
    of battles fought behind this screen's cold light.
    Tasks I loathe, they demand persistently,
    chipping away, till dreams are out of sight.

The digital hum, its drone so relentless,
    hours morph into days, then weeks, then years,
    the once vibrant soul now feels defenseless,
    drowning quietly in silent, unseen tears.

. . .

Endless cycles of pointless tasks, no end in view,
in this gray world, where joy seems obsolete,
a heart once hopeful now feels shades of blue,
yearning for rest, but finding no respite.

More than anything, I'm tired, I can't deny,
of promises made and dreams left unmet,
seeking solace, no more tears left to cry,
in the monotony, where hopes are set.

For in this life, where days feel all the same,
there's no reprieve, no glimmer, only disdain,
lost in the cycle, caught in the game,
everything is pointless, it's all the same.
More than anything, I'm tired.

51. Endless Night - Monday September 11, 2023 09:10 MST

Sore tired, I feel all but expired,
    lost in an endless, consuming tomb.

Each day bleeds into the next,
    an endless cycle, forever vexed,
    the weight of despair drags me under,
    thunderous sorrows, tear asunder.

The silent screams of the night,
    echo in the void, no end in sight,
    promises broken, dreams turned ash,
    hope's fleeting light, gone in a flash.

In the grip of a relentless frost,
    all warmth, all love, appears lost,
    the world turns, indifferent to my plight,
    engulfed in an eternal, starless night.

. . .

No solace, no reprieve, no end,
   only darkness, my only friend,
   in this void, where emotions decay,
   all hope has withered, faded away.

The wind howls, a mournful song,
   a reminder of all that's gone wrong,
   in this realm of endless night,
   there's no escape, no dawn in sight.

52. Distaste - Tuesday September 12, 2023 19:47 MST

Over it all, my spirit bends,
    a life of monotony, it never ends.

The beat of life, grown cold and numb.
    Promises eagerly sold, now just lies,
    devoid as hope dies.

Tethered to memories, slipping 1940s tunes are cast.
    In the silence, even tears won't fall,
    for they too, are over it all.

The world spins, but I remain still,
    haunted by an unyielding chill.
    All aspirations, cruelly destroyed.

No solace, no comfort,

only the dark, and shallow puddles that grow long.
In this desolate depth, where I tread alone,
all warmth, all love, irrevocably gone.

Tired of the cycle, the endless repeat,
    where even heartbeats feel like deceit.
    Over everything, though here I stand,
    lost in the grip of desolation's cold hand.

53. The Seventh Glass-Wednesday September 13, 2023 18:47 MST

In the heart of Brown's Manor, vast and grand,
    Evans, the loyal butler, did stand.
    A lifetime he served, proud and true,
    but this evening brought mysteries anew.

"Evans!" uttered a voice, frantic and deep,
    from the parlor's dark corner, a secret to keep.
    Mr. Brown, aged and frail, pointed with dread,
    at the grandfather clock, where time's path inevitably led.

"They've returned," he whispered, voice low and hoarse,
    eyes haunted with memories, filled with remorse.
    But Evans saw naught, save for the clock's sway,
    seeking to soothe his master's dismay.

From the shadows, a voice did creep,
    cold and disembodied, making time leap.

"You knew," it hissed, chilling the room's core,
as the manor's secrets began to pour.

"Pour the wine, Evans," Mr. Brown implored,
    "For the guests from my past, can't be ignored."
    "To the cellar," thought Evans, "to fetch the brew,"
    but ghostly footsteps followed him too.

Emerging from below, to his sheer disbelief,
    wine glasses filled on the mantle, causing him grief.
    A figure in black, with eyes that could sear,
    crossed the parlor's threshold, confirming his fear.

Urgency took hold, escape they must seek,
    but Mr. Brown's voice, was soft, and beyond weak.
    "This is my reckoning, Evans, let it be so,",
    for the sins of the past now cast their grief.

Evans fled, police sirens did ring,
    in hope they'd uncover the truth of the thing.
    They found Mr. Brown, lifeless and cold,
    six empty glasses, a story untold.

One glass remained, untouched, set apart,
    a reminder of the night- a broken heart.
    For in Brown's Manor, where shadows do lear,
    lies the mystery of "The Seventh Glass,",
    life's only true fear.

54. Fraught - Thursday September 14, 2023 19:46 MST

Darkness descends, consuming the room.

Thoughts whirl and spin, a tempestuous sea,
  grasping for air, for a place to be free.

The walls close in, breath grows thin,
  silent screams, where to begin?

Anxiety's grip, cold and tight,
  everything uncertain, nothing feels right.

The weight of the world, pressing down,
  hopes buried deep, threatening to drown.

Lost in a maze, no way out in sight,

overwhelmed by the endless, consuming fright.

Tonight is the night, so it seems.

Dreams of terror, only Armageddon gleams,
it seems the end- though I know it's not.

Time stands still, I'm fraught.

55. Failed Resilience - Friday September 15, 2023 20:00 MST

Where failure lingers, thickening the air.
　　More than one miss, errors galore,
　　a heart persists, craving something more.

Everything seems amiss, out of place,
　　chasing dreams, in a relentless race.
　　How many times must I stumble and fall,
　　before I hear victory's beckoning call?

Every attempt, every tear shed,
　　adds to the weight of the dread.
　　Within the depths of this abyss,
　　resides a spark, a hopeful wish.

For isn't every mistake, every wrong,
　　a step towards where I belong?
　　In the symphony of life, each note awry,

builds towards a crescendo, reaching the sky.

The road to success is paved with trials,
    each failure a lesson, spanning miles.
    With each setback, with every fall,
    grows a determination, breaking every wall.

One hit away, or perhaps even two,
    success remains, though sometimes out of view.
    Hidden behind the veil of strife,
    awaiting the moment to burst into life.

So, weary traveler, do not despair,
    in the face of failure, take a breath of fresh air.
    For the journey is long, but the destination is sweet,
    and the tales of your battles, they'll be hard to beat.

56. My Soul to Take - Saturday September 16, 2023 22:55 MST

In a forgotten corner of the mind it dwells,
   a taste, a memory, a place that tells
   of times gone by, obscured by haze,
   A moment lost in life's vast maze.

A scent wafts in, both distant and near,
   replications of laughter, susurrations of fear.
   I've known this place, walked its shores,
   it eludes, always just behind closed doors.

Balancing on life's precarious knife,
   I've battled through sacrifice, endured the strife.
   All for a glimpse of that fleeting scene,
   a moment, a look, what could it have been?

Is this memory real, or just a cruel pest?
   a fabricated tale, or a forgotten quest?

Yearning to grasp it, to hold it tight,
it burns away, just out of sight.
It's embers I chase through the night.

For the heart knows truths the mind might fake,
in the silent depths, where memories quake.
And in that space, between dream and wake,
lies the memory's reverberations, for my soul to take.

57. Harbinger of Change-
Sunday September 17, 2023
13:13 MST

In dreams where mysteries unfold,
    a Shoebill Stork appeared, so bold.
    With eyes that held the ancient tales,
    and wings that soared where no path trails.

A messenger from realms unknown,
    in moonlit skies, its silhouette shown.
    A rare sight, this bird of night,
    a harbinger of pure delight.

It's beak held stories forever untold,
    of treasures rare, and fortunes old.
    A guide to places we can't see,
    a beacon of what's meant to be.

From heights above it shared its view,
    of horizons vast and skies so blue.

Mumbles of secrets of the deep,
promises the world might keep.

In dreams, where wonder intertwines,
the Shoebill's call forever chimes.
For in its gaze, a world anew,
a symbol of the good to ensue.

58. Tread of the Dead-
Monday September 18, 2023
08:13 MST

We tread,
 dread's umbrage ever darkening overhead.
 Endless cycles, draining life's very breath,
 an unyielding march, a tango with death.

Each coin earned, a fragment of soul fades,
 time's cruel grip tightens, dreams wade in shades.
 Moments lost, never to return, never to gleam,
 in this nightmare world, where hope can't beam.

Woven in sorrow, life's fabric so unfair,
 tangled like twine, ensnaring in despair.
 The world's weight heavy, pressing us fine,
 our only refuge, the bitter embrace of wine.

There's no respite, no golden dawn's glow,

only endless nights, and sorrows that grow.
For in the abyss of life, all happiness is deceased,
and all that remains is the longing for release.

59. Tomorrow's Fire - Tuesday September 19, 2023 21:38 MST

Apprehensive, in the stillness, I lay,
    eyes transfixed on the ceiling's gray.
    In this silent room, all seems astray,
    save for a smoke detector's dim display.

Weary bones, aching for rest's embrace,
    sleep eludes, in this quiet space.
    For even in dreams, penumbras trace,
    the looming dread of the coming days.

The sun might rise, a new day might break,
    but what solace does a new morning make?
    When every awakening, every little shake,
    reminds of the cruel week I'm about to undertake.

Days blend into nights, in monotonous flight,
    each passing moment, a dwindling light.

Hope seems distant, out of sight,
in this endless cycle of day and night.

The world spins, and I'm trapped so tight,
in a web of obligations, an endless fight.
With every dawn, comes the stark invite,
to partake in another bleak transaction, try as I might.

I'm but a pawn, in this grand theater,
no say, no will, just an aimless wanderer.
My spirit, once free, now feels the tether,
sold, bartered to the whims of paper's clatter.

In this vast expanse, where dreams once soared,
now lies a landscape, barren, ignored.
Though deep within, a flicker stored,
a silent plea, for a life restored.

For now, in the dim glow of that singular light,
I lay and ponder, through the weary night.
Hoping, praying, for a future bright,
free from the chains, and life's endless plight.

60. Life - Wednesday
September 20, 2023 19:50 MST

Profound in its place.

In life's embrace, we're both lost and found,
    from the first cry to the last sound,
    the pull of love, the sting of wound,
    a quilt of emotions, tightly wound.

With hearts that yearn and hands that touch,
    seeking love's warmth, its gentle clutch,
    amidst the joy, pain's biting crutch,
    reminds us of life's delicate touch.

Strife, the fire that forges our soul,
    makes us brittle, renders us whole,
    in its crucible, we pay the toll,
    we emerge stronger, with a clearer goal.

. . .

Death, the horizon we cannot see,
the final verse in our life's decree,
but a transition, can't you agree?
To another chapter, vast and free.

In this journey, brief and defined,
a fleeting silhouette, a thought in mind,
in our hearts, a light does bind,
bearing witness to life, ever entwined.

For in every step, from birth to rest,
in every sigh, in every quest,
lies the mystery, both jest and test,
of love, pain, strife—life's fervent fest.

WORDS ARE SNAKES WITH ARMS

61. My Mind - Thursday September 21, 2023 08:19 MST

In a city of obscurity, where gloom does reside,
    the ground quivers beneath, nowhere to hide.
    Buildings once robust, now crumble and slide,
    by the weight of a mind, where demons confide.

Steel's once firm grip, now feels so weak,
    against the relentless hushes that bleakly speak.
    For within his mind, darkness does peak,
    bringing forth nightmares, making knees go weak.

The very essence of thought, corroded and rotten,
    memories of contentment, all but forgotten.
    In this abyss, where all is misbegotten,
    his soul feels trapped, ensnared, and downtrodden.

Water's shallow edges, he feels he could drown-
    in puddles of despair, where hope is weighed down.

Every step forward, his fears further crown,
as king of a mind, where anguish is renowned.

Chains forged of anxiety, bind him so tight,
keeping him captive, in perpetual night.
With every reverberation, his internal fight,
the escape seems distant, far from sight.

In this desolate landscape, no solace he finds,
for the demons are cunning, weaving their binds.
Every glimmer of light, the darkness rewinds,
leaving him lost, in these infinite confines.

Trapped in a maze, of his own mind's making,
every turn leads to despair, ever heart-breaking.
For in this realm, there's no awaking,
only the endless torment, constantly raking.

In the sound of silence, his mental prison,
he searches for an exit, but none is given.
For the chains of his thoughts, have deeply driven,
him into depths, where light is forbidden.

WORDS ARE SNAKES WITH ARMS

62. WHO? - FRIDAY SEPTEMBER 22, 2023 19:23 MST

Where angst and longing rarely depart,
a glimmer of hope, dim and slight,
emerges from darkness, yearning for light.
Puzzled and torn, in life's intricate game,
seeking the pieces, to a picture unnamed.
Fragmented thoughts, scattered and loose,
desire the wholeness, life's elusive recluse.
My vessel of dreams, only half full it seems,
reflects silent battles, and muted screams.
Lost on a path, unknown and gray,
wishing to wear another's role in the play.
The weight of identity, heavy and profound,
seeking an escape, where solace is found.
For today, in this moment, I wish to sway,
to be anyone, just not who I am today.

63. Poisoned - Saturday September 23, 2023 9:51 MST

Anticipation of the day makes my sanity severely sway.
    Each ticking moment on the verge of irreparable pain,
    I tread the paths where few would dare.

Fires of sorrow, every shade casts a long stare,
    my musings and thoughts, so heavy, so un-profound,
    make me wonder beyond fraught, where no peace is found.

The horizon stretches, vast and bleak,
    every promise, every secret they speak.
    In this world where night devours day.
    I search for an answer, my own way.

The sun, it hesitates, reluctant to rise,
    for it too has seen through life's cruel guise.
    The winds carry tales of miseries untold,
    of ambitions shattered, and souls grown cold.

. . .

Mourning the passage of countless years.
　　Only cement sidewalks caked in lament,
　　for promises made, and moments unspent.

My faucet endlessly drips, a flammable sludge,
　　a foreign substance that bleeds, not water.
　　A toxic cocktail, I feel my pulse totter.
　　It serves as an incessant fodder,
　　a consistent and unrelenting bother.

Every sip, more sour than the last,
　　chained to memories, bound by my taste for the past.
　　Seeking solace, losing my grip by the hour.
　　In this realm, this poison has won- I have no power.

64. The Billboard - Sunday September 24, 2023 12:59 MST

Upon a city's sprawling scene,
    three pigeons perch, silent and serene.
    On towering billboards, they sit so grand,
    selling souls, on this vast urban land.

Not for gold or treasures of old,
    they watch stories, both timid and bold.
    Silent witnesses to life's rushing facade,
    observing the world, night and day.

Their gaze unwavering,
    sweeping vistas, every sight, every sound.
    The needles seep a dull echoing thud,
    as they fall from junkies arms to the concrete,
    and into the mud-
    bending their hypodermic facets;
    they know the city, inside and out.
    It's coursing through their veins.

. . .

The clang of their spoons, so vile,
　　a necessary component of drawing up their vial.
　　Cocktails of drugs inseminate our streets
　　with the walking dead.
　　The birds remain silent, watching our defeat.
　　Nothing escapes their keen avian view,
　　every secret, every rendezvous.

In their stillness, a mystery surrounds-
　　tales of death from the ground.
　　For what might they think, what might they see?
　　In our human decline, our unavoidable fee.

Amidst the clamor, hustle, and race,
　　they see the yearnings of the human chase.
　　Behind each sour face, each pair of bloodshot eyes,
　　lies a world, a myriad of sighs.

Beneath their gaze, life unfolds,
　　stories of nothing, and tales of old.
　　A jaded mosaic of life, in all its hues,
　　sorrow, old and new.

Though they sit high, seemingly aloof,
　　they are privy to every truth.
　　For in their silent, watchful stance,
　　they capture the essence, the city's glance.

Walk the city's groove,

saunter past the dead, avoiding their angsty,
empty views, eyes falling from their head.
Feel the pigeons' silent, watchful move.
In the pulse of life, in its endless spree,
remember always, the eyes that truly see.

65. The Disease - Monday September 25, 2023 20:54 MST

A disease, esquisse to life - it stalks us;
    keeping us living on the edge of a knife.
    Its dual edges, our own evils and good.
    This sickness is shrewd and keeps us veiled
    under the lies cruel hood.

Our fear steers our impedance to the light,
    we consciously choose each day to fight.
    Though it is not noble; it's against the truth.
    An honest man?
    That must be a crook; a devious sleuth.
    We grow sicker each day.
    Every hour, our souls pay.

Pails of the poor, we rob our fellow man blind;
    simply because it's more expensive to be kind.
    We want, we need-
    the sickness itself continues to feed.

We serve the plates of our doomed fate.
Our toils coil us in foils of folly.
We hang the honest in public, in the square of the trolley.

It's the lies upon which we feast,
  eating much more than we can eat.
  Our sanity wanes, our fames gloat.
  We are the ones drilling holes in our own boats.
  We choose to be sick.
  We wanted it this way.

At least that's what they told us;
  we really have no say.
  For tomorrow- everyday; we poison ourselves further.
  Always intentionally going out of our way.
  It eats us alive, slowly whittling us away.
  We eek out an existence yearning to be sicker,
  with each day.
  Morality is nothing but a parable of frailty.
  We choose to cover our eyes.
  We chose this disease as our reality.

66. Forget - Tuesday September 26, 2023 22:34 MST

Today, memories fade,
    I forgot to remember to forget,
    like a deep darkness cast by the day's charade,
    in twilight's net, my thoughts are set.

My answers, where truth lies,
    my life is lived in the dark,
    a stark reminder to an outlet with no spark.
    Beyond the peace, a nothingness of bliss,
    there, an unconsciousness grants my every wish.

Each night I dive into this embrace,
    a world where sorrow has no place,
    I see the face,
    not only alive, but there to thrive.
    It is my reality, there is no triviality.

. . .

My waking hours are all but fake,
  it's more than I can bear to take.
  It's winner take all- and I'm the clear loser
  crime, education, works deep, state set
  it leaves me yearning to forget.
  To dismember every notification.

My true location, though tracked-
  is gone.
  I'm nothing;
  but a pawn.
  Like sheep, we march in a numb state,
  to the steep hill, at the end of which is our fate- an addictive pill.
  I choose the hill, but will not follow.
  Though I have forgot to remember to forget,
  I will always remember what shall follow.

67. The Puppet- Wednesday September 27, 2023 20:12 MST

It lays still in silence, encased in a box-
  until it's supplanted with our minds.
  It's fuel, your soul.
  It's the Soylent of our toll.
  We see their strings and hear their murmurings,
  it's master close behind, lips squirming.
  We know the answer but believe the fake.

It's garb is of our own artificial make,
  even so, we lay into the lie we watch them make.
  As the hoi polloi we ploy from the truth,
  stretching our fiat dollar in overpriced suits.
  They make the laws.
  They determine our flaws.
  Our morality.
  Our totality.
  Our reality.

. . .

Puppets, we are their true muse.
    The attack looms from behind our backs.
    We see the fear in the mirror,
    it's us that will disappear.
    They supplied, we demanded.
    We never really wanted it,
    but it was branded-
    to ensure we all become left-handed.

Backwards we crawl,
    searching for our answers in flesh dolls.
    They pander propaganda we are hungry to hear,
    it's evident- the words are clear.
    Spoken from the rose veranda.
    The issue is us.
    It's me.
    It's you.
    The puppet- a consequence we choose.
    We allow the toys to spew;
    our ends are all in view.

68. My Haze- Thursday September 28, 2023 08:35 MST

A haze that lingers,
   my grip tightens as it just slips between my fingers.
   An eerie everlasting fog,
   keeps me in this perpetual cog.

Shallow breathing and my heart barely beating,
   my existence is teetering.
   I feel it down to my marrow,
   my soul aches but is kept under the foot-
   that of the false Pharaoh.

I drag the hunks of limestone through sand,
   only logs rotating beneath decrease the demand.
   A slave I am not- so he insists.
   But a slave I am, my "work" persists.

Under the sun, my thin skin blisters,

paid only in drink, doled out from his listers.
A generous, righteous leader he is-
so they say-
only those he decides shall not pay.

For today my coils are but small toils,
I am only a small brick.
This pyramid's foundation stones,
are but the beginning of what made me sick.
My mind groans-
but these stones I must place.
Until I eventually have no place.

I am free, so he says.
Even the flow of the Nile,
is under his spell of denial.
A vile existence, I search for subsistence.

This pyramid's existence?
It is not a mystery,
it's built upon my back-
my misery.

69. The Shutdown - Friday September 29, 2023 13:18 MST

In dark and damp DC alleys, screens glow blue and cold,
    the heartland's pulse, now muted, once bold.
    Steel jungles rust, their sheen turned to grime,
    in the age of excess, hope's fallen behind.

Dark clouds gather, no shelter in sight,
    in cities once bright, now choked by the night.
    Capitol Hill looms, casting a shadow of greed,
    the many left wanting, while the few feed.

In hallowed halls, where falsehoods are spun,
    drowning the voices, the many made none.
    Bars of gold bullion changing hands,
    along with grips of hundred dollar bills, in rubber bands.
    The American dream- lost, it's done.
    Dead to a scheme in which we pay the ultimate sum.

. . .

Streets erupt in protest, from souls left behind,
chasing illusions, to dreams unaligned.
Misinformed by talking heads;
We believe their lies, as we adjust the noose of our ties.
The rich grow richer each day,
while the world outside slowly decays.

The nursing home on that hill,
has all but robbed us of our choice.
They have given us a cyanide pill.
We clamor just to have a voice,
these dreadful old men- it's us they kill.
As they celebrate, even rejoice.

We have lined their pockets with our pennies;
while they create imaginary enemies.
Their positions, a stark juxtaposition,
against the people's mission.
Their evolution of our Constitution has left us
in dissolution.

70. My Rest - Saturday September 30, 2023 01:28 MST

Bequest- that is my rest,
    for the lot, for all the rest.
    In a drowning society, I pity-
    that I am privy to the sins from within.
    They start from the spine and lay deep in.

In dirt I follow,
    I am my own fallow.
    Our harvest is weak but promised thick,
    in this drought, our hearts firmly stick.
    No rains from the heaven,
    not even an ounce of leaven.
    We starve, each of us- all seven.

Four they say,
    will release us from this day.
    Some dread but we have no option other than to tread.
    To the dead, we cheer.

Salud- to all our living fears.

It's the night that follows.
    Our curtails, our hollows.
    Dread from deep within, we let the evil in.
    The chores of stores keep us tilling until tomorrow.
    In rivers deep and dry, we drain our sorrow.

Our land is unable,
    to protect us from our own fable.
    No food, we sit empty at our table.
    All seven, we stare blankly- unable.
    The promise of more,
    guarantees galore.

Nothing is here upon our shore.
    We have but seven until we wait for four more.
    Torn we grasp at our bleak soil.
    To the almighty, we promise, we're loyal.
    When will our sun set?
    Will we ever finally get- the solace, the truth?

We're broken, forgotten;
    this is our unyielding truth.

71. The Devil or Director - Sunday October 01, 2023 22:25 MST

The gold atop the hill promises boundless wealth,
    beyond what's known, no more toil in stealth.
    No more desires or yearning cries,
    their taunting humming no longer tie.
    You'll have it all, and own each string,

"The world is yours," he crooned clear;
    "Just a small price, have no fear."
    Quid pro quo,
    for every gain, something must forgo.
    It cost your essence, your honor's glow.
    "To me, your soul," he said, "and want no more."
    The pact is sealed, inked in blood's core.

You traded your soul,
    to escape life's cruel toll.
    A steep price indeed, yet hunger's now freed.
    The feast is yours for this simple creed.

The bargain struck, unique to your stake,
in this one life, only one soul to break.

Was it worth the fleeting peace?
The temporary comforts that soon annoy?
It healed your scars, showed who you are.
Desires gone, hunger afar.
Though in the company of giants, you stride,
your spirit's no longer tied.
Is a soul's worth truly so much?

A dilemma, a thirst, a consuming clutch.
Yearning for life, for a vibrant drive,
what do you price your honor, to feel alive?
It's hard to believe,
that this deal is all you'd ever need.
For we barter our time, our very line,
to faceless figures, in suits so fine.
The gains we hardly ever reap,
instead, a paycheck, a short break to keep.

See, you gave your life not to the devil, but a firm's plea,
which of the two is truly free?
For with the first, a settlement's clear,
while the latter breeds reprimands and fear.
Before you commit, here's a thought to confer:
The devil you know or an unknown employer?

WORDS ARE SNAKES WITH ARMS

72. Words are Snakes With Arms - Monday October 02, 2023 22:19 MST

In the verdant meadows of the vocal, slither,
    words like serpents, their arms tenderly wither.
    Gently they weave, through thoughts unspoken,
    ensnaring, caressing the very hearts they've broken.

Crafty and quiet, they wind through the grass,
    their arms embrace gently, though they can strangle en masse.
    A comforting croon, or a dangerous hiss,
    in the arms of alphabets, lies both peril and bliss.

Tongues of politicians, they flicker, lie and tease,
    words constrict, comfort, disarm, and please.
    With syllabic scales, through the halls they slide,
    in expressions, they curl, where secrets abide.

They grip the earnest, cradle the serene,
    coil around anguish, in veiled shades of green.

Nestled in their clasp, the love tightly wound,
through the lithe, sinuous verbs, emotions are found.

Underneath the soft belly of their lexical charm,
rests a potent force, to comfort or harm.
Winding 'round heartstrings, with tenderness they warm,
oh, behold the might, of words- snakes with arms.

Entwining through fingers, these serpents of speech,
extend arms of meaning, our souls they beseech.
To understand them, we must gently unfold,
the layers of stories, in their coils, are told.

Wield them with caution, these creatures of phrase,
in their undulating bodies, our human soul weighs.
For they are potent, these serpentine forms,
with arms to enfold, in a multitude of norms.

Ink bleeds on parchment, though the serpents don't weep,
in slumbers, their split tongues speak, in awakening, they creep.
With arms they write tales of love, anger, and charms,
in an eternal stance, we're enfolded in their arms.

Conjured from voids where silence does dwell,
the snakes bleed from the mouths of all,
ushering the sirens call.
What truths we hold near and are taught to fear-
all a facade- but letters stabbed betwixt a dreaded kabob.

Both good and evil,

a moral righteousness we are taught.
All from theories of utters, words not fought.
These omnipresent syllables have us all caught.
We pen stories, even of those who are already bought.
Our fate- a distinct smell, rancid and rotten.
Only time will tell- for words are quickly forgotten.
Winds of wisdom or torrents of harm,
such is the duality of diction,
in deeds we must sow,
for it's action that truthfully depicts our conviction.

73. Lost in the Clatter - Tuesday October 03, 2023 21:10 MST

Lost in the clatter of menial tasks, the devil croons,
    urging I sip from his flask.
Sailing through the weary spirit, drowning, somehow persisting.
I continue to drink it in,
with each taste, my soul dims.
Endless to-dos, persistent batters,
the devil outstretches a platter.

A saucer of morsels, of obligations, an unending feast,
    should I just eat a small bite from the red beast?
It's smells entice me, appetizing the buffet sits.
"Just one bite" he hisses.
I outstretch my palm, fighting all my might.
Though my reality persists.
I give in, an accept the sacrifice.
A pastry, so delicious.
My mouth salivates, my morality misses.
Shrouding my essence, the first bite lasts,
a muffled scream, squandering my past.

Threads of vitality wane, beneath the menial strain,
in the abyss of the mundane, I begin to strain.
Drenched in disdain, from the tasks that enclose,
Satan offers me warm clothes.
Away from the cold I seek.
I hesitantly accept the garments.
he says they're mine to keep.

To-do lists become chains, relentlessly confining,
in the endless sea of tasks, my spirit is sprained.
Through the drudgery, a silent plea,
it's only evil that answers me.
My obligation, my only true toll.
A lull of silence resists.
My soul the devil wants,
but he forgets;
my soul is gone, nothing persists but lists.

74. The Ghost - Wednesday October 04, 2023 20:23 MST

It haunts me night and day,
 seeping into every thought,
 it's all my consciousness can display.
 It terrorizes me beyond dismay.
 Even so, there's nothing more that I yearn for,
 than to see this ghost today.

A figment of my past: this horror will forever last.
 It's voice so seductive and elusive,
 it takes from me all hours; I am never lucid.
 It chases me throughout the day.
 It pushes me past my path, I've lost my way.
 I owe this ghost: for what I'm not sure.
 Maybe it's the debt itself that's the allure.

The ghost persists no matter how my thoughts exist,
 there is no escape,
 I search for the date, the time;

when the ghost's presence and mine,
will once again align.
One thing of which I'm certain,
is that this specter is the Oz behind the curtain.

The truth?
It's all but moot,
the haunting, for me, is my best suit.
Why do I need this horror?
Why must I give in to the allure?
The spirit is intertwined in mine,
I've drank the wine; it was at one time divine.
I know in my bones,
these groans and yearnings,
are searching for something already dead.
nothing is churning.

Possessed I cannot rest,
the facts are disgusting; but beyond the best.
The spirit itself potentially never existed,
though it's by that ghost that my very being has grown into what I
detest.

75. The Descent - Thursday October 05, 2023 20:51 MST

Engulfed by the bitter bite of binary disdain,
   in this boundless abyss of data, I wane and sustain.
   Relentlessly engulfed, a phantom, a digital stain,
   adrift, silently sinking in the remorseless main of cyberspace.

In this inevitable digital doom, I find no splatter,
   ceasing not, the keys clap with a soulless clatter.
   A maddening melody of mindless, ceaseless chatter,
   my spirit, once resilient, now hopelessly shattered.

In this binary abyss where my thumbs numbly dive,
   devoid of vitality, into an abyss, I submissively slide.
   My integrity shreds with every resigned swipe,
   reality obliterated beneath the virtual, glowing hype.

Neither a zero nor a one, in this matrix, I am undone,

in the cold, endless digital void, my essence is none.
Within these skeletal hands, devoid of any mark,
extinguished are the embers, dark is the once feeble spark.

Images, posts, specters forever secco,
behind each pixel, a forsaken human shadow.
My voice, silenced in the voracious virtual flow,
seeking truth in a realm that refuses to bestow.

In the infinite binary, a relentless brutality,
devouring, shattering through fictive virtuality.
In this synthetic sea, I find naught but disgrace,
no semblance of connectivity in this boundless digital space.

In this paradox, my existence incongruently grieves,
tethered to circuits, within the wires, my soul heaves.
Amongst the digits, my genuine breath it thieves,
my spirit, once robust, now only silently grieves.

Amidst the noise, my silent plea remains unheard,
in the infinite code, my vision incessantly blurred.
Beyond the disdain, no sight to be conferred,
lost is the glimmer of shared humanity, once assured.

Forever lost in the emotionless digital cocoon,
an off-key melody, out of tune with the human boon.
And so I type, beneath the impersonal, cold synthetic moon.
A lost wanderer in the endless, unfeeling electronic dune.

. . .

In this ceaseless search for a shred of truth so aloof,
 I find not but a spectral, unforgiving sleuth.
 In the abyss of ones and zeros, so uncouth,
 emerges a frailty, distinctly, inexorably humanproof.

76. The Road to Hell - Friday October 06, 2023 21:37 MST

In the path where fiery reckonings dwell,
　　walked I, wary, on the serpentine road to hell.
　　A vial of salvation, so they boldly tell,
　　in its liquid depths, clandestine agonies swell.

Piercing through my vein, the metallic sting,
　　a promise of salvation; dread it would bring.
　　Into my being, the alien fluid did cling,
　　a symphony of promise, with an ominous ring.

Fevered dreams wrapped around my weakened frame,
　　in this toxic salvation, I found no one to blame.
　　The path to safety alight with feverish flame,
　　in every aching bone, hissed the devils name.

Winding through my cells, an unwelcome guest,

my body contorts, in unrest, it would protest.
In the quagmire of agony, my spirit compressed,
in this suffering, a paradoxical quest.

For though my body trembles, ensnared in pain,
the serum wages war, this ailment to detain.
In the crucible of suffering, hope is not in vain,
for from these dire straits, strength I might regain.

Veins coursing with pain, in this venomous swell,
each heartbeat pulses through my personal hell.
But with every pulse, arises a tale to tell,
of a survival, born from a venomous well.

Desolation courses through, an insidious stream,
within its tumultuous flow, glimmers a dream.
A distant hope that amidst this ghastly theme,
lies a latent strength, a luminous gleam.

Through fevered nights, under despair's dark spell,
a survival uttered in every agonized cell.
This road to hell, a paradoxical well,
wherein seeds of resilience silently dwell.

Thus, in hell's depths, my spirit rebels,
against the looming darkness that forcefully quells.
For in this torturous path, my essence gels,
into a formidable might, that quietly swells.

.   .   .

My form staggers under the venom's vicious spell,
in my resolute steps, a stoic resistance dwells.
Through this horrid path, tales of endurance tell,
the road to hell, a reluctant salvation does sell.

77. My Train - Saturday October 07, 2023 10:55 MST

The whistle wails, a haunting tale,
  dark smoke veils the gleaming sun so pale.
  Coal is fed, fire's fury unassailed,
  steel wheels screech along the rail.

Conductor calls, his voice a somber wail,
  "Last call, all aboard," resounds the final sale.
  My train, it veers from its stable trail,
  left behind, a track now frail.

I stand, decision wrapped in time's firm veil,
  heart tethered, dreams unassailed.
  Back I tread, slow, on life's platform, frail,
  to catch the train, in fate's tight grail.

My hand grasps the rail onto the last car's trailing tail,
  clutching fast, against the wind's harsh flail.

Outside perched, on platform thin and stale,
rebel I stand, against the conforming gale.

Moments pass, resolve begins to pale,
    I open the door, to a future, unassailed.
    Shuffling of shoes, on wooden floors unveil,
    the train now mine, in destiny's wide vale.

Inquiries rise, where shall this journey sail?
    But destination's repute, to me, so stale.
    I care not where these iron tracks may trail,
    but that I boarded, in pursuit of the crescendo of my tale.

My liberty, beyond the confining jail,
    one day to be free- that's all I want from destiny.

78. War Torn - Sunday
October 08, 2023 22:34 MST

The buildings all stand eerily still,
    until the bombs descend, executing their will,
    urban landscapes drowned in a relentless smoke,
    peace, an illusion, and now, irreparably broke.

For centuries a rift, cavernously deep, persists,
    a tale told incessantly, through war's suffocating mists,
    destruction, death, an eternally escalating toll,
    a ceaseless torment, consuming each soul.

It never halts, this grotesquely unyielding war,
    a merciless devourer of all that was, before,
    the disease of conflict, insidiously spreading,
    through realms of despair, its dark wings are treading.

Hate, manufactured, orchestrates the doom,
    rockets weep devastation, singing a tragic tune,

the world, crumbled, utterly spent and ended,
no more bends left, every semblance of serenity upended.

Seizing futures, renewing a boundless, aching pain,
a uniform agony under this cataclysmic rain,
all are enmeshed, ensnared in this human catastrophe,
entwined in a dark tapestry, bound by despair's apathy.

Manufactured hate pervades, source of perpetual strife,
rockets shriek overhead, extinguishing all life,
the end is not nigh - it has cruelly arrived,
humanity, utterly fractured, has not survived.

Through ghostly cities, the wind howls mournful tales,
of unity shattered, of love that perpetually fails,
the abyss gazes back, into the void we descend,
no resurrections await, no wounds to mend.

This is our collective human pain, eternally profound,
an abyss of perpetual despair, where no solace is found,
a morose symphony, with notes so tragically sharp,
a boundless void, where death is the only harp.

All creation muted, under this all-consuming despair,
a universal suffering, a void, we're condemned to bear.
The saga ends not with a period, but an ellipsis, incomplete,
an eternal silence reigns, in defeat's unyielding seat.

79. The World Bleeds - Monday October 09, 2023 09:08 MST

Weeping mothers cradle memories, not sons,
all the streets reverberate with silent cries, no guns,
rubble, where once there stood homes and dreams.

Innocence lost in the explosive screams,
nurturing no more life, only death's searing seams.

Impoverished lands, no hope shall sprout,
silenced voices, that once held sway, now barely shout.
Ravaged cities lay bare, testament to a ruthless bout.
Ailing hearts seek solace in a world that's gone insane,
endless night, where sunshine never follows rain.
Lost futures, buried beneath the battle's persistent stain,

Widowed lovers stare at horizons, dull and plain,
arid fields of joy, now fertile with unyielding pain,
ravens caw, amidst the melancholic rain.

In cities crumbled, children's laughter forever bane,
    nations, once prosperous, now under strife's chain.

The universe watches, indifferent to the earthly strain,
    keening winds whistle through the hollow remains.
    Ruthlessly, humanity drowns in a sanguine sea,
    abyssal despair stretches as far as eyes can see,
    innocence forever tainted by violent decree,
    no thoughts of peace on this desolate, barren lea.
    Elegies are written in the blood of the innocently slain.

Wandering souls seek solace, but find none to gain,
    hopelessness embeds itself in every crevice, every grain,
    eternal are the scars imprinted by war's disdain,
    nurtured are the seeds that propagate the conflicts.

Wasted lands stretch across the horizon, bleak,
    infinite sadness, of which no words can speak,
    lamentations flow through the desolate creek.
    Lingering spirits of the departed, eternally seek.

Where peace is elusive, it's hate we easily find,
    entering us all, eating our hearts and minds.

Silence envelops, where once was vibrant life,
    the landscapes now host only bitterness and strife.
    Oblivion, the only respite from the perpetual rife,
    pain, a constant companion, cuts through like a knife.

. . .

Tales of happiness, now buried under layers of grief,
hollow eyes, searching for an elusive relief,
eternity weeps for the stolen, no justice, no thief.

Punctured by sorrow, the universe sighs,
aching, the earth under war's weight lies.
Infinite screams of the never-ending goodbyes,
numb, the world, under the war-torn skies.

80. Spectral Ethic - Tuesday October 10, 2023 23:01 MST

I stand, amid the stained glass light,
    as history unfolds the ghastly sight.
    A helpless soul, betrayed by one so dear,
    her essence seeks a friend to lend an ear.

Beseech I do, the specter, "What seeks thee?
    What justice served for pain, and death to flee?"
    She bids me to seek the truth and share her tale,
    that peace might find her in the lifeless vale.

Returning to the realm of present tense,
    I ponder deeply on her last defense.
    Shall I unveil the secrets dark and dire,
    expose the woman, bloodied in the mire?

The ghostly child, her vengeance mayhaps find,
    in silenced truths to those of open mind.

Caution taps upon my rattling heart,
to reckon with a specter's murderous art.

Silence or speak, the moral coil turns,
inside me, a flaming conscience sojourns.
A mystery enshrouded in misty air,
of Victorian homes, and maidens fair.

A ghostly belch from forgotten hymns,
in solemn churches, where the light grows dim.
Mingles the scent of old, forsaken dreams,
where nothing ever is quite as it seems.

81. Hopeless Toil-
Wednesday October 11, 2023
22:20 MST

In the murky abyss of labor's futile grasp,
    where endeavors wearily in vain hands clasp,
    I tread the barren soils of ceaseless toil,
    sewing seeds of hope in unyielding soil.

Grimly I press, in endeavors turned to naught,
    seeking fruit from the battles, tirelessly fought.
    The boughs hang barren, efforts unrewarded,
    into the void, my pleading cries are recorded.

A gamble, stark and perilously thin,
    is the spectral hope I shroud my dreams within.
    Into the abyss, my aspirations tumble,
    as through the dark, I blindly grope and stumble.

Even faith, a beacon faintly gleaming,

offers not salvation, but mere dreaming.
I clutch to its ethereal strand,
whilst sinking further in the mire's demand.

Through empty days, my toil's blisters resound,
seeking salvation where none is to be found.
In a vicious cycle of empty pursuit,
my spirit withers, and my pleas fall mute.

Faintly flickers the flame of undying faith,
guiding through the dark, a wraith amongst wraith.
In its fragile glow, I discern my plight,
a spectral journey through perpetual night.

What is left when even hope dares not speak,
when the vessel is shattered, the future bleak?
A melancholy tale of futile strife,
a somber journey through the wasteland of life.

In obscurity, where aspirations decay,
I dwell, entrapped by shadows, led astray.
There, the resonance of desolate despair,
howl tales of sorrow, dreadfully bare.

A tableau of drudgery, endlessly spun,
a tale of desolation, hopelessly unsung.
Within the murky caverns of despair,
resides a glimmer of hope, starkly bare.

. . .

For in the bitterness of unrewarding strife,
    often we discern the veiled truths of life.
    And though my endeavors shuck fruitless calls,
    sometimes light most brightly falls.

82. In the Desolation of Want, Quietly I Die - Thursday October 12, 2023 08:26 MST

Within the sullen caverns of disdain's embrace,
    screeches a mournful dirge, a melancholy case.
    "They must have needed it more than I," narrates fate,
    a self-elegy painted in despondent taint.

Upon the altar of liberty, my toll was laid,
    Shackles persist, in dolorous parade.
    For them, the golden dawn of freedom gleams,
    whilst I, still entwined in despondent dreams.

Their chains dissolved, into the ether parted,
    leaving me herein, woefully not started.
    They sail on waves of newfound liberty,
    I remain, bound by invisible decree.

A bitter taste of iron, the cost I bore,

lies heavy within, a relentless sore.
They are unburdened, in a jubilant glee,
in the distant realms of their stolen spree.

Through the barren fields of inequity I tread,
bearing the weight of wishes, painfully dead.
They, perhaps, did clutch it tighter, the cherished prize,
as into the abyss, my forsaken spirit flies.

Endless corridors of despair, starkly extend,
as they bask in freedoms, on which I cannot depend.
"I paid," I mutter, through the hollowed dark,
my voice fades, an unheeded remark.

The cost, engraved upon my soul, so weary and torn,
manifests a specter, of hopelessness born.
They revel amidst the liberties I sought to see,
indeed, they must have needed it more than me.

So onward, into the void of sorrow, I sink,
with nothing but lament as my bitter drink.
Enshrouded by loss, of forfeited dreams,
a spectral form in despair's relentless streams.

Thus, I dwell, amid the specters of could have been,
condemned to wander, sightless, through scenes unseen.
Faint stains of freedom, in the distance cry,
as I, in the desolation of want, quietly I die.

· · ·

Here in the abyss, where lost aspirations bleed,
my spirit, broken, succumbs to the ravenous feed.
In the bleak, forsaken realms of boundless night,
my hopes are swallowed, extinguishing the light.

And there, I dissolve, into nothing, bitterly free,
a specter, enveloped by the abyss, ceaselessly.

83. I Live my Truth - Friday October 13, 2023 10:26 MST

In the cold embrace of truths solemnly, I've died,
  witnessing my demise, where quietus and soul collide.
  Repeatedly, through the spiral of ephemeral breath,
  I've beheld the lifeless, courting a silent death.

With a vessel emptied of its sinful, sanguine wine,
  a sacrifice of vice, upon conscience's damned shrine,
  into a cave of nothingness, I descend, so desolate,
  clawing through the opaque, towards an uncertain fate.

Lying supine, my form caressed by void's eerie balm,
  a specter amidst darkness, swathed in haunting calm.
  I fade to black, the tales and glories forsaken, sold,
  a form, cold and old, submerged in silence, bold.

The abyss does not claim the entirety of me,
  a sudden voice, singular, resonates in potent plea.

Incomprehensible hymns stroke the hollowed air,
I discern a figure, glowing, laden with all the world's
love and despair.

He advances, a luminous presence in the oblique,
a maelstrom of emotions through the cavernous quiet does leak.
With each step, a symphony of pain, love, and wrath,
carries through the desolation, illuminating the path.

Closer still, he speaks, "Feed my sheep," his demand,
then vanishes, leaving solemnity where he did stand.
A tranquility, strange yet palpably true, takes steer,
as words and meditations in the sacred quiet leer.

"May the murmur of my lips, and mind's silent ode,
be embraced in thy sight, O Lord, my fortress, my abode."
Laboriously, from the cave's maw, I emerge anew,
into a realm forgiven, beneath a celestial hue.

The verdant expanses call with distant, eager bleats,
my flock, amidst the meadows, the morrow's bread greets.

A shepherd reborn, beneath the forgiving, azure sky,
guiding towards sustenance, where the rolling pastures lie.

With hope, now an ally in form gentle and fair,
I lead them forward, through the valley's cool, crisp air.
Thus, begins a journey, in the light of redemption's sun,
where truths, once a burden, now victory, has won.

84. Total Eclipse of Morality - Saturday October 14, 2023 19:12 MST

Amidst the quivering bounds of fearful guise, it swells,
a churning cauldron of terror, where silent horror dwells.
An impossible dread, a calamity, fervently astir,
engulfing serenity, in its formidable, ghastly blur.

Behold, the ring of fire, an eclipse, darkening the sphere,
shrouding our existence under it, hauntingly near.
War, it blossoms, upon sacred deserts, and within our homes,
through the corridors of ideals, a sinister tempest roams.

Democracy, once aglow with liberty's fervent sun,
now withers in the dusk, its vital light undone.
The finale, it murmurs, through the silent, despairing fear,
spilling tales of doom, into the collective ear.

With pockets barren and no shimmer of coin in sight,
hunger gnaws at our essence, in the relentless plight.

To nourish becomes a luxury, far from our desperate grasp,
as sustenance slips through fingers, in a faltering clasp.

The very air we consume, sullied, a toxic breath,
and water, once life's elixir, now a harbinger of death.
Thick and black it flows, through veins of once verdant lands,
a morbid reflection of decay, slipping through our hands.

At the precipice we stand, eyes fixed upon the abyss,
where hope is swallowed, by a spectral, venomous kiss.
The world, it teeters, on the brink of frightful despair,
engulfed, we are, in the maelstrom of a global scare.

Within this darkness, mayhap, flickers a feeble light,
a testament of resilience, amidst the cataclysmic plight.
In the footsteps of doom, the spirit, perhaps, finds its way,
to carve through the nightmare, seeking the break of day.

85. 6,294 Days Alone - Sunday October 15, 2023 22:46 MST

A sea, unforgiving but actions full of valor,
  isles besieged, where seas and sorrows meet,
  a lone mariner embarked on a quest so pallor,
  fleeing the chains, in heartbeats discreet.

A vessel, unsung, on waters obscure,
  sailed through the night, in silence it tread.
  Against ominous winds, and fortunes impure,
  through passages haunted, by spirits unfed.

Haunted tides on the ghostly horizon,
  chants of the brave, in the theatre of strife.
  Mysteries woven in the fabric of the crimson,
  threads of survival, in the quilt of life.

The chariot of escape kissed by hostile skies,
  in the theatre of the abyss where the raven flies.

A symphony of survival, in silence it lies,
an odyssey marked by the oceans howls and cries.

In the corridors of history, the waves break and resound,
a tale of the intrepid, where legends are crowned.
In the heart of the abyss, where life is confound,
there lies the saga, in mysteries profound.

86. A Wasted Life of Work - Monday October 16, 2023 21:26 MST

In the hallowed halls of toil, where the soul's dusk unfurls,
   haunted boomings resound, as relentless hours unfreeze.
   Mired in the murk, where the flame no longer burns,
   chains of drudgery bind, in blood so thick, hearts cease.

Morning's cruel herald, a tyrant bell's icy chime,
   sunders sleep's embrace, in the cold light's brutal theft.
   To the altar of anguish, feet march in sorrow's rhyme,
   offering lifeblood's hours, to gods of greed they're left.

In a coffin of concrete, where the weary spirits dwell,
   ghosts in empty vessels, eyes hollowed by despair.
   Heartbeats sync to the rhythm of a lifeless, tolling bell,
   a symphony of suffering, in the cool, merciless air.

Windows veiled in gloom, shut eyes to the sky's embrace,
   barren walls absorb the screams of dreams that slowly die.

Clock hands, executioners, sever hopes with torturous pace,
life's colors bleed away, leaving a world desolate and dry.

In the chambers of torment, where creativity is slain,
ideas imprisoned, in the fortress of rigid rules.
Passions perish, beneath the weight of a monotonous brain,
drowned in oceans of apathy, where sorrow's current pulls.

Evenings wear the shroud, of the day's departed soul,
returning to a hearth, where warmth of love turns cold.
The night, a brief respite, in the endless, crushing role,
before the dawn drags the damned, back to misery's hold.

In this eternal cycle, where the spirit is consumed,
days devolve to ashes, in the furnace of affliction.
Hopes, like dying embers, in the darkness are entombed,
leaving naught but the reaper, in life's tragic depiction.

Thus, in silence suffer, the souls lost to this plight,
invisible chains ensnare them, in a reality so grim.
Working to the call of death, in life's fading light,
a sorrowful symphony, a harrowing, hopeless hymn.

87. In her Scales- Tuesday October 17, 2023 20:50 MST

In chambers dark where justice carves its tale,
    an advocate in her veil, prevailed.
    In hallowed halls where the people bear the weight,
    of battles fought behind the gilded gate.

A mantle worn, with unyielding embrace,
    he walked the paths, a labyrinthine space.
    Misguidance masked in tender's deceitful guise,
    against the tides of falsehood, he'd arise.

The ancient scrolls, their letters cast in stone,
    in their embrace, the seeds of truth were sown.
    A journey tread with meticulous care,
    through stormy bouts, the advocate did fare.

Silver tongues of compromise entwined,
    in the stark confines of the law, their fates aligned.

A settlement in the silent vaults entombed,
justice's fire in victory's arms resumed.

In tales unwritten, his resolve shall gleam,
a warrior's spirit in the legal stream.
In the symphony where integrity sings,
his odyssey, a legacy it brings.

In the heart where fairness takes its stead,
and accountability's threads widespread,
He forged a path, a paragon's quest refined,
in the tapestry of justice, his saga intertwined.
I am my own justice- you will find.

88. Jaded, A Life Wasted - Wednesday October 18, 2023 21:15 MST

Jaded souls in silence wade.
  No care for the morning dew's embrace or light,
  weary hearts, in endless night.

Burdened shoulders, heavy, bent,
  time, a thief, in hearts spent.
  In halls of toil where all good is erased,
  despair's bitter taste is embraced.

Coins they toss, so scant and worn,
  bills like storms, relentless, scorn.
  Thrills of life, a distant shore,
  in poverty's grip, we soar no more.

Seeking paths where dreams take flight,
  a life beyond this choking night.
  Trapped in walls that bind the soul,

in life's harsh grip, we pay the toll.

Breaths we take, mere seconds bare,
in a realm stripped of purpose's care.
In a sea of tasks, meaning drowned,
hearts are lost, where hope's not found.

A plea for escape from chains so tight,
to quit the trade, seek the light.
In the heart's silent scream, hear the call,
in the forrest of pain, leaves as curtains fall.

89. Your Decision to Leap, is Mine to Keep - Thursday October 19, 2023 20:14 MST

The lie, the deceit,
    a truth in which you cannot pay,
    you can't defeat.
    Veritas always comes with a receipt.
    Deception, denial, your only resurrection.
    You live your life without any direction.

It claws incessantly at the back of your head.
    It crawls from the floor into your filthy bed.
    The ghost lies with you, laying in state.
    Trapped in a cathedral of your own fate.
    Decisions made, paths crossed.
    The blood dripping from your palms-
    it's not from loss.
    It was a conscious thought to sever that horse's head.
    Bleeding in silence, it lays in quietly beside your pillow-
    but that horse- is not dead.

. . .

It treads calmly through the green grasses,
  bleeding in an alien fashion, slow from its neck.
  Trampling rocks with unkempt hooves- your greed.
  It feeds on your darkest innermost thoughts.
  A mouth or teeth- it does not need.
  You ignore the stench, though it has burrowed,
  into your spoiled nostrils; in your spoiled souls it furrows.

It's life you took- so at least you thought.
  It's inescapable, a palpable thought.
  You hear the screams, see past the decay,
  To know that horse is you- just not today.
  It will ride full bodied atop a hill from a distance.
  You will stumble to it, remiss of what you did.
  Inaction is as much of an action as an act itself.
  This is not something in which you can just place on a shelf.

It boils your mind, there's nothing left to find.
  It's only you that has created this bind.

90. Dead Aspirations - Friday October 20, 2023 19:47 MST

A palpable feeling of peeling,
　　my sense from reality, in incessant jeering.
　　My thoughts collide against one another,
　　a juxtaposition between hate and endearing,
　　this disgusting feeling.

A visage of potential, what once was there,
　　now dulled by the hands of time, the unfair...
　　I glance at the past, its scorn is leering,
　　a garden of dreams, now withered and reeling.

The ghost of what could have been, quietly sneering,
　　an effigy of hope, in the dusk disappearing.
　　A labyrinth of regret, my soul is veering,
　　towards a horizon of mediocrity, bleak and unyielding.

Each morning's mirror reflects a facade, so deceiving,

the candle's wick of ambition, faintly flickering.
In the quiet despair, I search for meaning,
a battle with self, in silence seething.

In the mire of disdain, my spirit is floundering,
even the sliver of hope, in the abyss is dimming.
Each tentative step towards change, fear is smothering,
the quest to reclaim the lost self, futile and blurring.

Though the road is endless and the night is leering,
in the core of despair, merely defeat is stirring,
The tale's ink has dried, no chance for rewriting,
a futile fight to regain the essence, now disappearing

91. The Nothingness Analyst - Saturday October 21, 2023 13:21 MST

A screaming inside, a loud noise I cannot hide,
   it triggers me, pushes out rationality.
   This anger, this disdain, is my reality.
   It breathes not of one source,
   instead it's born of many.
   The cry of the alarm clock each day,
   the ding of emails showing up on my display.
   The bleeding clacking of keys, wrists wrought in pain,
   my elbows no longer bend, my back numb in pain.

In this grey cubicle, my dreams slowly fray,
   a mosaic of monotony, colorless and grey.
   The ticking of the clock, a relentless decay,
   a sick reminder of life slipping away.

The screech of the chair, the hum of the screen,
   an orchestrated cacophony of the unseen.

Invisible shackles, a silent, soul-crushing routine,
a prison of triviality, where hopes lean.

Each stroke on the keyboard, a stab at the core,
a gaping void grows, it's hard to ignore.
The mirage of purpose, farther from shore,
a numbing surrender to the mundane chore.

The buzzing of fluorescents, a cold sterile light,
cast down the essence of plight.
A labyrinth of worthlessness, no end in sight,
an exhausting battle, with no will to fight.

The clamor of expectations, a heavy chain,
bearing the weight, I endure the strain.
The allure of escape, a desperate refrain,
but the cycle repeats, an endless, draining drain.

A cry for release, but bound by the dread,
of a future tethered to this thread of lead.
A yearning for the sky, but I am anchored to the bed,
in the realm of repetition, my spirit is shred.

The final bell tolls, the end of the ride,
a surrender to monotony, dreams cast aside.

In the stale air, even hope has died,
in the relentless mundane, my soul is tied.

. . .

So I drift in the abyss of the everyday grind,
  a ceaseless loop, a prison of the mind.

No way out, no solace to find,
  in the cold clutches of monotony, I'm confined.

92. The Endgame of Time - Sunday October 22, 2023 13:21 MST

An ethereal emphasis on reality,
    my subsistence questions my own triviality.

On the last day of dark, will the next dawn yield any proof?
    Is my entire existence a futile persistence?
    The point is moot.
    My tomorrows will not be written in a way so acute,
    for the next to remember.
    My troubles today are excruciating but-
    in one hundred years, they will be erased.
    By new faces, new lives burdened with the existence of their own
    lies, their cries will veil the skies, as mine fades into the ties,
    of a corporate disguise, where no stockholder replies.

In the grand illusion of life, our acts are but brief shows,
    a blink amid eternal throes, a quiet cry no one knows.
    The monuments of pride, the castles in the air,
    will crumble with the tide, in time's unforgiving glare.

WORDS ARE SNAKES WITH ARMS

the happiness we chase, the fears we face,
will vanish without a trace, as new sorrows replace.

Our legacies are mere fantasies, fleeting sparks in the dark vastness,
    in the endless cosmic tapestry, our lives are but a fleeting, fading
    gloss. The indelible mark we yearn to engrave upon the face of
    eternity, is but a feeble wave, lost in nothingness' serenity.
    The world will move, with or without our proofs,
    our essence will dissolve, as the ages evolve.

The ink of life will dry, the tales of us will die,
    with nary a sigh, under the indifferent sky.
    Our dreams of enduring fame, are but fuel to the flame,
    of the everlasting, unyielding deadly game.
    The names we strive to etch in stone, will be overgrown,
    erased and overthrown, our existence disowned.

So, in the face of eternity, we stand, transient as the shifting sand,
    our lives but a single strand, in the unending, infinite land.
    As the future unfurls, and swallows our world,
    we're but stardust hurled, in the abyss twirled.
    Our cries of despair and hope, are but a transient trope,
    a fleeting, elusive slope, in eternity's vast scope.

93. A Hunger for Finality - Monday October 23, 2023 20:57 MST

In abyssal waters, immersed I dwell,
a domain of desolation, a soundless yell.
Overhead, the sinister currents flow,
drowning in the darkness, in depths below.

A realm so dull, a monotonous gray,
where my doppelgänger and I have lost our way.
Hope's flame extinguished, the fire dead,
filling the vast void of the soul with lead.

The world, a menial triviality,
where only pain holds true, all with breath shall decay.
Each breath, a burden, heavy and cold,
in the icy arms of despair, enfold.

In humanities embrace, where light recoils,
a heart withered, in sorrow's soils.

In the leaders chambers, where love should tread,
resides the ghost of happiness, long dead.

The skies weep tears, in torrents they fall,
resounding the heart's relentless squall.
Vistas of gloom stretch far and wide,
in the dreadful silence where souls collide.

Heaven's melodies in agony twist,
a symphony of suffering, in the mist.
Endless nights woven in the fabric of time,
a passionate crime of torment, a mountain to climb.

Forlorn spirits in the chasm lost,
on tempestuous seas, forever tossed.
In the paralyzing grip of dread's frost,
in realms of nothingness, forever crossed.

In every corner, darkness breeds,
a pestilence of void, where light recedes.
A bleeding of the consciousness, sin is oozing out,
a melancholic orchestra, from cage to cage.

In the crucible of existence, spirits are tried,
where dreams are murdered, and hopes have died.
In over my head, in the quicksand of despair,
sinking in the silence, gasping for air.
I want nothing more, nothing less. I reside to my fate.
Please grant me peace- rest.

94. The Incursion - Tuesday October 24, 2023 20:44 MST

The hairs on the back of my neck stand up,
    it's looming, there is an impending storm grooming.
    The hate is the diagnosis, war an irrefutable symptom,
    in ancient lands where olives and histories bloom.

The sky weeps ashes, as ancient stones bleed,
    a collision of faiths, torn by creed.
    Where prophets once walked, now drugs with legs fight,
    silent cries call through the enduring night.

Beneath the veil of discord, humanity's face grows pale,
    as embers of hope struggle against the hateful gale.
    The wall, a silent witness to the raging storm,
    yearns for the soft hymns of peace to transform.

Amidst the fallen leaves, memories of peace are but faint,
    in every heart, the desire for solace paints,

a picture of unity, a dream of a land serene,
where olive branches mend the gaps, unseen.

The rhythm of bombs disrupts the ancient chant,
as faces of innocence bear the brutish rant.
In the heart of turmoil, resilient seeds sow,
in the cradle of civilization, hopes daringly grow.

In every sunset's glow, the weary pray,
for the dawn of understanding to alight the fray.
May the winds of change gently sweep,
and heal the land where history sleeps.

The righteousness of those whom protect truth and life-
the monsters shall feel their full might.
The city of the damned will crumble,
it will fall in a gradual but swift stumble.
Our cause- one of veritas and light.
We must never yield- never surrender from this fight.
There may be foes among multiple fronts- but
the might of Israel will always stand upfront.

95. The ill-Gotten Gains, Welcome Mr. Speaker - Wednesday October 25, 2023 21:02 MST

An all consuming weight, a petrifying terror,
  silent to all- lest the bearer.
  The warmth of a forgiving solitude, ripped violently away,
  leave the holder cold- out in the fray.
  The toil laments, even the spoils of the bent.
  The ill-gotten gains become the only truth of the politician-
  their true common cents.

A liar brews in the cauldron of political stew,
  blackened skies pour sorrow's viscous ooze.
  Floods of despair drown the house of hope,
  mountains crumble under the bleakness of nihilistic throes.

In the hallowed halls of tragedy, the Senate does perform,
  a morbid ballet, where lost souls squirm.
  The canvas of existence, smeared with the grotesque,
  painting images of doom, where no heart finds rest.

. . .

Winds taunt the laments of forsaken spirits,
　　trees bereft of leaves, stand as lifeless hermits.
　　A sun, once radiant, now shrouded in perpetual eclipse,
　　bathing the world in an apocalyptic abyss.

Oceans churn with the bitterness of a thousand tears,
　　waves crash against the shorelines of fear.
　　Each tide, a messenger of tumultuous throes,
　　where love sinks, and only the anguish floats.

Blossoms of joy wither in the rose garden of the mind,
　　petrified petals fall, leaving happiness behind.
　　Thorns of torment entwine the pathways of thought,
　　as democracy once vibrant, in sorrow are caught.

Nurturer Earth, now a barren mother,
　　her womb desolate, as one forsaken by a lover.
　　No seeds of tomorrow in her scorched bosom lie,
　　only remnants of life, under a mourning sky.

In the crucible of chaos, humanity dissolves,
　　in a solvent of suffering, where no problem solves.
　　The symphony of existence, now a discordant sound,
　　rocks dropped into the void, where only dread is found.

Buildings stand like tombstones, marking dead aspirations,
　　streets, the arteries, bleed the pain of desolation.
　　Windows, the eyes to the soul of the city, shattered,
　　reflecting the fragments of lives, hopelessly battered.

· · ·

A merciless night, eternal, devoid of dawn's embrace,
stars flicker out, leaving the heavens a darkened space.
Each thread of life's being, unraveled and torn,
in the loom of loss, where despair is born.

Life as we know it is torn, a reality unwoven,
where promises perish, and truths are broken.
In this realm of ruin, where the honest descend,
existence ebbs away, in a sorrow without end.
Welcome Mr. Speaker- will your gavel rule in truth?
Or shall it sadistically bend all the way to the voting booth?

96. We Feed the Beast we Fear - Thursday October 26, 2023 08:15 MST

It rolls in, cloaked by the fog.
　　It hides in plain sight, no need to retreat back to the bog.
　　It wears sheep's clothing but cannot hide its yellow eyes.
　　Its snout peeks from beneath the wool.
　　How can we be fooled by this beast drizzling drool.
　　Its intentions so clear.

It speaks in a hiss, a tongue of the venomous snake.
　　In the garden of mind, where our fears and insecurities rake.
　　Casting shades long and eerie, darkening the soul's terrain,
　　an orchestra of despair plays the symphony of pain.

It walks among us, a malevolent specter, in daylight's cruel test,
　　its footsteps resound with the sorrows of the oppressed.
　　In the hollows of hearts, where the cries of agony reside,
　　it builds its abode, in the darkness, it does hide.

. . .

It feasts on the spirit, a voracious, insatiable leech,
  sucking the marrow of hope, leaving the bones of desolation in its
  reach.

In its wake, a barren landscape, where life is bled dry,
  leaving the fields of dreams, under a merciless sky.

It wears the mask, a grotesque visage of ill intent,
  in its eyes, the flames of turmoil perpetually ferment.
  In its presence, the air thickens with the weight of dread,
  a suffocating silence, where words of comfort flee and fled.

It etches its legacy, in the annals of souls with a caustic quill,
  writing tales of torment, in the ink of despair's spill.
  Its chapters unfold, a never-ending saga of relentless plight,
  pages filled with shadows, obscuring the realms of light.

It stitches it's fabric, in the looms of psyche with threads grim,
  crafting garments of sorrow, wearing the spirit thin.
  Draped in its creations, the souls wander lost and forlorn,
  in a maze of misery, where they are relentlessly worn.

Its a puppeteer, manipulating the strings of fate,
  in its guise, where hope is brutally desecrate.
  The stages set with scenery of ruin and dire straits,
  where happiness is held, behind impenetrable gates.

It extends its dominion, a kingdom built on sands of suffering,
  its towers loom, casting shadows, chilling and smothering.
  Its ramparts guarded by the legions of fear and doubt,

in its dungeons, the flames of hope are mercilessly put out.

In its rule, the sky weeps tears of relentless woe,
　　rivers flow with the currents of sorrow's undertow.
　　Through the realms of reality, its ominous winds blow,
　　leaving the landscape ravaged, in the afterglow.

97. By This Tempest of Fear - Friday October 27, 2023 18:45 MST

Each rustle of doubt, a lash, severe.
    The storm, a relentless overseer,
    it's every gust, a mocking jeer.

The clouds of dread, they coalesce,
    in the chambers of my mind, they press.
    A relentless siege, an eerie caress,
    each moment a burgeoning, boundless stress.

The mirror reflects a face, so pale,
    beneath the storm's relentless gale.
    My resolve, once sturdy, now frail,
    each hope seems destined to fail.

Amidst this tempest of despair,
    lies a haunting dead face, fair and rare.
    It speaks of nothingness and dread, floating in air,

urging me to bear, to collapse and pair my existence with theirs.

I reach within, the storm to quell,
  but the weather is not what it seems;
  it's a conjured being from Hell.
  Lurking and luring.
  To break, enrich- embrace this self-imposed spell.
  With a breath of chalk-dust thick smoke, my head immerses itself in
  the cloud, drudging deep in the doubts of my spine, it coils my
  mind.

In the eye of the storm, my own hesitations, my fears lay bare,
  a chance to slip away, to engulf myself in a blanket of sullen-rich
  despair. Between the sheets, the tempest continues to relentlessly
  stare. There are no eyes looking back through the glare,
  only a looming inflection of my own fire.
  a calming chaos of a soul in disrepair.

The voice continues, "Oh, I've been waiting for you...",
  a haunting melody that leads me like the calls of a siren.
  My knees violently buckle, colliding with the concrete in a
grotesque
  thud.
  The voice seethes, "...yes...",
  I relentlessly draw my last breath.
  It sullies me into a breadth of itself.
  The mirrors surrounding grow lips.
  I can't do this alone.
  My burden carried, added within the pool of souls.
  I am part of the pulls.
  I crawl into the night,
  into the tempest's storm, I no longer can fight.

98. October's First Snow - Saturday October 28, 2023 21:22 MST

Snow blankets the earth, my spirit conceals,
    a somber silhouette in the icy fields.
    A chilling unease, through my heart it steals,
    in every flake, life's harshness reveals.

Frosty winds bellow with the sorrow I feel,
    a cruel, relentless, unending ordeal.
    In the heart of winter, where happiness kneels,
    my jaded soul, in coldness, it reels.

Working in vain, in the merciless chill,
    thoughts of warmth, the cold continues to kill.
    Each effort made, a battle uphill,
    a fading hope, in the frosty wind's shrill.

Dilapidated dreams, in the snow they lie,
    buried beneath the cold, sorrowful sky.

An unredeemed share, as life passes by,
in the bitterness, dreams wither and die.

A labyrinth of sorrow, in snow's embrace,
where all is lost, in the cold's vast space.
Tired eyes look for hope, but none they trace,
in the icy grip, where heartaches replace.

An enduring night, in the cold's harsh regime,
where the canvas of life paints a sorrowful theme.
An eternal struggle, a shattered dream,
in the frosty silence, where sorrows scream.

In the unyielding cold, hopes continue to fade,
in the vast, merciless, and endless shade.
Where warmth and love are forever delayed,
in the heart of winter, where sadness is laid.
It's myself, not the snow, that I want to evade.

99. I Desperately Need a Small Win - Sunday October 29, 2023 11:18 MST

Surrounded by invoking perpetual failures,
    every time I stand, I am knocked back again.
    My grin flashes orange, teeth stained from blood's tint.
    If only life could give a small signal-
    I need but one small win.
    Something to keep me going, in this daily chagrin.

In this relentless life of despair,
    where only anger stands thick, it lingers in the air.
    Each morning heralds a battle, a sorrow to bear,
    an endless throbbing in the hollow of fair.

The cruel hands of fate, tightly wound around the throat,
    each gasp for hope, a desperate, futile dote.
    The mocking symphony of destiny, a relentless gloat,
    in the barren streets, despair freely floats.

. . .

With every cracking of my eyes, the cold reality stings,
    a reminder of broken dreams, and relentless pings.
    The mirror reflects a face, sorrow clings,
    a silhouette of defeat, only silence it brings.

The world turns its back, the heavens scorn,
    in the abyss of the forgotten, my spirit is torn.
    The cold, mocking laughter of fate is borne,
    in the heart of the beaten, dreams lay forlorn.

Each effort to rise, a defeat to the cruel sky,
    an endless maze of failure, as time whisks by.
    The mocking tick of the clock, a sigh,
    a reminder of the relentless hands of fate, nigh.

In the gloom of the night, darkness sneers,
    a companion to the lonely heart, it leers.
    The cold moon casts looming figures of ancient fears,
    a bitter serenade to the fallen tears.

The relentless grind of days, a bitter pill,
    a banquet of despair, served against my will.
    In the harsh realm of reality, I lay frozen still,
    a graveyard of hope, on despair's windowsill.

The world spins on, indifferent to the silent plea,
    an orchestra of failure, life's mocking decree.
    In the cold eyes of fate, no reprieve I see,
    bound to the wheel of monotony- mediocrity, my spirit not free.

. . .

So, with a heart heavy with tales of the grim,
   I tread on the path of dead outlines, at destiny's whim.
   The insult each day adds to my injury, so grim,
   in a body of disrepair, hope's light grows dim.
   I desperately need a small win.

100. Let Them Drown Themselves in Their Cowardly Tunnels - Monday October 30, 2023 21:06 MST

For their queries, they don a mask, a veil so thin, a daunting task.
In damp dank tunnels they lurk, in propaganda they bask, weaving webs in the darkness, an ominous flask.
Their words drip with honey, a venomous ruse, a symphony of deceit, in ideals of misuse.

In corridors of power, where swords resound, their footsteps tread lightly, where conspiracies abound.
A puppetry of pretense, in silence they tread, orchestrating illusions, in which many believe.

In my house of justice, our truths penetrate- ever corrupting the soil, not with malice and hate or revenge.
It's justice- which is our best defense.
Their lies twist and turn, in a suffocating embrace, choking the truth, in a disheartening grace.

. . .

But fear not the evil, or the lies they have spun, for in the light
    of integrity, their deceit will come undone.
    In the hearts of the just, a resilience is found, an unwavering spirit,
    where truth does resound.

So let us stand firm, against pretense and deceit, in honesty's abode
    where diverse souls meet.
    We welcome with open arms—the poor, the elite, the artisans in
    foundries, where heart and metal greet.
    Our hearts harbor no malice, in love's warmth they bask, diversity
    our creed, in its richness, we bask.
    In the arena of discourse, where ideas intersect, our debates outline
    respect, a symphony perfect.
    United we stand, our voices in harmony soar, banishing Hamas,
    embracing truth's core.
    They will eat their own lies- extinguishing their own lives.

WORDS ARE SNAKES WITH ARMS

101. Halloween's True Horrors - Tuesday October 31, 2023 20:14 MST

In a world awash with pain, the ink of the day bleeds,
  upon our consciousness of parchment, each headline leaves its
  seeds.

A tale of metal-rich realms, the sky's miners set their deeds.
  Down on Earth, the silicon trails demand nature's heeds.
  A mourning crowd seeks solace, for justice they still plead,
  in lands where memories of a crush, still heavily impede the telecom
  giant treads uneasy on Iberian stead.
  A clean exit yearned, tangles of past misdeeds. Mislead-
  in eastern lands, a tax ascends on black gold's creed,
  a visage of numbers, a tango of greed, the needy still in need-
  across the sea, a deadly chase ends, hearts still bleed; a tale of
  gun smoke and loss, the violent seed.

Rallies roar in ancient lands, for them- they intercede.
  A cry for peace, a quest for rights, in unity they proceed.
  The globe spins, yet at each turn, new wounds are freed,

in a grapple of power, the mighty oft ignore the meek's plead.

Amidst the chaos, the heaven's gaze, on mortal misdeeds,
    bound by the devils rules, they watch as the earthly garden thickens
    in poisoned weeds.
    In realms afar, the lunar clans with earthly kin accede,
    a fate of hope, mayhaps a balm for the earthly greed.

In lands of mystic rivers, the salty tides proceed,
    a crabber's woe, a symbol of nature's urgent need.
    From the celestial to the terrestrial, the tales of today lead-
    a mosaic of human endeavor, in joy and sorrow, life's bead.

As the stories weave the fabric of today, take heed,
    each stitch a choice, a chance for love to supersede.
    The horrors of life continue, as the earthly actors proceed
    in the grand tale of existence, every action is a seed.
    On this Halloween the true terrors are greed, war, lies-
    lore spread from the true demons- paid off policymakers, they
    commit treason.
    They even dictate the time; they change our seasons.
    We must band as one, to run, lift the daylight savings pun.
    They pit us against each other, one on one.
    To put us in a veil; protecting their pockets and taking our lives.

102. Humanity's Arc is Burning - Wednesday November 01, 2023 19:59 MST

A god that weeps and dead men that pray-

in the alleyways where dirty syringes drop,
   God weeps, his tears drown browned lawns.
   Brick-built barricades, where the hopeless huddle,
   dreams drenched in the deluge of disregard.

The marionettes march, strings pulled by power,
   their pockets lined with the poverty of the many.
   In their silhouettes, the cold creeps, a relentless raider,
   silent thieves in the night, swiping warmth from the weak.

Golden tongues of the deceitful, weave tales of silver,
   in the chambers of choice, corruption festers.
   Their laughter, a symphony that serenades suffering,
   playing the opus of oppression on heartstrings of the helpless.

. . .

The furnace of greed consumes the fabric of fellowship,
in its flames, the threads of trust and truth are torched.
A blanket of tumult, woven with the wool of wrath,
hangs heavy over the halls of hope, obscuring the divine design.

In the crowded bars where empathy is marring,
an escape of fraternity flourishes.
Malice, the malicious mower, cuts down the brown blades of dying
grass, no more belonging.
Only ceaseless longing.
Leaving Mr. Jones' landscape littered with the leaves of loathing.

Eyes, empty of empathy, look towards the heavens,
seeking signs in a sky obscured by suffering.
Hands, the footprint of humanity, now clenched in conflict,
in the silence of the souls, the prayers of the dead reverberate.

A God who gave the tools to build bridges, not barriers,
weeps at the walls wrought by wickedness.
The dead, their spirits shackled by sorrow's chains,
pray for the passage to a panorama of peace and purpose.
You see, our prayers are answered but only to the blind-
we search empty handed for answers clearly outlined.
A brining cauldron of anger, fear of the unknown.
We know the answers, we just cannot trust-
the words of truth sewn.

103. Destiny Leers in the Mirror - Thursday November 02, 2023 20:00 MST

A visage awaits, the specter of a soul I'm bound to greet again; my
soulmate.

In a world awash with déjà vu, our paths shall intertwine, amen- I
murmur beneath my breath- the clock strikes ten.
I strain to see, too fail to pierce beyond that lopsided leer,
a crooked grin that guards the gate to memories so dear.

A white line of sin, their silence loud as a mime,
miming the voiceless pantomime of a bygone, faded time.
Through the epochs, feet have tread a path so worn, so fine,
marching in spectral lockstep, along the precipice of time.

Onward I venture, into the arms of this phantasmal embrace,
with every step, their countenance dims, retreating from my chase.
Journeying beneath the burnished sun of a late November sky,
my skin bakes under its fervent gaze from the heavens high.

. . .

Leaves pirouette, waltzing to the tune of the autumnal breeze,
    a rustling murmur through the trees, a natural symphony to please.
    Weakness seizes, a subtle foe, my knees betray their former might,
    folding beneath the weight of a presence just out of sight.

In the distance, a cacophony, the world's relentless buzz,
    while my heart keeps time with a rhythm only a lost soul does.
    A wanderer's burden grows heavy, with every mile, every toll,
    for the reunion that beckons is a balm to the weary soul.

But the person I seek is a mirage of the one I once held dear,
    in this masquerade of time, everything shall disappear.
    Estranged and altered by life's cruel, relentless pace,
    all that was once sacrosanct has vanished without a trace.

The figure I first encountered in the naive hour of my birth,
    is the one I'll encounter last, when I part from this Earth.
    In this destined meeting, there's a strangeness in the air,
    it's them, though subtly not – an enigma, a visage eerily fair.

With every intention to peer through this mortal mask's guise,
    I find my vision thwarted, my efforts met with silent cries.

My entire sojourn through mortality,
    a tale soiled with Gossamer lace,
    reveals itself to be naught but a mirage in time's unyielding space.

Could it be, this mortal coil, this life's labyrinthine race,

is but a fleeting dream, a figment, a spectral trace?
And the soul I seek, that familiar face once so bright and fair,
is lost amidst the crowd of time, a lost wind in the air.

Thus, I ponder, as I traverse this temporal realm's vast sea,
is the journey more profound than the destination could ever be?
For in seeking that lost visage, that desperate tender hour,
I find the passage lined with lessons, growth, and inner power.

In every fleeting encounter, in each ephemeral embrace,
we find the endless cycle of loss and grace.
And as I walk this mortal plane, with faltering step and stance,
I embrace the walk of existence, life's eternal, fateful lance.
I tread forward, as I must. Though my eyes drip with tiredness, I've
lost even all lust.
My ambitions: from dust to dust.
I trace the path of those before me.
Continuing with this trance; I walk straight even though I have no
chance.

104. The Ethos of Humanity - Friday November 03, 2023 20:45 MST

It rolls in, like a wave of sin.
   It engulfs you, covering every inch of skin.
   A testimony that will result in no alimony,
   the stretch of being a phony- it burns like an alloy.
   A thermite bomb shall initiate an unrivaled calm.
   It must be gouged out of your skin,
   the pain is nothing akin to the sin.

The dim light never stops, it never begins.
   for in the darks of the parks, the sparks of addiction fly.
   The living dead meander weariless, in tattered garb,
   they refuse to dress.
   Their hair is a share, a testament to the crime,
   that civilization has decided to enshrine.
   You see, the life you envy is an envoy of destruction.
   An element of nothing- a facade of construction.

A lie is the truth if you decide it so.

We lie to ourselves in every single throw.
It burrows deep, the secrets we keep.
The shouts fall hollow, acquitting our sorrow.
We hide that we are the fraud.
No matter their strength, no matter how they prod.
It's the person in the mirror that reflects the fear.

We waste our time in haste serving the subservient ideas,
  they choose to steer us into tears.
A separation that is unclear, an evidentiary smidge,
  our tender Keir is full, but not of a soul.
It brims with a flimsy tie, dangling from our necks,
  catching the executioner's eye.
They say the killers wear masks- I disagree.
I plea that their veil is one of truth, ours of flee.

When will we ever accept who we're truly meant to be?
  Destiny laughs at our failed guise of cloths hiding demise,
  our own mortality stares directly into our tired eyes.
No matter our occupation or translation we cannot hide,
  our true nature is not able to subside.
Sure, there's fire and we even found a way to weaponize,
  our own sense of soprattutto; our egos all we can bear to follow.
When it turns, the oceans will churn showing our turn.
We will roll to the tides, no matter what you idealize.

105. Divine Intervention - Saturday November 04, 2023 14:28 MST

My diction is not a conviction, not a mention of the hole.
  An observer sees what others cannot.
  A fight between an old man and a park bench ensues.
  Imagining grandeur, his rambling to peruse,
  thoughts of greatness- what could have been.
  An improvisation destined to fall on his face.
  Is it better to accept mediocrity or take the opportunity-
  one where you may fall.

A premier, an usher of expectations stand tall,
  three-quarters disappear, confidence clears
  a way to the best day of one's life,
  it balances delicately on the edge of the knife.
  A riveting opportunity to blur the lines-
  destiny eventually finds the strength;
  to knock the opponent to the floor.
  A fairytale that opens a door.

.   .   .

No more private moments, no more bones.
Success unimaginable- it's calling from atop the stairs,
we cannot do anything wrong; a living embodiment,
an infuriating tale- to sell the wind,
to a faulty sail.
Jealousy and success- the price of the top.
The storm-front looms precariously from the peak.
There's more to seek as journeys start to speak.
Patiently the world waits in a three legged chair,
ability questioned, there is nothing that's fair.
In the odyssey that swings away,
to weather the coming force of righteousness to pay.

Our possibilities are limited to the fact that we are nothing- but
dreams built upon others backs.
A carnivorous carnival- clever and entertaining.
It's odd that we are the only ones straining.
A blind flight, it won't pass.
"I'm afraid of it." the old man admits.
Defeated, he takes a seat.
The park bench permits destiny in exchange for a promise- the
subservient dagger draws in.

106. Daylight Savings Crime - Sunday November 05, 2023 11:23 MST

Juxtaposed against deception and perception, the puppeteers atop
the sliver hill- manipulate time itself - just for the thrill.
The result?
The cost skyrockets up, so we ration our medications,
crush our pills, only half today - after all, it's less of a day,
but we have no say.

Why do they choose to hang us from our own neckties?
Taxation without representation morphed into a grotesque
requirement for college education.
A tea party not in Boston Harbor -
we no longer Wish to barter with hesitation. Our frustrations left
silent, drifting into the abyss from Plymouth Rock.

They tape our mouths shut - robbing us of our ability to talk.
The control leeches from the swamps into our skin, it boils us
something akin to sin. The action is not as pure-hearted and simple
as just changing back the hour of the clock- it's a control bleeding

WORDS ARE SNAKES WITH ARMS

our stock.

We are the animals in their zoo - these elephants and donkeys are
    our keepers too. Their intent is to enshroud us in a state of lament-
    burying us in layers of cement.
    From our strings, they move our mouths, pit us against one another,
    a grouse.

Underneath the House's silent gaze, we begin to part with our daze,
    question the puppeteers, their cryptic maze.
    Are we to be forever bound, our hopes cast into the ground?
    To be mere flesh dolls, ideas that what we could pronounce?

No! Let the strings that bind us fray and snap,
    refuse to be lured into their cunning trap.
    They've turned our schools into factories, our dreams into fallacies,
    made us pawns in their grand economies.

Let us unravel their legislation of lies,
    peer beyond their smoke, their mirrors, their disguise.
    Take back our voices, our rightful due,
    reclaim the narrative, start anew.

We shall not be mere ants in their halls of power,
    nor shall we let our vibrant hues to dully cower.
    Rise, though our pockets are empty, our spirits remain wealthy,
    against the puppeteers, we stand united, stealthy.

Let the Boston Harbor once again hear our plea,
    as we toss their tea, claim our destiny.

No longer animals caged by political zookeepers' will,
we'll stand tall, reclaim the hill.

For the hour is not theirs to take nor give,
in our time, by our rules, we choose to live.
So we snip the strings, cast off the yoke,
unveil the truth beneath the smoke.

Our stock won't bleed for their amusement,
we'll heal, we'll thrive, we'll seek improvement.
In unity we find our voice, in solidarity, our choice,
together we'll vote, together- our body's our choice.

Gone are the days of the silent grouse,
we are the tempest they cannot douse.
From Plymouth Rock to every street,
our march resounds, our drums beat.

We are not the puppeteers' toys to control,
we are the heart, the spirit, the soul.
And from this day until the end of the clock,
we'll be the change, the key, the lock.

107. I Might not Make it Through the Night - Monday November 06, 2023 20:44 MST

In the quiet fold of the evening's sigh,
    where light recedes, and day yells out goodbye;
    succumb, succumb to the numbing throbbing in my vest.

Though pages in their final chapter concede,
    embracing the finality with a silent creed;
    they succumb through the numbing throbbing best.

Forgotten souls, who've seen their filthy faces turn,
    fall deep into the holes of a dirty syringe's greed.
    Lament not the transient, for we do not feel or yearn;
    it's only the escape for which we kill to earn.
    Succumb, succumb- intoxication feeds our chest.

Restless dreamers, chasing our red hot spoons cry,
    we lack mortality- we cannot ever die.
    Realize too soon that existences claimed cannot be tamed;

our blown out veins succumb to the time,
each nostril spews blood with every line.
Recede from the plea, sit quietly in the dark.
the very substances our savior- over prescribes us stark.

Solemn watchers, with eyes burning vacant bazaars,
witnessing night unveil its ripping scars;
it's a haunting sound- akin to canvas ripping.
Succumb, succumb to the echoing gun's lies.

You, my kin, bereft the Capitol's soft lamp light,
they walked us on ropes, leading us until it's too bright.
We follow to their gallows, eyes shut and ears bludgeoned.
Succumb, succumb to the fight- an eternal quest.
Or decide that we the people shan't relent-
until truth washes the sullied halls where all our money has been
spent in ungodly ways.

108. My Dead End - Tuesday November 07, 2023 20:29 MST

In the consciousness of my mind lies a somber dead end,
a place where I wither, and hope cannot mend.
No roads lead beyond, no escape from this night,
at the dead end, we're trapped, in eternal twilight.

The street is a calamity of voices, none my own,
just relentless ramblings, as we journey along.
The sidewalks seem to weep, and the sky is red,
at the dead end, we're lost in the depths of my head.

In this bleak corner, where my sanity shall sway,
there's a chance for destruction, to quiet the thoughts,
even if just for a day.
Sometimes a dead end is where we must dwell,
to mourn what is lost, in a sorrowful hell.

For at the end of all things, when all hope seems to wane,

we can grieve for our losses, our hearts filled with pain.
In the silence of endings, we mourn what's no more,
at the dead end, we grieve for the closed, final door.
My head is my prison, my body keeps it tightly shackled.
It's only the devil's voice that emits the cackle.

109. A Prisoner of a Magic Circle - Wednesday November 08, 2023 20:44 MST

Ensnared we slay our truths to only delay,
all we want is to hear the lie,
the falsehood that allows us at night to lay.
To lay in a false sense of security in a blanket of leis.
We give not even a second thought to those who pay.

We pray away our sins, jeering our noses down on limbs,
those deemed unworthy- but to who?
Who manufactured these falsehoods that we hold true?
The fabric of our society, our perpetual glue.
we may have evolved but our thoughts are not new.
Our desires perspire beneath our linen skins.
Garb hides our physical flaws but not our sin.

"We believe!"- they chant in unison.
A rhythmic taunting, a systematic haunting.
I too believe, I'm not entirely a fool.
That is not evident from my drool.

I chant the same song, maybe I believe it too.
I'm unsure- the facilitation of parturition is the lure.
I bit- hook line and sinker; now here I sit.

On second thought I ought not taunt or front-
    I am but a facade but I believe and that's upfront.
    The ever burning why; the question we all ask.
    We forget exactly what's inside the flask.
    Gulps of sanity, lapses of calamity- it's insanity.
    This is our everyday, we all pay in our own way.
    It's evidence is clear, the piper is near.
    We need God- this is the truth.
    But what is it that God needs of us?
    Why are we here- what is our proof?

In barren barrels our spirits join with wood;
    creating an insatiable flavor, an alcohol of good.
    Each of us grains in the mash.
    We wait to be distilled, evaporated so brash.
    This fate of ours is it destined?
    Or are we simply lying still in the cask?

110. Beyond the Wire -
Thursday November 09, 2023
19:32 MST

Past the barbed wire fence and trenches awaits a forest,
    thickets of trees where the grass stands over your knees.
    Freedom so close you can taste it;
    within the confines of this wire, life is wasted.
    In the trees it lurks, you can hear each footstep it clerks-
    its eyes burn bright red as the Autumn leaves rustle.
    This imprisonment of time- our enemy in which we tussle.
    It tugs and cajoles at our leery souls.

For in those pits, in those deep holes lay our bodies,
    covered in lye, we open-face rot towards the sky.
    The eyes of our killers gleam with intoxication.
    They themselves are the victims- their manifestation.
    How can man sin and wash his hands?
    You see- it falls to the falsehood of chain of command.
    Empty orders carried out through their actions.
    a malefaction of fake moral traction.

. . .

The monster omnipresently lurks,
an impossibility that robs us of our shirts.
What we want today haunts us tomorrow.
The cost of freedom leaves us in fallows.
The weight of our chains are constant strains.
Leaving the barren dirt stained with the blood drained.
The monster feasts in the mirror, it is our own fear.
We feed the animal- foster it as our own mammal.

Beyond that fence, dripping silently into the trench-
we steer the evil of all beings.
In fact we've created the steel of the fence.
Our own prison - our creation never relents.
We can hide behind our rusty smiles,
our birthed truths beguile.

111. They're Coming for me - Friday November 10, 2023 15:29 MST

It seers in my mind- the continual bond lingers in my stinging fingers.
    The crux of my torn lore no matter feels whole.
    It's a robbing of humanity- a striping of my sanity.
    My consciousness wanes in the flames doused in my eyes.
    All my elephants are in the room- in this split reality's guise.
    My past re-lives; it circles in perpetual motion- it drives me mad.
    It drowns me in a scorned ocean.

Faces of these ghouls ensnare my soul in a low hell.
    Why must these specters haunt me, daunt me beyond counsel?
    One by one I feel my days number under the sun;
    my last day I do not fear,
    My hesitation lies in knowing they're coming for me-
    that day is near.
    I've done these souls no wrong, that is clear.
    Nonetheless we share an inevitable attachment in the light of
    destiny's spear.

· · ·

All of the calamity is so near, my skin sizzles and my blood boils,
a gurgling reminiscent of the entire world's toils.
I see their faces not only in my dreams but in all places.
The words they speak, leak like the vomit of angels fallen from his
graces. I can no longer hear their voices, yet they speak in a cloaked
meek teak.
Their words are so solid- the pain so real it's impossible for me
to un-feel.
For in their agenda I was but a part.

Make me sleep, but not dream. Remove me from this insanity.
If but for a moment I could lose myself in the leak- oh to escape this
calamity.
That freedom is what I truly seek.
It's the devil that's inside, he does not hide in isolation or sneak.
Instead she stands before us as the temptress of our eye.

112. Holistic Hell - Saturday November 11, 2023 22:07 MST

It weighs so heavy, it's the dam holding the levy,
    a burden unseen, in the depths of the weary.
    The sky, forever gray, mirrors our plight,
    as hope dies dimly in the endless night.

Gone are the days of my old home's face,
    now just a memory, a long-forgotten place.
    A place of refuge; built to be a home now cold.
    You damned me, refuted me so bold.
    It's because of you my soul is sold.

Beside the river Thames, my ethos dried,
    in its barren polluted bed, our dreams quietly died.
    New cities to explore rise- the Shard so high.
    In that towering colossal my ambitions sighed.

Under its gargantuan antique hands all is withered,

A clock off, war, time is scorn, torn and tattered.
My consciousness scattered, robbing my days
no matter what, nothing lingers in the haze.

Hope, walks in Hyde park- hung in the square at night.
The path there- I no longer gravel or fight.
Standing, protesting atop a stool untrod.
Your ambitions and mine- both fatally flawed.

I trudge along, each step a heavy cost,
along the way, my morals, my being- everything lost.
It weighs so heavy, this life we carry,
a burden, unyielding, forever we parry.

113. My Tavern - Sunday November 12, 2023 20:25 MST

An irrefutable gamble, an ensemble, a trammel.
    The noise riots into the night- poisoning our rights.
    This bet is beyond tangible needs- should it gavel-
    my entire existence shall crumble, be beaten to gravel.
    A smothering thought to engulf such risk shall travel-
    a persistent subservient throbbing cavil.

My heart beats a cry of need- my nerves scramble.
    This win is my only hope; I'm desperate enamel.
    I'm unable to handle the thoughts of the mantle-
    what lays atop is a trope of gold burning as a candle.
    My eyes are ales, drowning the cask in this scandal.

In my public house, the rats hurry beneath shambles.
    I see them scurrying, currying meals of rotten flesh-
    They consume their decaying bodies, souls enmesh.
    Their grotesque tails trail like a dead tress.
    How they went unnoticed so long: I'm grossly impressed.

Nonetheless I am the courier of poison administering fate.

I need to rid myself of these vermin, I am their theremin.
My voice falls to the floor, feeding them audible tears.
They eat death and sadness, emit the plague.
I find myself in my first encounter of the mess I made.

As the night lingers on, my hope further dwindles,
the gamble deepens, in darkness, my fear kindles.
The rats, thriving in decay, the rat's souls and mine mesh,
in this desolate tavern, my sorrows refresh.

The prospect of tomorrow, a sick tale to embellish,
in this pub of the lost, my thirst shall never perish.
The vermin, my kin, in dead piles flourish,
feasting on ruins, in despair I languish.

No respite at night, just endless scramble,
a life tethered to a risk, too heavy to handle.
Amidst this chaos, my spirit is trammel,
in the depths of despair, extinguished, my candle.

114. Eternally Unattainable - Monday November 13, 2023 20:56 MST

Suffering is a gift for the living, not the dead.

I see it now, burned into my sight-
forever etched into my clenched eyes.
I smell the burning of flesh,
it burrows into my nostrils- it smells not of Resh.
Instead it reeks of sin; akin not to a new beginning but of linen
soaked in gasoline, so fresh.
I shall dress my wounds in this flammable garb, this deadly mesh.

I welcome the fire deep down, it's my desire.
I wish not to burn, its sweltering heat I very much fear;
its for peace I yearn.
These insatiable fumes drown my senses, causing my stomach to
churn.

The potent liquid emits a visible haze under the sky- destiny before

me, a match shall adjourn.
Only the fire determines exactly when it's our time- our turn.

Desperately I grasp at straws but they crack audibly with each of my
flaws-
Oh how I desire the chance to earnestly live; instead I hastily prep
my flaming gauze.
A happenstance to lance this worldly boil and grimly bleed out the
toil- its evil laws.
This impromptu operation comes with great cause; I must release
myself from its jaws.
To hold a man's life in one's hand- its the act of a demon's paws.
I take pause at my laissez faire approach to quell my hemorrhaging,
watching the macaws.

They eagerly croak and crow at the behest of the surgeon of fates
applause.
Underneath the hospital the enemy lies cowardly with hostages.
A population stolen and murdered, the killers rummage the
refrigerators- brutal sabotages.
I beg of you please, bring an end to these violent meaningless
montages.

115. My Monadnock - Tuesday November 14, 2023 14:10 MST

Today, I've officially lost.

Everything is gone, iced over in the morning's idle frost.
    All my hopes, my prayers- to no avail.
    Forsaken, my decaying ship shall never again sail.
    Beyond reproach- a gala of falsehood; it's cost?
    Morphed my vessel into a failed tale of sale.

Nonetheless I must endure- continue to traverse, lost.
    Eternity did not grant my boat to sink- it lays embossed-
    in the peneplain; a graveyard tarred and feathered with carcasses of
    other ships weathered by time's exhaust.

While still alive, I'm unable to thrive on this desolate island I had
    hoped to have only crossed.
    Planted in the sand I wish not to stand, I desperately seek to sink
    into these grains- Lord let it be a reprimand.

. . .

Skin wrinkled and withered, I rise to my feet, pale.
  If only I had the frankincense and myrrh to allure a fate that could
  more contour to riches, gold overflowing my pail.

As I traverse the unknown; songs of my own voices accost my sanity.
  I walk until I reach a place of utter calamity.

Atop the monadnock where my place ends;
  it's the final destination of all my sins.
  God please rinse my soul of this sand;
  I beg you- wash away my thoughts and existence into some
  semblance of subsistence.

Subservience has mossed over my brain, it's evident that on this
  monadnock I have already missed my train.

Today, I've officially lost.

116. Wildfire of Embers - Wednesday November 15, 2023 20:50 MST

In the heart of the inferno, where secrets breathe fire,
   an orchestra of embers, a wildfire of desire.
   Unbound, unchained, the flames ascend,
   reflecting in eyes where wild dreams blend.

Like a spark to the night, so is fear to the heart,
   a silent humming, an unspoken art.
   The blaze roars, a story untold,
   in the lost alleys of my mind, secrets unfold.

A chaos within, where calm seas turn,
   each flicker, a memory, in solitude it yearns.
   A storm within, where silence roars,
   a residual haunting of battles, on unseen shores.

The fire's fleeting glow, a transient haven,
   a moment's peace, a soul unladen.

It burns away, a phantom in flight,
leaving behind a world, cloaked in night.

In its relentless quest, the fire molds fate,
an indomitable will, an insatiable state.
Amidst its rage, truth unveils,
a clarity born, as the facade pales.

Stories of fear, from the depths arise,
tales of a dream, in turmoil lies.
Its crackling laughter, a haunting serenade,
a bond of spirits, forever made.

The allure of the flame, a deceptive guise,
promises warmth, but in its heart, truth dies.
In its fervent embrace, a revelation waits,
in the crucible of fear, destiny creates.

For within the fire's core, lies a poignant lore,
in surrendering to the flames, we find more.
Though the blaze may wane, and the battle cease,
in the embers of courage, we find our peace.

117. Cyclical Musings - Thursday November 16, 2023 13:11 MST

In the quiet hours, I ponder what it means to truly exist,
    a question lingering like mist, a concept often missed.

It feels somewhat like this:

In the scar tissue of my being, where turmoil and tranquility collide,
    a journey through the ocean,
    where malignant thoughts of the soul reside.
    A silent cacophony, a storm of thought and feeling,
    reverberating against the canvas of consciousness, endlessly reeling.

Visions flicker, a montage of moments lost and found,
    a menagerie of memories, in their haunting melody bound.
    In the quietude of realization, a fleeting peace ascends,
    a fragile reprieve, until the cycle renews and bends.

. . .

The passage of time, a relentless and rhythmic tide,
    bearing away the remnants of what we hold inside.
    What they say of life's fleeting nature rings true,
    in the final act, the essence of self comes into view.

A tranquil acceptance, a surrender to the inevitable flow,
    in the ice of existence, the melting of our being is the glow.

It ends, but in the sunsets light, it begins anew,
    an eternal cycle of becoming, ever-changing, ever true.

118. THE TUNNEL BESIDE THE SEA - FRIDAY NOVEMBER 17, 2023 12:06 MST

In the tunnel beside the sea, the answer laid painted on the walls in front of me.

It rolled in with the tide, drowning the fish's urgings in the sand; washed ashore souls bared all our existences demand- the key.

They instinctively knew that far off from the shore is where they belonged, yet they chose their demise as their decree.

I should have paused but I refused to bend the knee.

The marine life knew the strife to come; even so I dismissed their drowning plea.

. . .

On that beach I walked hand in hand with a damned destiny, treading over their discarded carcasses without regard. I should have seen my tax looming, I too will pay their fee.

From that moment, now in perpetuity, their admonitions have become so true to me.

The juxtaposition of their prudence to the sea likens that of a now dead fearlessness that once lived inside so easily.

To this day their weathered bones litter that same beach; a testament to the remnants of what would one day come to be me. If only I'd accepted their blatant counsel, now all I can do is flee.

Anything to escape that day, anything to rid my thoughts of that September spree.

Now my directions lie burnt and smolders in a bonfire of desire fueled entirely from the fractured limbs of a singular tree. A tree that stood alone in the sand- beyond all natural happenstances to be. This synthetic arboreal plant's roots are coursing through my veins with a vicious veracity, leaving the viscosity of my lifeblood all but flimsy.

My crowded, tired eyes do not recognize the person staring back in the mirror at me. Instead I catch sight of a coward who cannot accept the decisions that were fated to see. The decisions made were mine, so they said, but at night when I lay my head, it's upon a pillow of sand and I cannot ignore the aquatic carcasses demand.

119. Cacophony' Reign - Saturday November 18, 2023 20:03 MST

In a world of endless clamor and cacophony,
    where sense is shackled, and madness is monarchy.
    A relentless din of disillusion, day by night,
    each moment a melee, an unending fight.

A parade of folly, a cavalcade of the absurd,
    words once profound, now utterly blurred.
    The grand crest of logic, unwoven, unfurled,
    in the theater of the ridiculous, our banners are twirled.

Here, wisdom weeps and folly holds court,
    each truth undone, each lesson cut short.
    A circus of chaos, where clowns wear the crown,
    and the music of reason is turned upside down.

In the raucous bazaar of the bizarre we dwell,
    where the currency is nonsense, and all goods sell.

A Babel of babble, where silence is slain,
and the echoes of senselessness forever remain.

Amidst this tempest of tiresome toil,
a sliver of hope stubbornly uncoils.
For in the heart of the hurricane's eye,
lies the tranquil truth that we cannot deny:

That beyond the ridiculous, reason still waits,
patient and poised beyond all our debates.

120. Bewildered in Time - Sunday November 19, 2023 10:49 MST

In this vast expanse, where laughs mock and sigh,
a wanderer's heart, under the watchful sky.
Lost in the maze of existence, profound,
a soul in search of the ground it never found.

The map of life, once vivid and clear,
now smudged by tears, by doubt, by fear.
Each step, a question in the silence of night,
each breath, a remnant of a forgotten fight.

The truth of destiny, undone,
under the indifferent gaze of the setting sun.
A journey with no end, no start, no aim,
in the endless search for a nameless claim.

Where once the fire of purpose burned bright,
now smolders a flicker, a waning light.

In the forest of thoughts, dark and deep,
lies the person I could have been, in eternal sleep.

A soul adrift in the sea of time,
in a world out of rhythm, out of rhyme.
Seeking solace in the stars above,
aching for a sign, for a hint of love.

In the voices of the wind, in the rustle of leaves,
in the quiet despair that the twilight weaves,
lies the haunting question, persistent, stark,
a lone ship wandering in the endless dark.

The melody of life, once sweet, now sour,
in the twilight of existence, the final hour.
A search for meaning in the grand design,
in the haunted house of fate, where destinies entwine.

121. Our Division - Monday November 20, 2023 18:19 MST

In a lackluster society where arguments turn to shots,
    where labels are cast, without a moment of doubt.
    First, they branded souls with a singular mark,
    a term of disdain, a divisive spark.

"Racist," they cried, with a pointed finger,
    in an atmosphere where such accusations linger.
    Then, cloaked in disillusionment, a new irony bore,
    accusers themselves, what they once deplored.

Corporations crept in, with a silent tread,
    democracy's fabric, quietly shred.
    In the name of profit, values sold,
    our collective conscience, left uncontrolled.

Then came the wars, distant and near,
    Ukraine's struggle for democracy,

Israel is violently attacked by a bloodthirsty kleptocracy.
The world watched, in horror and awe,
as principles crumbled, under the law of claw.
Sovereignty is apparently a hypocrisy.

Now, as conflict spread, puppeteers sharpen their strings,
the pain and sorrow that war always brings.
Hate, in all forms, a poison we taste,
in the name of 'progress', humanity laid to waste.

In this knife of strife, we all play a part,
in the blanket duality of life, where empathy must start.
Let us rise above, the labels, the greed,
in our actions, let love be the seed.

For in the end, it's unity we need,
to heal, to grow, to truly succeed.
Against the tide of hate, let's take a stand,
with an open heart, and an outstretched hand.

122. The Gallows in our Homes - Tuesday November 21, 2023 21:03 MST

In the silent chambers of the night, a closet inhales – a specter behind the gallows of the rod, its breath a subtle cadence of secrets kept and truths concealed. Within its wooden ribs, a coffin of unspoken words of hidden sorrows and silent victories.

With each slow, deliberate breath, it nurtures the words spoken, feeding on the unconfessed, the buried, the unacknowledged. Its doors, a mouth with teeth of brass hued hinges- the threshold, oscillate gently, as if moved by the sighs of restless spirits. Here, in this confined sanctuary, lies the repository of human frailties, the archive of our innermost contradictions.

The closet, a crucible of our internal struggles, mirrors the complexities of the soul. Each creak, a reflection of the heart's tumultuous journey; each silent rustle, a ghost of forgotten dreams. It stands, a monolith to the human condition, bleeding the inexorable passage of time and the undying quest for understanding.

. . .

In the quietude of its presence, one finds an unsettling comfort – a realization that in the embrace of the dark, in the heart of the enigma, we confront the essence of our being. This closet, with its rhythmic iron lung, becomes more than a keeper of secrets; it transforms into a beacon of introspection, a silent witness to the horrors of self. From the top shelf, the twine gleams a deathly shine, coaxing you to join in the decline. As the knot tightens, no longer is it frightening. Hell has been all too inviting.

123. Tantalizing Visage of Déjà vu - Wednesday November 22, 2023 08:32 MST

In my preferred reality, where indecisiveness is merely a triviality, life truly thrives. Here, unbound by the chains of consequences unbearable, everything unfolds with ease; I am relaxed, even in jandals. Memories, some long forgotten and others not yet born, are surfed at leisure. I find myself in my childhood home, the epicenter of a joyous celebration. Everyone dear to me, those I've loved or cared for, are present, alive and well. A long-lost friend is there too, radiantly different, carrying new life within, finally happy.

The gathering's purpose, it dawns on me, is a birth – the birth of her child. Intuitively, she knows, and so do we. Peacefully, she settles in a kiddie pool in the middle of the room, ready to welcome her child into the world. Despite not being the father – our past as lovers has long faded without any resentment – I watch over her, enveloped in a nervousness not my own. The birth is swift, almost effortless for an unassisted natural birth. I eagerly observe from behind until she lifts the newborn.

. . .

It's a boy.

He's healthy, and her eyes sparkle with years of joy; she's genuinely happy. I touch her shoulder, conveying more with my eyes than words can express, only managing to utter "Congratulations." Her eyes respond with a sincerity that surpasses any words.

The scene shifts; the baby is now swaddled in her arms, we're in the living room. I hug them both, a rare feeling of comfort without hesitation – usually, hugging anyone makes me uncomfortable, but not this time. It feels like the only genuine embrace I've ever known. The father is absent, not part of this picture. I assure her, with heartfelt sincerity, that I'm there for her, ready to love her child as if he were my own.

Leaving my childhood home, she's in the passenger seat with our son. In the back window of my car, I see an uninvited part of my soul arriving late. Rather than being consumed by dread, I drive past slowly, acknowledging this part of myself that I can now leave behind in peace.

I'm fulfilled, my heart brimming even as I leave behind a fragment of my soul.

124. The Macaw - Thursday November 23, 2023 09:36 MST

In an unending spiral, my essence slowly erodes,
  my skin is peeling away, but not from the sun's abodes.
  A constant battle, victories never known,
  pursuing opportunities, in winds that have blown.

My losses, lush as grass under summer's gaze,
  in this relentless cycle of failure, I'm ablaze.
  Soul aching, hollowed by a deepening void,
  bleeding from wounds, life's cruel asteroid.

A macaw in man's guise, yet bound to the earth,
  crass instincts guiding, denying my worth.
  Trapped within myself, in a shell so stark,
  wandering in circles, lost in the dark.

This existence, a dreadful weight to bear,
  in mundane routines, gasping for air.

Like a bird caged, in my own form ensnared,
a soul screaming silently, hopelessly impaired.

Each day, a reflection of despair's deep well,
in the mirror, a story too pained to tell.
Oh, for a moment's escape, a fleeting respite,
from this prison of flesh, this endless plight.

I endure, in this relentless fray,
a specter in life's play, faded and gray.
This Thanksgiving my hunger looms, unfed.
In this cycle of sorrow, where dreams wither and die,
I am a disease, a soul's desperate cry.

125. The Third Bottle of Addiction - Friday November 24, 2023 10:21 MST

In the whirl of the spinning wheel, a gamble of chance and fate,
where fortunes rise and fall in the blink of an envious slate.

A gambler's heart, ablaze with a feverish, insatiable thirst,
in the temple of chance, where the last is often first.

The dice roll, the cards flip, a symphony of risk and hope,
in this arena, dreams are tethered to a fragile, slippery slope.

For each win, a siren's song, sweet but deceitfully grim,
in the wonders of chance, where light grows ominously dim.

The table's allure, a magnetic pull, strong and unyielding,
where reality blurs, and the mind starts willingly conceding.

.   .   .

In this game, the stakes climb, not just for coin or fleeting wealth, the essence of time, sanity, and the gambler's very self.

Each bet, a leap into the abyss, a deal with deviled sprites, logic fades, and addiction's grip brutally alights.

In this gamble, a mirage of control, an illusion so bitter,
where the toll is the soul, in this relentless, gluttonous river.

For in the depths of this frenzy, where reason is lost and blind, lies the gambler's quandary, in the shackles of the mind.

A vintage bottle of hope, uncorked with each roll, each deal, in this dangerous slope, where the unreal seems so real.

The heart of the empty, where desires and fears collide,
the truth screams, a faint though persistent guide.

That the game is a mirage, a seducer of the strongest will, in its deceptive collage, a void it can never fill.

The gambler's plight, in the bottom of the glass,
of this unending game,
a journey through night, seeking a flame that's never the same.

For in the end, it's not about the wins, the losses, the strife, but the return to within, to reclaim a forfeited life.

. . .

Thus, in the clacking of the dice, in the shuffling of the cards, sewn a
lesson, cold as ice, as valuable as the worst vice.

That the greatest gamble, in the end, is not played on a velvet floor,
but in how we handle the heart's mend, and the spirit's core.

Why I ever thought I could win- I may never know.
It's the hope of a new chance, a potential for my existence to glow.
Until then I drown my losses in cheap alcohol, this I know.

126. In Chasing the Horizon: My Demise - Saturday November 25, 2023 19:36 MST

At the threshold of dreams, where ambition's fire glows,
in the garden of fate, where the river of longing flows.
A seeker stands, eyes fixed on a distant prize,
heart brimming with hopes, under the vast skies.

Destiny, a mirage, ever shifting, ever sly,
with every step forward, it hums a silent goodbye.
The chasm of reality, wide and deep,
swallows dreams, leaves promises to weep.

In the pursuit of stars, life's journey is wrought,
each leap towards them seems for naught.
The shore of achievement, visible yet far,
a relentless chase, under destiny's mocking star.

In this pursuit, the soul, weary and worn,
yearns for the crown of purpose, for which it was born.

Like a permeable burn in the cement at dusk, elusive and faint, is the
fulfillment of destiny, a picture no words can paint.
Etched in time by the radiation of the weapon that split the atom.
Is the destruction worth it- taking more lives than we can fathom?

Here, in this quest, where victories tease and taunt,
    lies the bittersweet saga, a haunting want.
    To touch the zenith, a dream so divine,
    in the end, no matter what I create- it's just short of the line.

127. Hostages Freed - Sunday November 26, 2023 10:33 MST

In the quiet aftermath of justice's toll,
　　cries from a nation's soul,
　　where a man in chains for another's last breath,
　　finds no solace, even in the depths.

Border's tragic murmurings, a tale untold,
　　of lives lost, young and old,
　　in the frozen embrace of fate's cruel hand,
　　a story etched in no man's land.

In the north, where earth shifts, stealing breaths,
　　a family succumbs to nature's depths,
　　under the weight of the world, silently they lay,
　　in the cold grasp of destiny's sway.

A threat, a fear, in a crowded space,

a heart races, a familiar face,
the mall's echoing halls, strangers collide by fate-
an unfortunate chance;
life, suspended in a moment's glance.

Accusations, of a past so dim,
  in the corridors of power, a haunting hymn,
  a city's leader, caught in time's cruel jest,
  in the court of public opinion, no rest.

Diplomatic words, a fake stance of might,
  in a world stage, dimly lit by fading light,
  leaders converse, while the world holds its breath,
  the eyes of conflict, life and death.

Celebrities, icons, under scrutiny's glare,
  a society grappling with what's fair,
  the courtrooms, dramas unfold,
  stories of pain, new and old.

Over lands afar, where conflicts rage,
  history's actors take the stage,
  soldiers, faceless, in a distant fight,
  under the shroud of the endless night.

In the heartland, where trains derail,
  lives upended by a chemical trail,
  a community's peace, shattered, undone,
  under the fading Thanksgiving sun.

· · ·

This unfolding of events, a world in strife,
    reflects the tumultuous nature of life,
    each pulse, a story, a shared human fate,
    under a cold November day, our truths resonate.

128. Sleepless Malaise - Monday November 27, 2023 21:32 MST

For nights on end, insomnia's grip, in a broken home where reality starts to slip. Hallucinations, phantoms in the night, the faces of the dead that taunt me- my plight.

A mind teetering on sanity's brink, I am a sea of thoughts, I slowly lose the ability to blink. Drops of blood crawl out from my face and drip in the sink while shaving. The pooled blood and water look back at me- hands emerge waving. The faces that now haunt me, my life's collar. Dreams and waking moments blend, an endless cycle, without an end. I can't decipher the real from the unhinged.

The voices in the dark, speak a silent plea- are they calling out, or is it just me? Their screams, blood curdling loud... my eyes jump to my wife lying next to me, she hears not even a sound.

It's not real.

· · ·

I've lost all sanity.

A world that wavers, trembles, and sways, in the haze of the sleepless malaise.

Each moment stretches, a timeless flight, in the realm of the restless night. Grasping for reality, slipping away, in the perils of a mind's disarray.

In this burning nightmare of waking dreams, nothing is quite as it seems.

The ceiling, unmoving, watches my flight with the eyes birthing out of the smoke detector as I stare blankly through an endless night.

129. The Ennui Beyond the Door - Tuesday November 28, 2023 21:31 MST

"Perhaps this is all there is," a hidden voice curdled incredulously from the vacant adjoining room of my home.

I answered it as if it were normal, like it was a friend: "The twilight to the dawn, mistaking weariness for wisdom, in the hour before morn. Like life, when stripped of its vibrant hues, becomes a monochrome existence, a path we did not choose. In other words- yes, this is all there is and all there ever will be.".

The voice relented, it no longer spoke. Inside my head, my thoughts are incessantly stoked by the iron hot words, no longer beneath the veil of death's cloak.

Is it merely existence, this routine we endure? Hardly living, merely persisting, in a world so obscure. Worth noting, perhaps, in the margins of our days, that we once felt, even if now lost in a tired haze.

. . .

I know my demons, as if that's my entire tale, perhaps that's sufficient, in a life where vivacity grows stale. Moved by intentions, noble but unseen, until we halt, immobile, in a world so serene.

In this quiet surrender, where dreams begin to fray, I wander, half-awake, through the motions of the day. Alive, but not living, in this monotonous chore, a specter in the daylight, yearning for something more.

Perhaps the voice from next door- is my own, a future me. One who has already fulfilled my destiny. In this time and place now is all I feel, the old me and the me of tomorrow- well it's all unspoken, all intolerantly hollow, fleeting and poor.

Please God, show me it's me, perhaps, behind that door.

130. 1565 N Colorado Blvd Denver, CO 80220 - Wednesday November 29, 2023 16:33 MST

I pass it in my car on a commute of drudgery and dread;
    in the footsteps of the Rockies, a structure stands,
    a remnant of dreams, built by hopeful hands.
    The Royal Palace, once a beacon bright,
    now a specter, in the fading light.

Its walls, a canvas of time's ruthless art,
    each crack and crevice, a story's part.
    Graffiti documents the horrors of crime and those slain,
    a staunch fleeting reminder of a city where pain remains.

A monument, not of stone, but of human plight,
    of dreams tarnished, lost in the night.
    Once a haven for the weary head,
    now a refuge for specters, hope long fled.

Within its crumbling embrace, society's mirror,

reflecting the woes, the pain, and the terror.
The stains of greed lie etched in bloodied mattresses, the dead lurk.
In its forgotten rooms, where darkness works.

Here, the streets screech tales of despair,
of souls lost to the night's cold stare.
The homeless, the forgotten, in its four walls find,
a moment's respite, from a world unkind.

In this Palace of broken dreams, resounds pains of a nation,
a testament to our society's lost station.
Where once stood pride, now only decay,
a mirror to our times, in disarray.

The drug's cruel grip, like vines, entwine,
through corridors of a once-grand design.
A symbol of a society, frayed and worn,
a reminder of what we have mourned.

This mausoleum of socioeconomic strife,
a testament to greed's corrosive might,
Where ambition's fire has lost its light.
Once a refuge, now a den of vice,
a mirror to our fall from grace, the price.

In its embrace, the discarded and lost,
a stark reminder of humanity's cost.
The walking dead, the forsaken, in it dwell,
dirty needles hanging out between toes sell us
a glimpse into our own potential hell.

· · ·

Here, the pulse of addiction throbs in the night,
in corridors haunted by escape's false light.
A microcosm of a society frayed,
a cacophony of lucidity, in ruin laid.

The Palace, people drive by,
doing anything to avoid the eye of the beggar, the addict.
Though it's only to ourselves to which we lie.
Now a graveyard of hope's remains,
a symbol of a world enthralled by chains.
Where once stood a beacon of prosperity's glean,
now stands a monument to a silent scream.

In this begotten page tells us of a forgotten age,
lies the story of our self-made cage.
A tale of a society, blind and torn,
a warning of what we may become, forlorn.

In its decay, a bitter truth we find,
a reflection of the rot we've left behind.
A requiem for a dream, once bold and new,
in the ruins of the Palace, our failures in view.

What scares us the most is knowing we are them.
We are the addict, we are the beggar, the homeless akin
to each of us and our fraught decay.
We are only one paycheck away-
from joining our fellow brothers and sisters,
we shall all sleep under the Palace's roof.
Bedbugs and drugs- our hearts design;
we pretend to ignore that we are that man with the sign.

131. The Unwilling Voyager - Thursday November 30, 2023 18:06 MST

In the silence of existence, I found my unintended path,
a life unscripted, swept in destiny's aftermath.
No dreams adorned my cradle, no star to guide my way,
merely drifting in the current, in the sea of the everyday.

I wear masks not of my making, tales spun from other's threads,
fables woven around me, heavy crowns upon my head.

I am, regrettably, a mosaic of many things,
a gallery of titles, each a bell that never rings.

In the calamity of life, I've stumbled into roles,
accidental accolades, filling unforeseen holes.
My purpose, an elusive calling, darting from my grasp,
in the warning of labels, I find no solace to clasp.

. . .

From the strings of society, my spirit dangles, frayed,
saddled with burdens, in debt's dark shade.
I never sought to carve a legacy in the stone of time,
only to taste each day, sour and sublime.

What pays me, you ask? A void, dark and deep,
swallowing the essence of the dreams I couldn't keep.
Still the scared child within, now cloaked in sorrow's shroud,
these labels, my chains, in their weight I am bowed.

Will I heed the call, the summons of the unseen?
Or will fate, in its cruel test, intervene?
In the forgotten steps of my journey, a tale untold,
the story of a soul, neither bought nor sold.

132. My Paradox of Existence - Friday December 01, 2023 21:08 MST

In the consciousness of nature's whims, a curious happening unfolds,
   where hail argues with rain, but with snow, it refuses to withhold.
   Attributed to capricious turns of the seasonal wheel,
   beneath lies a deeper pulse, a more profound feel.

A rhythm that endures, relentless and unyielding,
   Through time's fabric, quietly threading and wielding.
   The aqueducts, marvels of human ingenuity's birth,
   twist reality, quenching humanity's ephemeral thirst.

Conceived in civilization's nascent dream,
   a testament to our societal scheme.
   In our hubris, a thirst insatiable grows,
   leaving us parched- exsiccate, as no life-giving river flows.

Our transgressions, a burden more burdensome than gold,
   undeterred, through the tempest, we boldly hold.

I stand, a sentinel at the brink of my own undoing,
unyielding, unwavering, my purpose pursuing.

In the face of annihilation, my essence won't falter,
for it is not in my nature to kneel at the altar.
Shatter my foundations, I shall not cease,
in the shards of my being, a relentless yearning for self derived peace.

Driven by an unquenchable thirst for existence,
defiant, I traverse the path of most resistance.
My being, my longing, a flame that never wanes,
fueling the fervor that in my soul remains.

This odyssey of existence, a paradox so profound,
in the rules of life, my story is bound.

A narrative of resilience, against time's ruthless tide,
in the canals of eternity, my spirit shall reside.

133. So it Goes, George - Saturday December 02, 2023 21:52 MST

Voices clash and merge,
    a tyranny looms, a majority's surge.
    Or perhaps, in the quiet, the suffering's hue,
    of a party of two, under the sky's vast blue.

An eviction, a life uprooted and tossed,
    or a conviction, where truth is lost.
    Amidst these trials, a due so true,
    we, the nexus, in the world's shifting view.

In the suffering of the many, a silence profound,
    where the meanderings of the few, resound.
    A struggle between the thundering herd
    and the soft-spoken word, seldom heard.

Are we but pawns in democracy's grand charade,
    swept along in the current of the majority's sway?

Or are we the keepers of a quieter faith,
in the poverty of the crowd, a wrath?

This dichotomy, a pendulum's relentless swing,
between the roar and the howl, the king and the West Wing.
In this consummation of power, a delicate balance,
a tale of the silenced, their quiet defiance.

We are the bridge, the unseen tether,
linking the disparate, through stormy weather.
In the cacophony of voices, a harmony sought,
in the leaves of existence, a plant wrought.

The tyranny of the many, the agony of the few,
in this inevitable march of destiny, a story anew.
An eviction from normalcy, a conviction so deep,
in our collective consciousness, secrets we keep.

Thus, we stand, in the twilight of choice,
in the symphony of life, finding our voice.
A connection, a bond, amidst divergence and unity,
in the heart of the struggle, the essence of community.

134. Don't Scream, I'll be Right Back - Sunday December 03, 2023 10:06 MST

This unease, this persistent relentless restlessness.
    The panic- every ounce of my being, manic.
    I rock silently back and forth, even though I'm standing.
    The ground is calling; urgently demanding.
    Whether or not I will fall on my face or back, my body has no
understanding.

The voice- I think it's mine, repeats "Don't scream, I'll be right back.".

This request, this lapse of brevity to which there is no remedy,
    A sinking ship in my mind's stormy sea.
    Screeches in the void, an melodiousness of despair,
    a chorus of chaos, spiraling in the air.

The walls, they breathe secrets, dark and deep,
    in my house of madness, a twisted leap.
    My thoughts, once a river, now a torrential flood,

drowning in the depths, a mind caked in mud.

Reality blurs, my mind unravels at the seams,
  in this puzzle of lunacy, where nothing is as it seems.
  I grasp for sanity, a phantom in the night,
  in this twilight of reason, lost is the fight.

The clock ticks, a harbinger of time's cruel test,
  in this prison of the psyche, there is no rest.
  The mirror reflects a stranger, a soul unmoored,
  in the eyes of the beholder, sanity ignored.

  In the gallows of thought, no peace to find.
  Each second, a lifetime, in this eternal descent,
  into the abyss of madness, my will, bent.

The voice, now a distant bottle, its message lost at sea, a forgotten plea,
  in the silence of the void, a desperate decree.
  Lost in the maelstrom, the sense of the self,
  a mind unraveling, put upon the highest shelf.

A brain of ruin, where hope dares not tread,
  lies the remnants of a being, a psyche shredded.
  The darkness, a truth, stark and bleak,
  In the canals of insanity, my gondola sinks,
  a tale unfortunate but not unique.

135. My Last Supper - Monday December 04, 2023 21:13 MST

In the dimming light of my inner sanctum, a table is set,
a gathering of disciples, a pantheon of regret.
I, the weary host of this spectral feast,
stand as a savior, but feel the least.

Around this table, my vices, in their ghastly might,
each a disciple of my darkest night.
Greed with its gluttonous, grasping hands,
envy, green-eyed, in its silent stands.

Anger, with flames in its unforgiving eyes,
lust, draped in desire, a master of lies.
Sloth, languid in its unyielding yawn,
pride, vainly preening till the dawn.

As the prophet among these facets of my soul,
I ponder the price of this unholy toll.

WORDS ARE SNAKES WITH ARMS

The Holy Grail before us, brimming with a bitter wine,
promising eternal life, a curse in a divine sign.

Who among these grotesque men shall betray me tonight?
Which part of my being shall extinguish the light?
In this last supper of the self, a reckoning so dire,
I confront the fragments of my own internal fire.

The bread of my soul, broken, shared,
in this communion, my deepest fears bared.
Each vice takes a piece, a part of my essence,
in this twisted ritual, a grim convalescence.

Greed lunges first, its hunger never sated,
followed by Envy, forever frustrated.
Anger's fiery bite, searing and raw,
lust's lingering touch, a flaw in the law.

Sloth, indifferent, partakes without care,
while Pride feasts on the adulation in the air.
Amidst this macabre supper of my sin,
a realization dawns from within.

The true betrayer, not one, but all,
each vice a nail in my soul's eternal fall.
The Holy Grail, a chalice of ceaseless strife,
who would wish for such an endless life?

In this moment of truth, a decision so grave,
to surrender to vice or my spirit to save.

In the last supper of the self, a choice to be made,
to embrace the light or let it fade.

Thus, I stand, a Messiah of my own demise,
a savior seeking salvation, under the starless skies.
In this twilight of existence, a path to tread,
though I see Judas' eyes reflecting back at me in my chalice-
but it's the reflection of my own head.
I am my own betrayal, I have snuffed out my own light.

136. It's all Wrong - Tuesday December 05, 2023 21:30 MST

It swells in, a sour somber embrace,
    it lies in a soul, weary, at time's relentless pace.
    A silhouette against life's fading light,
    bearing the weight of an endless night.

In the corridors of thought, gunshots pose a silent plea,
    bookings of destruction, a longing to be free.
    A journey through despair's deep sea,
    a damned voyage in the void, where the heart longs to flee.

The windows of the soul, shatter to pieces, no longer whole,
    now shuttered, in the wake of life's unseen streams.
    A calamity of glass, gripped by sills, rubber thread,
    in the loom of existence, where hope has fled.

Now stands a wasteland, by doubt consumed.
    a broken house of regret, under this desolate roof,

guard the remnants of a once radiant tooth.

The chalice of life, brimming with bitter tears,
  holds the essence of the yesteryears.
  In its depths, a reflection of a soul in strife,
  Contemplating the enigma of a weary life.

In the mirror of the night, a fractured self I see,
  a prisoner of existence, yearning to be free.
  The chains of reality, heavy and unkind,
  bind the fragments of a shattered mind.

In the quiet before the dawn, a decision dire,
  to succumb to the void, extinguish the fire.

This moment, on the precipice of fate,
  a dying within urges me to wait.

137. A Fractured Polity-
Wednesday December 06,
2023 19:50 MST

On the stage of power, a lament seethes, bleak,
  where voices of the just grow ever meek.
  A government, fractured, on corruption's throne,
  sits blinded to the seeds of despair it has sown.

Once guardians of trust, now agents of greed,
  draped in the guise of public need.
  In Congress, the pacts are silently made,
  principles are bartered, and ethics fade.

Behold the closing statements of the partisan divide,
  truth is a chameleon, and justice denied.
  A polity splintered, in disarray and scorn,
  bearing the weight of promises worn.

In the boardrooms of government contractors, the deals are struck,

under golden chandeliers, amidst the muck.
No Republican or Democrat to challenge the sway,
only the hymns of the corrupt that play.

The specter of healthcare, a tale untold,
of exemptions and profits, brazen and bold.
Pharmaceutical giants, untouchable, unchained,
a world where morality is feigned.

A reckoning looms for the COVID plight,
for the choices made, in the dimming light.
MNRA shots, a hope, a fear, a debate,
turned mandates, shackling freedom's fate.
Common sense, a vaccine did save.

Voices silenced, rights eroded in the night,
in the name of safety, extinguishing the light.
Nurses, our healers, pushed to the brink,
a world on the edge, forced to rethink.

In the Sunshine State, a stand was made,
against the tide of overreach that pervaded the glade.
A cry for autonomy, for the right to choose,
in a time where there was much to lose.

This elegy, a reflection of our times,
of a system riddled with silent crimes.
A call for a return to foundational truth,
to restore the spirit of our collective youth.

. . .

In the looming demise of democracy, a hope remains,
for a future where integrity regains.
A polity united, in purpose and vision,
breaking free from corruption's prison.

138. The Last Train to Nowhere - Thursday December 07, 2023 22:14 MST

In the dimming carriages of my fractured mind,
a train speeds on tracks it cannot find.
The landscape blurs, a world unseen,
my thoughts, the passengers, unquiet and lean.

Through tunnels of doubt, the engine roars,
over broken bridges, past forsaken shores.
Each station passed, a memory fades,
in the whistle's cry, my sanity parades.

The conductor, a version of my former self,
navigates the rails of my diminished health.
Two pills, three, tickets to a hazy peace,
a desperate bid for a moment's pharmaceutical lease.

The rhythm of the wheels, a heartbeat lost,
a journey without end, no matter the cost.

My existence, a carriage in perpetual night,
trapped in motion, fleeing from the light.

In this train of thought, I'm a prisoner confined,
to a seat of despair, in the recesses of my mind.
Each turn, each jolt, a jarring reminder,
of a life off course, a perpetual wanderer- I will never find her.

Her image, a graffiti on the wall of my soul,
a constant companion as the dark landscapes roll.
A number, etched obscured above the urinal.
Tattooed in my psyche, a number, a name,
in the depths of my being, an indelible stain.
It's ink forever visible on my forearm, staking me tame.

Through the window of my woes, the world is a blur,
a canvas of pain, monochrome and demur.
This locomotive of lament, on a track of torment,
rides to oblivion, its fuel spent.

I am the lone passenger on this spectral train,
a journey through madness, in the realm of the insane.
The destination unknown, the path unclear,
in the whistle's melancholic note, it mimics my fear.

In the metallic clatter of wheels, the universe speaks,
of a life derailed, a spirit that seeks.
The calling of the tracks, a hollow refrain,
I am but a muselmann, aboard the last train.

139. The Lights Burning my Mind - Friday December 08, 2023 23:36 MST

In the caverns of my head, where thoughts wage their war,
   burns a relentless light, a beacon of inner gore.
   Behind my weary lids, a fear rages, fierce and wild,
   a spilling of alabaster and blood, untamed and undefiled.

Visions seared upon the base of my sight,
   a bleeding night, with no respite in flight.
   A battle waged within, no victor, only sin,
   a duel of the self, where darkness seeks to win.

Oh, for a moment's peace, to dim these glaring lights,
   a brief reprieve from these internal fights.
   My soul, a weary collier in this hellish mine,
   yearns for a pause, a silent, sacred shrine.

The walls of my mind are but crumbled dust,
   leaving me exposed, in my fears and distrust.

No solace found, no ear to hear my desperate plight,
alone I stand, in this unending, cursed night.

With a shovel turned rubber, in these tunnels, I toil,
a Sisyphean task, in my mental soil.
Trapped in corridors of thought, a labyrinthine bind,
a relentless pursuit, with no exit to find.

In this inferno of my making, a landscape bleak and bare,
lies the death of a spirit, caught in despair.
Each stroke of my rubber spade, a futile attempt to flee,
from the chains of my own making, a longing to be free.

The light, a cruel sentinel, never dims, never fades,
a constant reminder of my mind's relentless raids.
In this purgatory of thought, where hope dares not tread,
I navigate the mazes of the living dead.

In the ashes of my sanity, a truth stark and dire,
in the pyre of my mind, burns an unquenchable fire.
The battle within, a journey with no end in sight,
a solitary wanderer, in the abyss of night.

140. Days Melt Together - Saturday December 09, 2023 12:35 MST

Time's relentless march,
  blurs days into silent grey,
  dreams fade, unremarked.

141. So I Hear - Sunday December 10, 2023 11:37 MST

What's it worth? I may never truly know. Everything is a stone's throw away from calamity. The entire human race, all of humanity- could so easy drift out to tow. We've garnished our souls, trying to fill empty holes, but we have forgotten. The downtrodden, those who were and are here begotten.

The best didn't make it out alive, so I hear.

Still, each day I look for a way to pay. I wander aimlessly into the fray though these debts shall never sway. We lie to the man in the mirror seeing a reflection that's infallible; it soothes us, in our minds what we want to hear. We know it's a facade, the ugly brutal side of a rake. Even so all we can muster is the thought to take, take, take.

What's it worth? I believe this actually not to be a question; it's a condescending contradiction that peels itself away from our ultimate introspection. There is no real value, all just fiat fragments of thought. In the end, the most treasured commodity, time, cannot be bought.

So I kneel at the altar regardless of my convalescent falter. Grasping for coins, cash or cards to buy my way out of this cloture. Unfortunately my pockets are filled with shattered glass, there is no money, only sharp edges that relentlessly pass.

I bleed, crawling out on all fours. It's not fortune I'm chasing, it's more time, this I cannot ignore. I salivate at the thought of finally getting that closure. Instead there is a leach inside of my mind sucking all of my life, all of my time. The signs proclaimed that it would set me free; it was a lie, it's all consuming and all I'll ever be.

What's it worth? Ultimately, you tell me. All I can tell you is that this freedom, is by no means free. All I have is a rattling, an enigma-survivors guilt. So I hear. I will remain on my knees, all I can do is pray.

The best didn't make it out alive, so I hear.

142. The Helper - Monday December 11, 2023 21:51 MST

Everyone wants something from me;
    I help them all, I get no fee.
    I'm overwhelmed, stretched beyond my seams.
    The world takes advantage of me.

143. It Leads to Gilligan's Island- Tuesday December 12, 2023 22:10 MST

This constant barrage of desiring a mirage,
    it amounts to nothing more than a cheap corsage.
    Gleaming under the desert sun, it looks so real.
    Deep down I know it's nothing- far from the real deal.

I should know better than to continue this journey,
    with each step my blistered feet sink into the sand.
    Eventually I will be wheeled out in a gurney.
    Even so, I cannot help myself, I must continue to go.

Each forward movement, a waste, a cantonment of my war weary soul.
    This grand illusion seems within my reach.
    If only but I try once more, my consciousness continues to beseech.
    Onward I tread, though my fortunes cast a shadow much farther
    than the word of the gospel can even preach.

I collapse underneath the heat of the devil, that damned desert sun.

Though I've reached a foreign lagoon, the evil has won.

I hear cars clamoring, horns are sputtering engines.
    My eyes reveal it all to have been an illusion.

A desert? I am not; I find myself crawling behind the
    Studio City Los Angeles lot.

144. The Frayed Rope - Wednesday December 13, 2023 21:20 MST

The twine of my spine pulls at itself violently in opposite directions,
   this rope of my being is hanging on by a meager string;
   meandering reflections.

Those around me cannot see or hear the tears.
   I am the only one witness to the ripping.
   It's my very essence being pulled apart, no one cares...
   I am on a medieval rack, my shackles once cold and black.

Now the irons are warm from my body's heat and
   stained with my blood.

The iron shackles never relent though my dying soul does.

My torturer laughs as he pulls, cajoling the wheel tighter, first
   popping out my joints in a sickening crackle.

Then comes the ripping of my skin.

It burns like a cauldron of boiling sins, each tear, each turn of that
　　wheel. My spine is the fraying rope, my life will no longer congeal.

The tension, so immense I cannot fathom why my damned
　　consciousness relents.
　　Please, I beg you God, let this torture end.
　　Cut my fraying rope of existence, allow my soul to descend.

145. The Midnight Juggernaut - Thursday December 14, 2023 21:00 MST

It prowls unseen,
    a juggernaut in the midnight's gleam.
    a daunting force, relentless, obscure,
    through time's fabric, it endures.

With a hiss like milk's hot steam,
    it weaves through the world, a waking dream.
    A cry that pierces the silent veil,
    an ephemeral burning, a dire tale.

Its scent, a miasma, ungodly, untold,
    in the darkness rolled.
    A presence felt, in the heart's deep well,
    the story no lips could ever tell.

Through the ether, it moves with grace,
    leaving tracks in its haunting trace.

A force that bends the will of fate,
in its wake, the threads of destiny wait.

In the hush of the nocturnal tide,
the juggernaut moves, where secrets hide.
An empty cry in the wind, a shiver in the soul,
in its path, life shall unroll.

A creature of the abyss, of our forbidden place,,
moving in patterns, with ghostly grace.
An entity of mystery, of fear and awe,
in its presence, the world withdraws.

This midnight juggernaut,
the Grim Reaper's fleeting glance.
A force beyond our mortal ken,
In our doomed existence, it writes in no chance.

In the quiet of the night, it roams free,
a guardian of secrets, a key to the mystery.
In the stains of reality, it bleeds out its tale,
a juggernaut in the night, eternal and pale.

146. Ode to the Unseen - Friday December 15, 2023 23:39 MST

In shallow gap, a stage unseen,
    beneath the feet where musicians tread,
    Lies a chasm deep, where light has been dead,
    a silent story, unsung, unread.

Here in the dark, a mop alone stands,
    its strands splayed out like a star's bright arms,
    a sentinel in the underlands,
    guarding against unseen harms.

Not a prop, but a player true,
    In the Ball Area's pulse, it plays its part,
    a quiet custodian, out of view,
    cleansing the canvas for art's new start.

This mop, a symbol, simple, sure,
    of all that's done away from cheer,

the work that makes the spectacle pure,
the hidden toil that brings us here.

In this cavernous, concrete hold,
    where notes reverberate of the final scene and fade,
rests the untold tale, bold,
    of the mop's quiet serenade.

The lights above, they shine,
    and musicians bask in their applause,
but remember the mop, its humble line,
    for in its fibers, lies the cause.

It's not the grand, but the small and still,
    that holds the world firm and right,
A mop in the dark, a testament of will,
    that sweeps the stage for another night.

This ode to the unseen, let it be known,
    a tribute to the silent lives,
for every misnomer that has ever shone,
    needed a mop, and a chance.

147. My Forever Deluge - Saturday December 16, 2023 17:36 MST

Sometimes I wonder whether or not my soul will eventually clear from this thunder. Under gray and red skies that rage, ear shattering explosions drain the blood from my veins. I love the rain, though this thunder is my plight. With each strike of lightning, the clouds smother my existence, snuffing out my light. From the shrouded cover of the clouds this precipitation brings to light my hesitation. Another whipping crack travels through the night, my fingers are bloodied and raw, no more nails left as the monster continues to bite. Living in the eye of the storm I feel my grip quickly slip. This storm is my reality, a deadly weather that shall never cease. Instead I find in my bloodshot eyes only the resolve to quit. This monsoon has left me in a daunting state of buffoonery and spite. Despite the flower moon crying out of human sight, the squall continues to relentlessly pound my Earth with all its might.

How I desperately wish this rain would fade to oil, lining my pockets, softening my toil. My ethos is packed up, bunched in a heap of tightened coil. I know that fate will only continue to foil my height, leaching poisoned water into my soil.

. . .

WORDS ARE SNAKES WITH ARMS

Sometimes I wonder whether or not my soul will eventually clear from this thunder. It's a moot point, a lost thought- water left out that will never boil. This deluge will continue to drown me from the inside out.

148. The Evil Max Heiliger - Sunday December 17, 2023 21:49 MST

The ill gotten gains robbed of those that arrived in heinous ungodly trains. The arrival on those damned tracks was just the beginning of an odyssey beyond smoke stacks.

Max of Kanada was just the start, he took more than the souls of the innocent that were so viciously forced to depart. The countless murders- an unforgivable crime. It's the hate, the misplaced manufactured hate that is twisting minds and alters our fate.

The sheer ignorance of such poisoned propaganda, history unfortunately repeats itself- and if this poison continues, it will be the world's last stanza.

Hate in any form is a festering mutation of misinformation, a grotesque inexcusable castration of moral decay. Any being with hate in their heart shall inevitably drift into the fray. Their transgressions against us all; luckily for us, as a collective humanity, we decline hate's vengeful call.

. . .

Still, Mr. Heiliger continues to linger haunting us all from the bridge. This man, these men, deserve no salutation. Max- you're eternally wretched and shall forever traverse a purgatory worse than hell without any destination. On Earth, you attempt to bleed us dry, but you've forgotten we will never bow to your disgusting riches, your lies.

While you stole and murdered, we fought back. Relentlessly we shall never falter in our peaceful combat. You see, we are not like you Max. We refuse to profit off of anyone's backs. You're robbed riches, bricks of gold shall rain down from the heavens pelting you, opening up your evil. Not even a million stitches shall heal your wounds. Instead you will pour salt into them yourself- you racist buffoons.

Take your Swiss bank accounts and try to flee. No matter your worldly wealth, there's no escaping destiny.

149. My Biggest bet - Monday December 18, 2023 21:34 MST

My entire existence is a preamble to a nonstop gamble.

With each decision, each bet- I feel my heart slip from my chest
and fall like a steak from a discount meat cabinet.
Even so, I call my bookie, I place my wager.
Without this cheap thrill, all I have is perpetual danger.

The house agreed to my wager, taking my bet.
My odds are extremely thin, though I do not fret.
To actually win?
That's an inconceivable gambit.
I'm a loser, so my expectations must be met.

The fourth quarter rolls around,
My money lies in a coffin, sports books surround.
They clamor in in a desperate craze, each yearns to be my bookie, my
pallbearer. They wish to watch as I seethe and sink into the ground.

. . .

I lost, though that was my expectation.
 I intentionally lose, it's an attempt to garner some semblance of
 frustration, a blood let.
 The truth is I'm numb, not even the prick of a needle
 into my thumb can help me feel something; I'm vercome.
 Glum- I am not. I'm a hollowed out body of rotten flesh in destiny's
 empty lot.

So when tomorrow rolls around, assuming it still does.
 I know I will place another wager- my soul dares, it does.

150. Turmoils Burn - Tuesday December 19, 2023 20:08 MST

It creeps in, an undeniable invincible sin.
    It starts to boil underneath my skin, a feast for the devil,
    something akin to a last meal.
    This hole left in my soul, there's nothing left to feel.

My disposition, a deal.
    It flows over me, every hair on my body erect,
    my consciousness demands that my very being shall insurrect.

My strength to fight off this squall is menial compared to the
    tempests call.

I relent.

My spirit falls to their evil intent.

Against all odds, to sail the other way across the world my soul laments.

I am now an unnamed figment, a fragile fragment of broken cement.

Now all consumed, I have no option but to plea,
    I cry out but there's no avoiding my destitute destiny.

151. The Offer - Wednesday December 20, 2023 16:10 MST

It watches me intently from the corner of the room, its eyes droop like sinking balloons.

What it wants? That I do not know. Though it's apparent its presence is here only with maleficent intents. It erupts a scream, one in which only I can hear. The words are nonsensical though its meaning is entirely clear.

I watch as the specter fumbles around; from its pockets it produces bloodied gold coins, from which it found. They clank and clink together with a tin on tin like clamor. The blood drips as the entity continues to stammer.

The figure grows larger as it begins to encroach. I'm not fearful of the ghost, instead I eagerly await its approach. It outstretches its claw with the gold coins in the open palm. A clear gesture for me to take them, an evil invitation.

. . .

Though I know that nothing is for free- by taking this bloodstained currency my soul shall flee.

152. Time's Light - Thursday December 21, 2023 22:06 MST

In the quiet hours before the day's first light,
    breathes a world in chaos, a realm caught in night.
    Eyes wide open, in the silence they keep,
    a mind racing forward, denying sweet sleep.

Each tick of the clock, a reminder so stark,
    of moments slipping by, in the profound dark.
    Anticipation stirs, a restless guest in my bed,
    spilling secrets of the hours ahead.

In this kingdom of wakefulness, thoughts intertwine,
    of nightmares in waking hours, they're mine.
    The night, a canvas for my unspoken fears,
    painted in the hues of my unshed tears.

Awaiting the sun, a promise yet to bloom,

the quiet anticipation of a world to resume.
In the hush of the night, under a sky so deep,
I find myself lost in the space before sleep.

153. The Ride - Friday December 22, 2023 21:41 EST

On a reckless path,
    control slips away, heart pounds,
    destiny's wild ride.

154. The Tumultuous Tread - Saturday December 23, 2023 23:11 EST

In the depths of my soul, a desperation brews,
  a dollar store of emotions, in shades of blues.
  It widens and crashes in relentless waves,
  in its tumultuous grasp, my spirit craves.

Feeling overcome, adrift in this storm,
  seeking a lighthouse, a sheltering form.
  Lost for days, in this internal sea,
  yearning for a shore, even though no land shall set me free.

The swells of sorrow, the tides of despair,
  in each crest and fall, a silent prayer.
  Beneath the surface, where dark currents flow,
  lie the secrets, only the depths know.

155. The Christmas Eve that was- Sunday December 24, 2023 16:39 EST

Beneath the weight of years now gone,
    I wander through a world withdrawn.
    The laughter and tears of days long past,
    mourned in silence, lines since cast.

Ghosts of me and sorrow intertwine,
    in this solemn march of time.

So I run, under grieving skies,
    from memories that never say their goodbyes.
    Each stride, a leap from yesterday,
    but the past, in persistence, chooses to stay.

In the death of what was, a life depleted- gray.

156. The Pull - Monday December 25, 2023 22:18 EST

In the silent struggle of existence,
    the push and pull, a constant formidable pressure,
    a force that shapes with quiet insistence,
    the intricate patterns of life's advance.

It tugs at the core, a sculptor deft,
    in every moment, its presence felt,
    a silent duel, a forgotten craft spelt,
    in time's embrace, our fates are dealt.

With each fierce pull, a lesson learned,
    with every push, the spirit's yearn,
    an endless cycle, subtly spun,
    until the final hour is done.

157. The Insatiable Current - Tuesday December 26, 2023 21:24 EST

The call resounds from heights untold,
a yearning cry for more, so bold.
In ceaseless caves, it implores,
for lavish dreams on distant shores.

In its wake, a hollow ring,
of endless wants, a burdensome thing.
A siren's song that never sleeps,
it claws and gnashes, through the deep.

The more we grasp, the less we hold,
a grim pursuit, as days unfold.
For in this race, no prize awaits,
just fleeting rushes and empty fates.

A nothingness that cries, ever vast,

of all that's sought, none shall last.
In this pursuit, we're left bereft,
desire calls, and we are left.

158. Repose - Wednesday December 27, 2023 17:12 EST

In the gray calm of a stormy sky, where souls rest,
   the world in hushed repose.

A gentle breath, the day's last vest,
   as silence 'round us grows.

Beneath the sky's soft fading light,
   all turmoil finds release.

In stillness holds the quiet night,
   a moment's sweetest peace.

The earth itself lays down its head,
   on night's cool, soothing lap.

. . .

A tranquil pause, all words unsaid,
    time's soft, unfolding wrap.

In repose, the heart may find,
    its rhythm is slow and deep.

A sanctuary for the mind,
    in restful, healing sleep.

159. To the Gallows they call - Thursday December 28, 2023 15:47 EST

To the gallows, from the shallows- the sickness follows.
  It rolls in with the tide, there's nowhere you can hide.
  The transgressions follow in each aggression of the sea.
  No one will answer your calls, hear your plea.

From the cold cobblestones of your cell to the greased rope upon
  which your neck will sell.
  All you can hope for is a quick break.
  Praying that your weight is more than your spine can take.

To the gallows you walk.
  The crowd and the passerby gawk.
  Soon, your soul will take stock. You failed to lead your flock.

On the platform of death, the squalls spill out through the night. This
  rope, thick but each strand bridle- shall lead you to the hymn of the
  devils fiddle.

. . .

The executioner reads out your crime- it's benign but enough to rob
you of your God given time.
The floor beneath falls, only the rope catches your calls.
Though the rope sat behind your left ear, you're not given a clean
break- your last moments are spent in perilous fear.
The only thing that's never been fake.

160. Sailing Mechanical Vices - Friday December 29, 2023 21:06 EST

Smoke contrails pierce the night like spiral stairs through a veil. They twist in a mechanical belch following slowly, trailing behind in forgotten tails.

Their pollution significantly degrades our Earth's constitution though we seem to care not.
We prefer to shoot ourselves in the foot, forgetting that nature will not.

These hazardous toxic winds follow our desires, cast in sorrow's powwow. Despite the hour, our needs call.
We feed them; like a mother nursing a child.
Though our grotesque human meanderings are much more callow.

From planets far away, I witness alien ships glimmer in the clarity of oceans night.

. . .

They wonder why we choose to create our own plight.
    For even creatures divine and far flown, cannot understand why
    humans choose the unknown.
    I know not why we do what we will. I waste my days under the sun
    reenacting memories of the past- maybe just for the sheer thrill.

Though the truth remains, we board our fate like passengers of a
    plane. This pollution ultimately is our evolution- we call it green, act
    like we are righteous.
    Though the ocean can see through our sick mechanical vices.

161. Airport Purgatory - Saturday December 30, 2023 12:23 EST

In transit's purgatory, where time and patience fray,
we're herded, cattle-like, through gates that lead to gray.
A symphony of shuffling feet and sighs compose the score, while
human glaciers drift and halt on polished terminal floors.

Here, in the vein of travel's heart, where frustration's roots take hold,
impassive faces weave and dart, in patterns brash and bold.
A sudden stop, a vacant stare, amidst the hurried swarm,
a blockage in the artery where haste and languor form.

These wanderers, in selfish arcs, care not for flow nor form, in their
idle drift, they leave behind a wake of a silent storm.

Annoyance blooms, a bitter bud, in this human maze,
where common sense and courtesy are lost in transit's haze.

. . .

Each step, a trial, each pause, a curse, in the airport's hum, a
   labyrinth of lethargy where wits unravel, come undone.

We're marooned in this no-man's-land, where time's a thief, unseen,
   among the aimless amblers who wander as if in subservient
   standards.

In this nexus of departure, where paths and people cross,
   the world's absurdity unfolds, humanity at a loss.
   So here I stand, an island firm, in the river of absent minds, awaiting
   the boarding call, leaving the thoughtless behind.

162. New Year's Grieve - Sunday December 31, 2023 07:37 MST

As I sit pondering the failures of my year, I dread the next one to
   come- continuing is my fear. I'm tired, mired down in thick mud.
   Another year squandered, signaled by a ball dropping, a fake thud.

I sit, chewing on my cheek like a cow chews its cud.
   I'm nervous, hesitant- helpless in the eyes of this new year, I have no
   more blood. The talking heads on the TV pretend in grandiose that
   they're enjoying sitting in a square with millions.
   I know the truth- so do the billions.

Facades of famous acts, notable celebrities are paraded about. The
   clout of the evening, it's a lie I refuse to tout.

I'm not entirely sure exactly what my sadness is all about.
   I'm overwhelmed, another year is foreboding enough to make my
   soul shout out.

.   .   .

The clock ticks down; even though it's prerecorded. It's just
   another reminder of the lie that time pretends to be.

When the clock strikes twelve I'm sure I'll be on my eighth drink.
   Anything to numb my mind, dampen the dead smelling rot that this
   new year shall brink.

163. Dreamer - Monday January 01, 2024 14:02 MST

I've seen it happen a million times over in my mind.
    From the deepest depths of my psyche it is my bind.
    I've tasted the wine, felt my fine silk suit tear as I caught the thorns
    of the roses walking in the garden of disrepair.
    It's behind that home, that false throne so kind that I share.
    I've seen it happen a million times in my mind.

I'm a powerful dreamer, that's a fact.
    The most frightening part is I know my dreams will impart.
    Each will come to fruition- it's an inevitable increment of my
    mission. My vision carries on in perpetuity; destiny's pact.
    It is my future, my futility, my vice- my immunity.
    I am the ultimate leader over my own ant community.
    I've seen it happen a million times in my mind.

Slowly I watch my age progress as an outsider but blind.
    I know my years are just a damnation to remind.
    It burns in a forever ember, slowly sleeping the fire stays lit.

My eternity is written, etched in stone so unkind, unable to quit.
My dreams amass together, our coincidence of time.
I've seen it happen a million times in my mind.

It shall never cease until it's done. I'm inching closer, I've all but
    won. These dreams morph to my reality, my new existence. It's one
    in which I've achieved through only my own resistance. I've gone
    without any substance to arrive at the open door of the future,
    which silently continues to implore. I will reach the top of every
    single mountain behind that door.

I've seen it happen a million times in kind.

So I breach the epochs of success, boundaries all but pushed past the
    brink. I have made it to my finality, I am the ship that they could not
    sink.

That is the degradation of my inescapable plea. My dreams are now
    no matter what- my forever reality.
    I now sit upon broken piles of my own success.
    Onlookers gawk, beguiled at my beautiful mess.
    Each spiderwebbed shatter of glass looks to each of them, their cost
    will never surpass.
    I am hungry, unsatiated, I squirm. Achieving my destiny is
    something that I am forever damned to earn.

I've done it a million times.

164. Frenzied - Tuesday January 02, 2024 22:18 MST

Amidst chaos crying in my mind, I fumble, desperate hands grasping at the ethereal, seeking a fragment of solace in this relentless hole. I dwell in a coffin of steel, buried in the abyss of the unspoken, muted, my only consort in this earthen tomb.

My skull throbs with the drumbeat of despair and palpable pain, my eyes dimming in the relentless march of agony.

Inescapable, this torment that weaves its web, tying me to a world where farewells are all but unsaid.

Behold this shroud of sartorial deceit, a noose of silk and tweed, suffocating in its embrace. Each breath, a battle against the tightening yoke, my psyche drowning in an arid well of mania.

In the frenzy, I reach for the intangible, grasping at the straws of hope, wealth, affection – each attempt, a collapse into the chasm of futility. No elixir, no flight, no dalliance offers reprieve.

This collar, my albatross, weighs upon me, a relentless reminder of a personal purgatory. In my lost existence, I am the minotaur, a leper, seeking an exit that eludes my grasp.

165. The Relentless Pursuit - Wednesday January 03, 2024 20:09 MST

I find myself on a journey far away from home all in service of an unknown stranger sitting high on a golden jewel encrusted throne.

It's no secret that I've lost my way. In fact, I'm not even sure if I ever knew where home was anyway. My path has taken me through pastures of deep green grass fast overgrown. I go unfaithfully wherever the king calls.

I do his bidding, not out of loyalty or fear. Instead I'm his errand boy simply because I have no other option- this he makes clear.

Though I may work for the crown, I yearn to spit at his feet. His monarchy is tyranny; everyday I watch it repeat. Every dirty deed I perform at his behest leaves my soul squandering; at least what's left. The more lost I become in my head the clearer I see that I have no home. I have longings for something that never existed, something that will never be.

. . .

Daily I try to flea, but there's nowhere to go. The crown and his men
    deliver me my orders, I carry each of them out- just for the pay. The
    evil I've chosen, it cannot be undone. Nothing matters anyway; the
    king is always the one who won.

I carry my spade, the holes I dig... eventually I know one will be my
    own. In the countryside my corpse will eventually rot.
    Though this in the grand picture, matters not. Until that day I
    meander under the clouds, walking facelessly through his servants'
    crowds.

I found myself on a journey, without any home or purpose. My entire
    existence is a quiet, pointless spell.

166. The Trial of Self - Thursday January 04, 2024 21:48 MST

Inside the public court of my psyche a trail wages war.
    I am the lawyers, defendant, plaintiff, judge, jury and onlookers
    galore. My crime, disgusting and existentially corrupt,
    the judge does implore.

The striking of his gavel on the lectern oozes out an attempt to reign
    in my insanity. The defense's lawyers spill out their case,
    their turn at the urn. Rat looking men, small and disheveled - they
    speak hastily about why I must live, my crimes slowly beveled.
    Though my crime, all but nonexistent to others, even the state, must
    still adjourn.

The plaintiff's lawyers, with greasy slicked back jet black hair, call
    out, as if it were fate,
    "The defendant is an evil man, one who should
    be locked away forever in a small wooden crate."
    They continue to throw their claims, "He's a failure, he has
    irreparably ruined the life of our client. His actions are unrelenting,

with malicious intent he consistently self-harms!
He drinks to excess, smokes, works himself beyond reproach and
pulls fire alarms."

The judge's lips furrow downward in a frown of intense curiosity, a
sign to proceed. My defense lays out their case,
"The facts, simply, you cannot heed. Our client has never
committed any crime- not even a dirty deed. He's guilty only of
living- if that's a crime then call in the executioner now; let him be
trampled by justice's stampede!"

The judge calls the court to order, the trial shall proceed. I take the
stand against myself, for both parties, as I lay into the fire of all
questions. I am hesitant as to where this path shall lead. Though I'm
innocent, I plead no contest.

Oh how I desperately want to be found guilty- if anything for my
greed.

We retire to the court's inner chambers while my soul laments. I
desperately wish this trial to end, I wish to be locked forever behind
that barbed wire fence. We stare at each other blankly across an
inordinate mahogany table, but we each are looking into a mirror.
A knock at the chamber door interrupts our scrying.
The verdict has arrived but we know it's lying.
Hidden inside the envelope, violent words silently tucked away.

It reads innocent, but the words are stretched ineptly across the page
in a nonsensical splay. I'm damned to be tried another day.

167. Trapped in the Spider's web- Friday January 05, 2024 14:00 MST

In the evil reach, where poisonous spiders have spun,
    I flee from a foe that cannot be outrun.
    My eyes sealed tight, though visions persist,
    seared into my soul, a relentless mist.

A name, a curse, etched in blinding light,
    haunts my every step, a perpetual blight.
    Stench of decay, a scent so profound,
    marks the path where no peace is found.

Desperate, panting, I forge ahead in despair,
    a race against evil, through a nightmarish snare.
    Each breath a gasp, a struggle for life,
    in this twisted game, with peril rife.

The devil's melodic humming voice, a song of dread,
    burns in my mind, a chorus of the undead.

Invisible chains bind my frantic pace,
in this macabre waltz, a fiendish chase.

Through desolate streets, under a mocking moon's glare,
I sense his presence, a cold, suffocating air.
No sanctuary in sight, no haven to claim,
in this endless pursuit, a sinister game.

With every stride, the fiend draws near,
under the guise of smiling faces, my greatest fear.
A date with the devil, a fate entwined,
my soul's lament, in people's lies confined.

In the final stretch, my strength wanes,
succumbing violently to their pain, where evil reigns.
A futile escape, a destiny sealed,
in the devil's grasp, my fate revealed.

And so I falter, my resistance undone,
in the grip of the beast, my battle lost, not won.
In this haunting lament, the spider's tale is spun,
of a soul that fled, but was never truly gone.

168. Cairn - Saturday January 06, 2024 21:00 MST

In the ridge, deep between the rocks lies thick veins of gold.
Civilizations throughout the ages have tried to mine it, to master
nature, mold their worldly fate. Did they actually succeed- history
spins a debate.

Their existence, all but gone. Through the pond, we watch the
trespassers as if we were the pawns. The wildlife follows,
besmirching ponds, the fawns continue to follow.
Its riches they seek, though only sorrow will be all they swallow.

You see, the ridge-line runs deep beyond their morrow.
The riches are actually bleak, the claws of destiny are all but hollow.
Carvings in the rock claim to pave the way.

The wildlife heed their calls, towards the deserts' watchful eye. The
seven sisters will mark the cave, a landmark to the lost road's mine.

The path they tread- will be their ultimate fine.

In the end, damn the stories, there is no gold- no glories. All that lies
in wait is a false bait. Something that keeps us fools salivating, lying
in wait. We will find nothing, only a missed date. No matter where
we dig, our pond is sullied with our floating carcasses- it's fate.

169. Persistent hum - Sunday January 07, 2024 19:19 MST

In the hum's persistent drone,
    lies a hope that's never known.
    A false light in darkness shown,
    leaving me forever alone.

170. Sisyphean Mirror - Monday January 08, 2024 19:42 MST

In the crest of ambition, a solitary figure toils,
    pushing a boulder, a testament to lifelong spoils.
    Up a steep incline, where the moon's light reflects a swine- evil does
    intertwine, a life's work ascends, on a path by fate's design.

The stone, heavy with the weight of unspent years,
    rolls skyward, baptized in silent, unseen tears.
    Each push, a measure of the heart's ceaseless strife,
    a cycle unending, the labor of a single life.

In the cold sweat of the unforgiving wind, a silent narrative spins.
    Of endeavors and aspirations, now worn thin.
    The summit looms, a mirage of triumph so close,
    but with each step, the distance morosely grows.

The boulder, a quiet keeper of damnation and pain,
    bears the scars of a journey, both brazen and bold.

A monument to efforts, futile but sincere,
in its roundness, the passage of each year.

The figure pushes, muscles straining under the load,
    on a path of solitude, a singular, desolate road.
    The summit, a siren's call, luring with deceptive grace,
    in its pursuit, a life rendered a relentless chase.

At the hilltop, a moment of harrowing clarity prevails,
    as the boulder teeters, a balance so frail.
    The laborer, now weary, beholds the impending fall,
    a life's work descending, breaking against nature's wall.

Down the slope, the stone crashes with relentless might,
    a rolling thunder, a spectacle of tragic plight.
    The cracking of stone bleeds out in a crumbling screech through the
    unforgiving night.
    It serves as a testament to the pointless grind,
    in its callous splintered wake, a trail of shattered hopes left behind.
    Everything, all of it- life is fake.

The laborer stands, a witness to the ruinous descent,
    realizing too late, the years misspent.
    For the boulder was not just stone, but dreams cast in lead,
    now lying broken, a legacy of dread.

So the cycle resumes, an Sisyphean plight,
    under a sky indifferent, night dies into day, a hopeless fight.

The boulder awaits, at the foot of the slope, so steep,

in its silence, a promise it cannot keep. Awaiting the next fool to glue all its pieces back. Another relentlessly pointless task asked by the mask.

For in this labor, where destiny and despair are sewn,
    lies the truth of existence, stark and alone.
    A life's work, like a rolling stone, unforgiving and cold,
    in its journey, a story of futility, forever told.

171. The Pawn's Lament - Tuesday January 09, 2024 22:59 MST

I'm just a pawn in the universe's game,
    tossed around, always feeling the same.
    At this ignorant game of chess I sit beguilingly reaching at my waist
    for a rusty dagger to bury into my chest.
    The game is tactful and lauded by intellectuals as a challenge. To
    people like me, it's just another interlocutory attempt at snagging us
    in their talons.

Sick and tired of being a plaything,
    in this worldly game, I'm just hanging by a string.
    Their rook castles and I just sigh perplexed- ogling.
    They manufacture these rules to keep using us as tools.

Angry, annoyed, fed up with the show,
    I'm the rich man's toy, just going with the flow.
    Each move of mine a repeat, the same old story,
    in this damned game, for simple minds like me- there's no glory.
    They act like they enjoy this parade of boarded pageantry but it's

apparent to me that it's just another means to depict and enact their royal savagery.

Trapped in a cycle, can't break free,
    this bureaucratic joke's got a hold on me.
    I have but one piece left- oh how ironic it's a king. They could have beaten me sixteen moves ago, but they like to watch us suffer, our pain lingering.
    But I'm done being played, done with the strife,
    a quick death please, over a life game of chess, I choose the rusty knife.

172. The Optimists Spade - Wednesday January 10, 2024 22:38 MST

Go ahead, grab your shovel. The peat won't wait long, it's calling for
you. The hollows of the ground sing a song in the dirt, don't worry
about it dirtying your shirt.

"You worry me." The shovel cries.
Nonetheless pick your weapon, dig your prize.
You could say I'm afraid, but my voice resonates through
your noise. You see, the fire of the world is fully surrounding us;
don't worry about coughing up the ashes.

So I grab my spade and dig tirelessly through the deep grave's steep
grade.

"Who's the hole for?" I desperately implore.
"It's a wayfaring waste in deserted land." The figure retorts.

. . .

It happens all the time, just embrace the crime. Where have you
spent all your time dying? A misnomer one-hundred million miles
away, ripping at the seams- it's all there ever truly has been.
It doesn't matter if the hole is for you or your kin, innocence will
choke you or smoke you. Pick your chains.

So I dawn my steel restraints and take my place in the hole. It's clear,
everything is evident. This dollar is the last I've spent. They're going
to have to drag us away into the abyss- the forever gray.

173. Operation Hailstone - Thursday January 11, 2024 20:00 MST

This wreckage. It tells my story. The diver hears it in each bubble
    wasting up from his breath; seawater eating my glory.
    I lie at the bottom of the ocean, but my spoils live to this day. The
    flared barrel of my plane's machine gun paid back the fiends from
    December 7th, a grotesque display. In fact, they're still paying- this is
    the enemy's leaven.

While my center of gravity now is a depravity below the sea, the sun
    and history still smiles upon me. It's at the hands of righteous acts
    that justifies me.

Funny enough- the enemy has the same
    righteousness, at least it's all they see. Regardless of facts, it's all an
    emotion. It sinks ultimately to the bottom of the sea.

What was all concrete is now a futile toil, everything reverts back to
    the soil. While they were there, not a single tree stood on the island-

a human foil.

Again- in the end, none of this matters, we all will boil.
So here I lay in my watery grave- but it's you that sits in dismay. No matter who or what you pay, the bombs ensure we all end the same way.

174. It's Outside Your Window- Friday January 12, 2024 13:43 MST

It starts as any other monotonous night, the lights dim at 9:15 and my medicated head hits the pillow at 9:30 in fright. I wait to go somewhere happy, where I live my best days. In my preferred reality, there is no malaise. Anxiously I wait for my woolen bedded craft to take off, carrying me into the next world hopefully soft.

Instead the voices start to surround. They call my name, though they speak of nothing profound. I try to ignore their murmurings but inside my blanket, my skin is squirming. I pretend they're not present- though my thoughts will not move them far. They stand at the edge of my bedside urging me to follow them to the hall.

I have but one choice, and it's already made. Uneasy, I upend my legs and follow them to the maze. I'm greeted downstairs by the watchers; my neighbors by trade. I ask desperately how they entered my home; is my security so easy to evade? They act as if this is their dwelling, like they belong. They unveil their entrance, a sliding glass door, it has been along. This throng of strangers is amassed in the streets outside my home. The wind rips violently, singing a dry sour song. This cold stale air makes me temporarily forget this gauntlet of a situation in which is now my spoiled fare.

My Adirondack chair wisps from my porch and careens silently through the air. It lands upright on my roof, on display like it has always been there. The voices of the animals in the streets belch an ephemeral call. From the open door, all my possessions are sucked out with the force of a vacuum; not even the floor breaks their fall.

In a silent tornado all of my home's contents lament as they land also on the roof, but not even a spoon is bent. My neighbors don their teeth in a hasty gritted grin. I realize this nature doesn't affect them, to their chagrin. Suddenly my chest erupts blood from a nickel sized hole. Like baby vomit, my blood spurts out as if it were my entire soul. I know that I cannot sustain such bleeding and live. I put pressure on the grotesque wound as I prowl in search of a towel. But all my belongings are out of reach, perched on my roof like an owl. There's nothing to stop the bleeding, no way to pack my wound.

Though I feel no pain, I know this ending hopelessness is all that will sustain.

175. Excelsior - Saturday January 13, 2024 23:05 MST

Sixty-one battles led before my exile.
  Regardless of my gaudy hat I could not get them in file.
  So here I sit on this isle.
  I need no trial to see what a man I am. It's reflected in the mirror, a
  bleak skeleton.

In the sand my shells sell thoughts of my crumbled mind's aisle. Clad
  in vain glory, adorned with ambitions so vile,
  in ranks of my own demons, I could not them compile.

So here I sit, in desolation, on this life's Nile,
  no need for judge or jury, no pretense of a trial.
  Still my reflection bares the truth in the stretch of a mile,
  A visage gaunt, a life's summary in a bleak skeleton's smile.

The mirror's cold gaze, an indictment of denial,
  I still remember the relentless conversations, a soul on trial. Words

like daggers, sharp and hostile,
each phrase a verdict, every silence, a file.

Carving out the substance of a spirit once agile,
    now a sculpture of regrets, a gallery of my own revile.
    This self-made purgatory, a heart's domicile,
    bleak and barren as a winter's tile.

Once sought salvation, through methods versatile,
    dreams of conquest, now memories juvenile.
    For in the end, I am nothing, an empty profile,
    a tale of loss, where darkness did reconcile.

In this realm of sand, where I serve my while,
    no more battles to wage, no strength to rile.
    In this somber twilight, no more reasons to beguile,
    just the quiet surrender to the night, ever so sterile.

A man once clad in armor, now facing his defile,
    with every setting sun, I inch closer to the final mile.
    Conquering demons, a quest futile, in the end,
    all that remains is the specter of a once hopeful smile.

176. The Winter Hike - Sunday January 14, 2024 20:00 MST

I tread, a reservation not needed- just walk ahead. My trail begins with ease, though I take it walking with shaky knees. My end destination, usually picturesque, Sprague lake in winter is frozen and the water seems to cease.

The frozen lake will be the only witness to my wake. A walk that's been eight years in the making, it's all so much more than I can take. I've been here before, to this very lake. Though it was July, it was not frozen, but my heart was pierced by the very same stake.

My feet guide the walk, it's so cold words cannot carry so there's no point to talk. Only the frosted pines would listen- they hear each frozen breath and they know my mission. Alone, there's no one else around- no one else who can hear- it's a weeping somber eternally bound. It reverberates in the valley, reminding me of the deadly dally. It's negative twelve degrees outside, the dreadful cold from which you cannot hide.

. . .

WORDS ARE SNAKES WITH ARMS

I'm seeking my past, trying to end the present. I yearn for a familiar spot, even so I'm hesitant. This march in the cold, I thought I'd never be here-I'd never be so old. Everything seems so foreign in the drowning essence of night, stars are my only light. First, I lose feeling in my hands and feet-it fades to a relentless pain that stings ever so sweet.

Before I know it, I am overcome with a glowing warmth. I know it's only a blanket over my senses, one that signals imminent peril commences. So I walk deeper but my memory proves to be a poor keeper. I no longer recall the destination of my path. I venture off to a rock that's covered in snow. I take my last seat on it. It's an ice cube of death. Though I died years ago, so this end is no behest. At least my last place will be one of eternal rest.

177. The Drifting Door of Fate - Monday January 15, 2024 22:48 MST

There's an unspoken lore that every failure offers a new opportunity, a door. Each lapse is a lesson that one can learn from and explore. Speaking from the experience of a perpetual failure I can confidently say firsthand that it's akin to rowing a canoe without an oar.

I am in that canoe today, without a paddle. My endeavors break the crest of each river wave, each offers another fiasco. Every setback and collapse, I'm tired of being mired down in this ridiculous wooden boat. I couldn't get anywhere, even if I just tried to circle in a moat. You see, there is no success for me, no accolades or parades. I'm a penniless rock, sinking my vessel and wasting my days.

It's true, my canoe has holes, it sinks steadily. At the beginning of my seafaring journey I plugged each eagerly. Each mishap bore another implosion in my dastardly bow. First I plugged them with my fingers and toes, it slowed the water but never fully clotted the gapping bleeding of water careening- if only I could row. I began to question whether or not my biggest concern was the water gushing in or my dead weight that would be the demise of my float.

After all these years, I have found my answer. I let the water rush in, I could give a damn about the impending sin. Though my weary head has been above water all this time, I have been drowning anyway from towing the line. I'm tired of trying, I'm done with it all. No matter what I try, no matter what I do- I cannot fight nature's call.

Maybe it could have been different, my journey. If only I'd had an oar to start with or a larger vessel. As my sinking continues, I am unconcerned about the lessor. The shore seems so much further as I drift. What once seemed in sight, now is nothing but a myth.

At this point it's futile to even try to swim. The water is freezing anyway and I've lost control of every limb. As the top of the wood struggles against the surface of the water I feel it rhythmically toddler. How ironic that now this canoe tries desperately to float. I hope it knows my toils. In my last moments I laugh as I gloat aloud to this boat. Just like me, it stands no chance to her might, the water sucks us both under in a white rising thunder. Under the river I keep my eyes open in a sick desire to watch what's fated. Floating eerily by is the remnants of a door; I guess it was just lore. We are all just another example of what destiny has in store.

178. Impulsivity - Tuesday January 16, 2024 21:37 MST

Impulsivity drowns me in a thirty gallon drum, just when I feel like I have a shot at crawling out, I realize just exactly how stout this barrel is. It won. I can't see inside, the oil is thick. It relentlessly gushes into my mouth and up my nostrils so quick- I forget that I'm stuck, just for a fleeting bit.

It drips down my throat like a post nasal drip. There is no remedy here- except hoping that I drown quick. There's just enough room beneath the top of the lid- it offers an outstretched hand at life's bid. More than anything, it's an overarching temptation to quit. It's not enough cubic air to sustain the fare of my life.

Gasping for breath in this confined space, I swallow more oil than air, a relentless race. I'm beyond panicked, I'm locked in death- this viscous case.

. . .

Suddenly the top of the barrel is lifted swiftly out of place. Without thinking I submerge my head and reach for the lid- locking it back in place. My impulsivity is the true bind. It's thicker than the oil and darker than my barrel's confines. I can't help it, I truly am under a slick treacherous spell. I inhale a deep breath of oil, I hope it's my quell.

179. OUR DISEASE - WEDNESDAY JANUARY 17, 2024 20:50 MST

I feel sick to my stomach from this disease.

It afflicts us all, it's a hungry monster impossible to please. I try endlessly to cure what ails. Instead the sickness drips eagerly from pales. There is no drink, no magic pill. This ailment is one we shall never kill.

It creeps up my collar, choking me at the neck. Its effects linger a paralysis so profound I cannot lift a finger. We are the walking dead. Like a chicken without a head- we continue. It's not a choice, it's a sinew of Earth that gently crafts our hearth. There is no warmth or guarantee, we are all cheap suits drifting with no warranty.

The working man must eat- it's no great feat. It makes my blood boil. To experience these worldly human desires causes me nothing but to ignorantly recoil. It makes me ill, not just visibly but to the depths of my core. The sores burst and ooze green paper that seems to make eyes light up in galore.

. . .

What we're doing here will be a grand trail. Our sins committed out in the open, though to the heavens our transgressions can craft no denial.

Still I have this itch that cannot ever fully be scratched. I scrape at my flesh with everything but it stands no match. I need a fire, to burn away this itch, quell these worldly desires. There is no end, we even pay to expire.

180. Derby Day - Thursday January 18, 2024 21:26 MST

It burns- the way this visceral world churns.

It imbues a cyclical cruise of news, each new story imprinting a forever bruise. I wish for an ignorance, any state of not truly knowing. That could satisfy my human state, leaving me un-showing.

The usher circles the crowd in this circus, showing each of us to our determined seats. It's a communist juxtaposition between capitalism and a metered feast. You see, they say we have the pursuit of happiness, but that's a sad lie. It's only an endeavor to hang ourselves by our tie.

It doesn't take long- it's just our end. Our evasiveness is futile, the opportunity is nil. Still we sit in our theater seats, at the edge waiting for the thrill. We all know well that it will never come, instead our hunger will spill. If you give a man a chance, he might actually fulfill.

. . .

This would consume their plot, devour their proposed constitution. So they leave us desolate, let only to fight over a proposed solution. The answer sits in the speaker's chair, looking at us as if we are devoid of any hair. The true limerick lies in the callous carelessness of a brick. It's these devoid stones that carve the position for these carless politicians to sit. We lack an overarching mission, we're too busy infighting for a pointless position. We jockey for better seats but we're all just an audience for this brief intermission. Nonetheless, we pay with our lives, day after day. Beaten by bills into submission.

181. Drones Lament - Friday January 19, 2024 21:33 MST

The fear. It eats me alive. It crawls in like a bee into its hive. Instead of honey it's money I'm plagued with making. A fate just as pointless as collecting pollen for a matriarch that is all taking.

All day my time is wasted forever on nothing, I'm so exhausted with faking. I never even see a dollar I make. It sits in an account- but it flies faster than leaves raking. No matter the season or the reason I am subject to living for no reason.

The fear. It eats me alive from the inside. I can't even take a breath without feeling it burning inside. It's everything and everywhere, there is no escaping. When will it end, I'm tired of faking.

These seeds are sewn into a dead soil. I plant each one by hand, no mules or tools, just my own toil. The bees buzz around my head in search for their dreaded spoils. There are no flowers or color in this dry barren land, it's no secret that nature is disloyal. Our mission is one in the same, our lives each carry the same lack of merit. Soon they will fall dead from the sky, I will lapse into the ground. Only the buzzards crying above our heads will be the last worldly sound.

182. My Last Hand - Saturday January 20, 2024 23:49 MST

In a dim-lit room where happiness and dread collide,
    the cards fall like fates, scattered wide.
    A pair of Queens, eyes sharp and keen,
    challenge the stoic King of Spades, unseen.

In their court, a higher card looms,
    the Ace of Spades, a harbinger of dooms.
    In this game, the stakes climb higher,
    not just chips, but the soul's mire.

Each hand dealt, a fragment of life's lore,
    each card flipped, opens a new door.
    To win is to lose, in this twisted limbo,
    every gamble, a stab at chance.

The King, in his silent, somber state,

battles the Ace, a hopeless romance against the cruel hand of fate.
The Queens watch, with a gaze so sly, in their eyes,
the reflection of a bottle of rye.

But the Ace of Spades, dark and profound,
    weighs heavy, a power unbound.

In its presence, the room's air grows thicker,
    a callous odor of malice, a perspiration of hate makes the
    gambler sicker. Time slows down, the candles flicker, the flop will
    reveal our fate.

The players hold their breath, as the final card descends,
    in its fall, a life's journey bends.
    The clatter of chips, the shuffling of decks,
    in their rhythm, a story complex.

The King is vanquished, the Queens sigh,
    as the Ace triumphs, under the Devil's watchful eye.
    Though the true loss, unseen, untold,
    is the player's heart, now icy cold.

In the game of life, the cards are cast,
    their fall, paints the insanity of our vanity.
    Each play, a moment of hope and fear,
    in this poker game, the end is always near.

As the room empties, and the night grows still,
    the cards lay silent, as if by will.

In their stillness, a tale of despair,
of a life gambled away, in the dealer's lair.

In this game of death, where souls are the prize,
the winner and loser, both wear a disguise.
For in the game of life, as the cards cascade,
we're all just players, in the charade.

183. I Wish There was no Seventh Day - Sunday January 21, 2024 18:45 MST

I wish there was no seventh day-
in the unbalanced chemistry of my brain, my hemoglobin ceaselessly
tries to cheat my mind.

A relentless carousel of pills, a prescription it holds.
"Take one every eight hours, for insanity." the label coldly but boldly
told.

A chemical waltz to mute the chaos that within me has only one
option: to unfold.

Each capsule swallowed, not a cure but a masquerade,
a temporary veil over a mind frayed.
In this medicated refuge, reality blurs and bends,
an illusion of peace, on which my sanity depends.

. . .

I am a marionette, strings pulled by pharmacological hands, jittering
    violently to a tune, not of my making, in shifting sands of a
poisoned
    lagoon.

Each dose, a momentary bridge over turbulent seas,
    beneath the surface, the storm will never truly appease.

The weight of existence, a relentless torrential rain,
    each drop a reminder of the unending strain.
    These pills, mere pebbles against a mountain of despair,
    in their futile defiance, an argument of a prayer.

In the mirror, a reflection of weariness, eyes that plead,
    for an escape from this cycle, a respite from this need.
    But the carousel spins, and the calamity ensues,
    an ego of two or three, I have no idea which one actually belongs to
    me. "It's true, go ahead." Says one of the voices cackling in my head.

I have no idea whether or not he's hungry or tired, I'm confused-
    completely mired. I seem to just be a host to parasites in my head.

These pills, a hollow armor against an unseen foe,
    in their muted battle, my only ally and greatest woe.

I'm not crazy- but then again the crazy never really know. So I butter
    my hands and put the toast on the counter, delicately placing plates
    in the toaster for an hour.
    I pour coffee into an upside down mug, on the top placing the

coaster. I sip air, but I think there's coffee there.

I wish there was no seventh day-
   I guess I'm making breakfast for another Monday to feed the
   dismay.

184. Lightning in the Snow- Monday January 22, 2024 20:39 MST

In this half-world, a liminal trap, where time drips slow, in a relentless sap, I stand seated, a smoke repeated, bound and tight, in purgatory's endless kite. I tie on my key to this string, preparing it for flight; I release it into the churning wind to find the electricity of the night.

The lightning proves itself to be living - bolts blind me as they violently explode, showing our plight. It's followed by a thundering crack that shakes my chest and steals my breath. It just isn't right, that even out here fishing for danger in the sky, I catch no break, just welder's eye.

I want this lightning to strike me down. I want to feel the bolts sizzle my skin and deafen my ears- cook me for the whole town. I know that not one resident, not one would care. They would light their cigars from my smoldering hair and laugh at my forever burned frown.

Maybe it's not the storm here that makes me so forlorn. Maybe it's not even the town. I think it could be that I shouldn't have ever been; I'm nothing but a dead weight, a mass of pounds wired together in sin.

I want nothing really, I have no desires. All I have is fear. So night after night, day after day I fly this kite. It's been done before but there's never been any bite.

So here I linger, a ghost, a sigh, under a lightless, starless sky. In purgatory's grip, I find no dawn, just endless twilight, hope forever gone. A prison of my own, where dreams decay, in this twilight realm, my kite and I forever stay.

185. Wandering Flames - Tuesday January 23, 2024 19:52 MST

In this ceaseless snowscape, where time stands still,
each flake, a silent witness to purgatory's will.
Endlessly falling, a cold, white shroud,
in this frozen limbo, thoughts scream aloud.

The fire crackles, its hunger unbound,
devouring logs, in its crazed blaze, profound.
An elemental beast, devoid of reason or thought,
spreading its reach, in the hearth it's caught.

I watch, entranced by its fearsome glow,
a paradox of warmth in the endless snow.
Though I've forgotten that it's fifty-two degrees outside
and I have no fireplace or chimney inside.
There is no snow but there is a fire.
It glazes over my eyes in an entrancing desire.
Even with the cold, I never cease to perspire.

. . .

My thoughts make no sense even to me.
> The idea of eating yanks tears from my eyes- it's a grotesque decree. I think back on things seemingly benign- they haunt me beyond all of time. I'm backwards, even in my words. Daily human activities claw at my utility, deadly stewards.

A double-edged sword, cutting deeper than a knife.

This is purgatory, not of fire, but of ice and flame,
> where each moment lingers, unnamed, untamed.
> The world outside, for me is lost in a wintry haze,
> in this trashcan of solitude, I count the days.

The memories, a relentless, suffocating plastic sail,
> in its ceaseless retrial, my spirits fail.
> The fire, I see clearly that it's not there,
> but it's heat burns me and I smell the sweet dry sour singeing of the keratin- my own hair.
> It's a caustic toxic smell that bears no description or name, but when it burrows in your nostrils- never again can you forget- it's a forever stain.

Here, in the heart of nature's indifferent might,
> I dwell in a chasm between insanity and the walking fight.
> A prisoner of elements, in a world so stark,
> where fire and snow leave an indelible mark.

In this purgatorial realm, where time loses meaning,
> I find myself between two extremes leaning.
> The fire's rage, the snow's blank face.

. . .

Trapped in a cycle of fire and frost,
  in this purgatory, my path forever lost.
  A landscape of contrasts, harsh and divine,
  Here, in the silence, purgatory and wine intertwine.

186. Aft Sinks Last - Wednesday January 24, 2024 10:18 MST

Today I poured into a glass, but it was bereft of a bottom.
  The liquid trickled out, not fast but in a slow seeping leak.
  I kept pouring, trying desperately to fill it to the brim.

I think I knew that it was an impossible endeavor.
  Even so, I continued to pour, I did.
  I have no other option but to try and fill that glass.
  My decanter steadily tapered off in it's weight,
  my shaking hands were just small components of the debate.

Why do I have to continue this effort? Why can't I feel the liquid
  spill? It demands it's presence be recognized as it splashes about,
  even into my eyes it did spill.
  Still I cannot feel it, there's nothing there.

I am in the wheelhouse, the captain of this ship.
  I have no knowledge of sailing, only failing.

Though sailing on I do, a prisoner of the bridge.
The liquid drowns out my radar and shorts the chart-plotter.
I have no compass on this trek.
Still I continue to pour until there is nothing left.

I know that all passengers aboard my ship have but one fate and
    we're all subject to it. When we try to cross the channel, I have no
    idea of the depths or path, we lay in wait.
    My fear is laid not in bricks of what I don't know- but instead the
    mortar of what I do.
    I'm overcome by everything, my tears could drown a moat, flooding
    the castle of my mind.
    All the world's sin and pain seem intertwined in a map
    that only I can find. I'm done, I resign to this glass.
    Slowly I come to accept that I will bottom out this boat-
    my only hope is that aft sinks last.

187. Icarus's Necktie - Thursday January 25, 2024 15:17 MST

I'm jumping on a trampoline suspended high in the sky,
    it's dangling from the Hindenburg- the sun is blinding my right eye.

From this height it's lighter but with each bounce only the clouds
    hear my cry. It makes no sense- none of it everything is nigh, a sweet
    but simple sour lie.

From the clothes I'm bearing to the lack of a parachute I'm not
    wearing. All of it is ridiculous, even the fact that I will die. Whether
    or not I miss a jump or slip from my suspended trapeze in the sky.
    None of it matters, because the hydrogen is flammable- we all will
    fry.

The whole charade will come careening violently down but for the
    press it will be like manna raining down newsworthy pie.

. . .

Tomorrow will caress another story, they think it's sly.
Nonetheless they will blame it on the balloon's painted dress.
Aluminum and iron oxide they shall decide. Even though it's all so
evident that it's the gas that made everything go awry.

Maybe instead the question should lie in why we felt it so
pertinent to float ourselves up for our own demise. As I'm falling
silently to the ground that's the only question tickling my throat.
Why did I do this? I'm helpless to my own actions and thoughts, but
this is not a gloat. I think we're only meant to exist for one reason
and it's not to float.

188. Luring Ashes - Friday January 26, 2024 21:45 MST

When it all fades to black I'll be silently sulking in the back. In
absurdity, I'll watch as it all sets fire.
They will keep passing around the hat, preaching to the choir.

In the smoke, I see all my desire. It's bleeding from my skin as I
perspire. Before I never understood the reprieve, now it stares me
back in the face, ever-clear and I'm the liar. In this century city, I'm
the one they actually want to be- to impress.

I gawk in curiosity at their seemingly alien dress. In the curiosity and
calamity of the moment, a clarity arrives all too late to undress.
Nonetheless, I surmise the mess.
This subservient fatality, my reality, is the ghost of my unrest for
worse or best.

Here in my steeple, I continue to watch my people. They will discover
the pollen of my flower, the truth of the hour.

I was shallow in my search of the earth, a sour hearth. This church has billowed into our fireplace, there's no unceremonious thought left to erase.

The soot and all the ashes, we will wear them as ceremonious sashes. This specter of my house has all along been residing beneath my shirt, my blouse. I'm the sole subservient to myself, placing my own endeavors high on the shelf. It's only myself that I've been trying to grouse.

189. Horizontal Obelisk - Saturday January 27, 2024 22:36 MST

A figure stands, on a precipice grand, grappling with a command.
   This obelisk of resolve, a testament to the problems we're meant to
   solve, within, a screeching urchin stews, a player in this manic storm,
   eschewing clues.

No compass in this tumultuous sea, no chart to plot a course to be.
   A vessel not of wood, but will, against the waves, obstinately still.
   Each crest, a challenge to surmount, each trough, a depth to
   discount, in this odyssey, the mind's own plight, seeking a landing in
   endless night.

Resistance, a mere fog, fades, as into the abyss the spirit wades.
   Persistence, once a noble steed, now a charge without a creed.
   In this corridor of fervor and fright, seeking solace in the flight,
   the quest not for a distant shore, but for meaning, something more.

In the heart of this maelstrom wild, dwells the soul, once a child.

Now a traveler, weary, worn, in the fabric of existence, torn.

This journey, a menagerie of trials, baked with tears, marked by

miles, a pursuit not of land or stick, but of dope-sick peace within the

manic.

This obelisk stands, not in stone, but in the breath of every moan,

a monument to the battle within,

a war not lost, though impossible to win.

190. Mantra of Mania - Sunday January 28, 2024 11:26 MST

I am safe, I am happy, I am healthy.
  I urgently repeat this decree in my mind as water to fight the fire of
  insanity. I'm weary that my consciousness buys my plea.
  Though it's my only attempt- my best attempt to be.
  I am safe, I am happy, I am healthy.

I am safe, I am happy, I am healthy.
  I hope with these repeated words, their weight will carry me into a
  slumber. My breathing heavy, each breath a plunder of sand
  leaching out in a thunder. For me- there is no last curtain call. My
  eyes are pasted open and even the walls are in motion. I feel them
  tugging at my feet, an attempt to drag me from my bed.
  I coil myself into a ball, like an infant's reprieve though they claw at
  my head.
  I am safe, I am happy, I am healthy.

I am safe, I am happy, I am healthy.
  Their voices are loud, clear as crystal. They're howling out my name.

There are no words that can extinguish this flame.
Sleep- its an impossibility in this damned game.
I'm beyond tired, mired in a drudgery of lead sinking down my head into this bed. So my urgent chant turns to a slow count, not of breaths but of heartbeats.
At first, it's only the rhythm of my heart- slowly but surely, theirs begin to join.
It's a harmonious snow of coins dropping like flakes, each an actualization of mistakes.
I am safe, I am happy, I am healthy.

I am safe, I am happy, I am healthy.
I pick up my prayer again, their hearts too flaunting, taunting.
By now hours have passed, my flag of rest sits juxtaposed at half staff. It's a white flag- I've surrendered but my captors will not render my resignation.
They wish not only to hunt but to haunt me- and so they do.
I am safe, I am happy, I am healthy.
I hunger for the safe soothing voices that always arrive before taking me by surprise.

Tonight, it's only the voices of their foes that call me to rise.
The light of day peeks into my eyes.
Another night without sleep, I realize.
I am safe, I am happy, I am healthy.

191. Cúchulain- I am not - Monday January 29, 2024 21:56 MST

Cuchulain- I am not.
    I'm fraught from battles others have since fought.
    I wield no sword, all my weapons are nothing against their rain.
    It falls from the sky in the form of burning arrows, tattooing the terrain.
    The arrows form around me, the fires burn with anger but they cannot compare to my own internal blaze, a wildfire in a hellish maze.

I stand, not a warrior of legend or lore,
    but a mere mortal, raw and sore.
    I tear off my armor, I'm done with this war-
    my battlefield here, I pray it to be my last.
    I wish to bleed out like a pig in this thicket of green grass.
    I cannot stomach the sound of another cannon's blast.

I tread forward in a steady pace, I've sheathed my sword and shed
    my mace. I grimace wildly trying to direct their arrows to my face.

. . .

The sky weeps flames, a celestial pyre,
    mirroring the inferno of my inner fire.
    Each ember in the air, a taunt, a jeer,
    a coaxing of my own thoughts, crystal clear.
    I walk with a fervor into the fire. It blisters my skin and bubbles me
    into a smoking denier.

No Gae Bolga to wield, no chariot to steer,
    just a heart heavy with unspoken fear.
    There's nothing this enemy can do to me now.
    I increase my speed as I run towards the tower.
    A thousand men clad in the king's armor gawk in disbelief, I'm am
    death and my legacy will bequeath.

Shocked, these soldiers are frozen in confusion, locked in place they
    cannot leer. Ablaze I sprint full speed towards them- I'm all
    they can see in this haze.
    I no longer fear my death- I'm so glad it's here. These lying excuses
    for soldiers will soon too feel it near.

Before the moat of the tower I explode into a booming laughter- I've
    silenced their cannons; I'm no longer under any master. They watch
    eagerly as my skin boils off; only my teeth are visible now and a
    vomiting white froth. As the heat consumes my vision I stand
    solitary alone, finally with no mission. There are no more lives to
    take, no fights to bait. The pain I feel now is nothing compared to
    everything prior I've been forced to take.

So I stand, amidst the fiery rain,
    not a hero, but not in vain.

My end is my only purpose; a fact everyone's fate will ascertain.

Cúchulain, I am not, nor need to be,
    for in my story, a different strength I see.
    A resilience that's uniquely mine,
    in the face of burning at the stake- I choose my fire;
    I will forever build my own spire.

192. Imponderabilia - Tuesday January 30, 2024 22:27 MST

My thoughts fall out of my head like drug paraphernalia from the
   pockets of the walking dead.
   This delusion, delirium- it's true source, imponderabilia.
   I cannot recall what I've done, let alone said.
   It's all consuming like flesh eating bacteria.
   I relish the thought of a permanence where all is fled.
   I cannot work, think, or exist according to their criteria.

I live in a fragmented reality.
   These people in my head dictate with totality.
   As their burdened servant I am a flesh frailty.
   It's lost- I've walked past the tracks of no return fallibly.

I am devoured, bit by bit, by this ravenous disease,
   a slow consumption, an unyielding siege.
   Craving the oblivion where turmoil is quelled,
   a silent harbor, from which those inside me are expelled.

. . .

In their world of order, I am but a dissonant note,
    a discordant melody that refuses to float.
    I am the disarray, the outcast, their inconvenient truth,
    in the rigid cadence of existence, I am the uncouth.

Still I drink their anointed fluoride water and paint my skin with
    gasoline, I'm but fodder.
    One of those inside my head struck the match,
    though it snapped and no fire elapsed.
    The stick fell to the ground without any sound.
    I stand drenched in oil- the true blood of the soil.

I cannot spontaneously combust since inside I'm already ablaze. I
    smell my skin smoking and see only though a thick haze. I have no
    hours, no days- all my time is digested in the bulging gut
    of corporate craze.

For a dollar- it's worth more than a soul. Ask anyone sitting high in a
    suede chair above Central Park. A stark reminder that when the rich
    bleed, it's green not red. Their reality is just as unimaginable as
    mine, but I'm poor and poisoned by their lead.

193. The Inquisition - Wednesday January 31, 2024 21:57 MST

"Why did you do it?" I retort.

He stares through me in silence, seemingly nothing to report.

"Was it worth it- what you did?" I sneer in a low snort.

He answers simply, "No- I came up short."

The fog of my breath hides the man in the mirror just for a moment. Not seeing him is the best, I hate this man, my life's inherit opponent.

Still, I smear away the dew to see the same man peering through- this pest.

. . .

"I don't understand you. You need to explain." Now I try to persuade. Though there's no getting through to this fool; it's like trying to get blood from a spade. My questions continue through the night. This interrogation has consumed my life's entire page.

Finally he spews, "No dice- I guess. I feel absolutely nothing, I have no desire to impress. You think I'm the fool? Look at you, lying in your own mess."

I berate this animal, yelling every obscenity I could think. It doesn't move him an inch- but it pushes me to the brink. This line of questioning is more akin to pouring salt in a gaping wound, festering.

I do not relate to this man in the mirror; we have absolutely nothing in common- not a single link. Nonetheless this man controls me and spills poison in my mind, telling me what to think. Today, he gave no substantive answers; tomorrow I'll bury his head in the sink.

Maybe this approach will coax the truth from this devil dressed in a grotesque flesh mink. I'll save my biggest inquiry for last- he will cave to my inquisition. He has no option, ending this fiend is my life's only mission; the righteous path.

194. No Absolution - Thursday February 01, 2024 20:29 MST

In a quiet abyss of a derelict church, I sit eagerly but alone in the confessional. For people like us, it's nothing personal- it was always professional. Regardless, there's no absolution for people like us.

We're the rotten crust encircling the outskirts of society. Were the ones in a persistent battle for sobriety. We bleed out in the streets and smoke sins from old mint tins. There's no absolution for people like us.

In this wooden box I peer through the screen, no priest beside me, no sane being. It's just me; I hear the cold wind cry through creeks of glass stained windows and old pews buckle, crackling as if the wood was alive. I'm not sure I have enough time to spill all my transgressions. This will be my last confession. It's more of a progression from a view above. I've watched in third person as I've ruined my life- everything snubbed. I wait for a voice from the other side- no mystic humming but I know God will provide.

. . .

There's no absolution for people like us. We toss away our lives, chasing our next rush. A dirty needle is the least of our feeble missions. Each of us will eventually find ourselves seated beside one of these thin partitions. I knock and whisper through the chicken-wire like screen; the only voice that talks back is the one in my mind hollering.

Even in my last hour I consider treading up to the pulpit in search of the wine chalice, silver and sour. I bet I could get a few dollars for it- I know it's callus but I have no power. The incense burned during the last service laugh their way up my nose; it's as if they knew I'm a man with no prose. I should get out of this confessional but my body already knows. There's no absolution for people like us.

The tired worn red carpet lining the aisles between the pews is the only one that will ever report my news. It looks back at me, so it goes. So I tie off my arm and poke around with a curved rusty needle until the drug flows. It warms me through my spine, a divine wine that curls up my toes. The blood of Christ- but for me only this grows. He's the last thing I see, crucified on the cross. Before everything fades to black, I can't help but wonder why our paths failed to cross.

There's no absolution for people like us.

195. And so we Exist - Friday February 02, 2024 23:46 MST

And so we exist, like a list that never persists.
    We cease to live, we only hunger to subsist.
    You see this list is one of none.
    It can never be completed- it's never done.

A ledger of life, pages worn and frayed,
    ink smeared by tears, the cost of the charade.
    We move as dead animals, mere outlines in the dust,
    chasing moments that crumble, dreams that rust.

We are pennies discarded into the void, copper clanging cents
    without a voice, bound to a cycle that offers no choice.

A perpetual yearning for what lies beyond reach,
    a lesson untaught, a sermon not preached.

. . .

Our days are the shroud of Turin, cloaked in despair,
   colors bleed together, a portrait of disrepair.
   Time, the thief, is cunning, and we are oblique.

In the end, we are but footnotes in a forgotten tomb,
   a story untold, a place unknown.
   Our existence, a lit match, a fleeting fire,
   in a universe indifferent to our birth, our death, our match will
   extinguish the unrest of our fire.

And so we exist, in silence we resist,
   the urge to be seen, to be known, to persist.
   But the list remains empty, a chasm unbridged,
   a testament to lives unfulfilled, spirits undistinguished

196. Room 1703 - Saturday February 03, 2024 18:46 MST

Sleep evades and my consciousness pervades my thoughts and reality
    into a nightmarish totality.
    Another seventy-two hours of fight or flight,
    all my nerves are completely shot,
    as my body continues the fight.

From a hotel bed I stare at the ceiling as it begins to drip.
    It's an upside down lake, my bed beneath it. I do my best to pay no
    mind to the man in the closet or the one waiting outside my door. I
    roll out of bed and crawl on the floor.
    My head becomes violently acquainted with the end of the bed, it
    rings a hollow echo loud enough to wake the dead. The lights flicker
    as my stomach churns in knots, making me sicker. As I crawl, a man
    enters from the window- pulling my feet; God is heeding my call.

I squirm violently and kick- perplexed about how an intruder entered
    from the seventeenth floor window; I'm vexed.
    Nonetheless I continue to kick, he crawls on top of me slithering

WORDS ARE SNAKES WITH ARMS

like a snake, it all transpired so quick.

In the struggle, I end up on top. I rain down on this specter with my
    fists, my skin blisters open with each strike revealing
    another cut. My blows lack the power that they should; each punch
    connects but are not hard enough to concuss.
    The man vanishes and-
    my splintered hand's joints feel like shattered rust.

I continue towards the door, but cannot make it passed the man in
    the closet. He steps out flashing a grin as he looms above me, he
    looks made of tin. My eyes close- maybe they were never open. I'm
    breathing heavily on the floor, bleeding and broken.

I look for my attackers but everyone is gone. I'm confused and
    shaking until I see the sun peek past the curtains, again- another
    sleepless dawn.

197. Chalked Fates - Sunday February 04, 2024 19:46 MST

In the dim-lit haze of a smoky hall,
  I thread the baize with a shark's cold thrall.
  Life, a table green with felted lies,
  where every shot's a guise, and truth belies.

With a hustler's grace, I play the game,
  each stroke at a temporal tempo, each mark a name.
  Balls clack and spin, a symphony of deceit,
  where angles lie, and the red chalk is the cheat.

Its dust smokes on the cue tips' kiss,
  plotting trajectories through the abyss.
  Life's pockets deep, its rails so slick,
  with every pot, the plot grows thick.

Banking hopes on a ricochet,
  watching dreams in rebound play.

The eight-ball looms, a specter grim,
in this parlor game, where lights grow dim.

A hustler's heart, a gambler's soul,
  where life's a break, and fate's in control.
  In the click-clack serenade of ivory orbs,
  I find my truth between spins and absorbs.

In this cornered sphere of slate and felt,
  where fortunes fade and pressures melt,
  I pocket not just balls, but moments, sheer-
  life's a hustle, and I'm the mark.

198. The Double Duke - Monday February 05, 2024 19:55 MST

It dangles a prospect of prosperity on a fishing line,
   luring me in. In my snow globe pond, it glimmers just long
   enough to attract me- it draws me in.

The lure is so enticing, and I can't see the perils until I bite.
   The hook of life jousts its way through my cheek.
   There's no escaping this piercing bleak peak.
   I struggle against the pull of the wire, it rips my skin,
   a cloth like tearing humming a choir of pain.

The cheat is one of life, one where it laughs at our disdain. It flashes
   signs of hope but gives us a damaged vessel, a boat that won't float.
   The hook breaks loose,
   but my neck tangles in the twine. This scam of life is one
   that eats us like rotten swine.

The pull of life tightens the line. It lets me fight- knowing that eventually I'll exhaust myself from my own attempt at flight. My existence is a damned tram with no end in sight. So I take to scam and continue to struggle. It knows that it's given me enough rope to hang myself- it know I'll drown in this puddle. Face down I gravel and twist with a gross unearthly urgency that none with eyes could resist.

It reels me ashore from the sewer and into the street. As I rise, I'm flattened by the bus of deceit. This mess is all I see- it's all there will ever be.

199. THE RED CASTLE -
TUESDAY FEBRUARY 06, 2024
20:07 MST

A slew of cues cry out as silent clues, forever etching my plunder.
    "Lead me to the rock that is higher than I." the green leaves of the
    English countryside briskly sunder.
    I follow the path, the landscape of my fate ends at a wrought Iron
    gate.

It takes me to the entrance of an underground labyrinth.
    They say that the riches await. The bounty lies not in fiat paper or
    gold, instead it's the secret of life. A minuscule scent jar, Roman and
    carved from alabaster. This grail is the final catcher of the world's
    greatest disaster.

They say the holder of this chalice is the world's master.
    From this very small urn I have drank. Immediately, my heart sank,
    mired in coagulated blood thick as mud drowning a tank.
    There is no healing elixir, no infinite amount of petrol in my tank.
    My limbs simmer with sciatica,

as my head throbs from the pains of
Attica.

My mind is all but dead, attached to a walking wanderer.
Damned to roam the Earth for all of time in search of that actual
glass that held the last wine. At the final feast, what will be my line?

200. The Opaque Mile Trial - Wednesday February 07, 2024 20:15 MST

A happenstance of chance looms, burning in eternity.
Why do I subject myself to this utter absurdity?
Nine tables of souls to which I must plead, I must stop at each, this
they beseech for me to make my case.
I must show that I'm worthy, I'm smiling as I approach but
my teeth curve inwards towards my face.

Only one candidate will succeed, there is no second place in this fate.
The words just slip past my lips as I take my turn at each table. I
make my introduction, I weave my fable. Their questions, pasted on
each desk. I must answer each of them, at their behest. My heart
gravels, my chest ties my own heart in a knot.
With each word, my only hope is my answers are the words they
expect they bought.

So I drudge alone to each trial.
This interrogation, its results,
determine the date of my trial. Some judge eagerly with

cocked heads and a plaster smile. Others stare through me,
uninterested in my guile. A few judges pass a remark or two, add
another question. To my dismay, I don't know if this is a suggestion
or success or succession.

I stand out here in this small murder of crows;
    it's evident I'm a goose,
    not among their prose. I'm the black sheep, an autodidact
    that oozed from society's crack. My sobriety, a figment of the past,
    stares up at my from my half empty glass. And with this stare, it's all
    the judges and myself can bear. It concludes in an all familiar rouse-
    "Don't call us, we will call you." say's the conductor with a blank
    meandering stare.

I search for the exit, knowing that among these species; my
    breed will not compare. They have already chosen their horse, I just
    needed to be there for the sake of other mammals.
    This didactic trick is another malefaction, a demonstration in
    nepotism and its attraction.

201. Her Sheer Terror - Thursday February 08, 2024 11:24 MST

The sheer terror.

It lasts but a few fleeting moments before you slip away.
    The agony seers into a warming comfort.
    A crude retribution of life's biggest wound.
    The key is to let your thoughts go, do not attempt to battle
    the reaper.
    In the end she is the fairest keeper.

She makes no mistakes, and guides us all into the fray.
    No matter your occupation, dedication or biggest frustration- she
    will arrive with a punctuality that time itself shall never even know;
    its grandest frustration.

The sheer terror.

.   .   .

None of us will be anything more than something that makes the
  grass grow. A duality that spins in our minds like webs of a spider,
  patterns only they truly know.
  There is a true war between Father Time and the Grim Reaper; it's
  the only fight that ever existed- the cell, the sleeper. An unfair
  advantage some may say- that we're inherently born with a debt and
  it's the reaper to whom we must pay.

The sheer terror.

Life's simple hidden lesson is our finality, our concession to her
  profession. She operates with great discretion, letting most of us
  choose our final progression.
  I sit today in this faux white leather chair pondering the choices
  granted to me; I must compare.

The sheer terror.

In this double life I lead, my loyalty lies with Father Time, this I
  gladly concede. Though I must admit, my fatal attraction. The
  Reaper is more than an end, she is my everything, my heart's reason
  for contraction. She comes to me every night in the brevity of my
  slumber. She reminds us of the times both seen and unseen- oh how
  I wonder. Now, she yearns for my soul- though before I was to her,
  all but forgotten plunder. She pretends that she never left, like her
  transgressions were simply bereft. Together, she introduces me to
  my son, the one she took. He's about seven years old now, healthy
  and dawning a happy lively look. In a house untold, her new
  decisions engender a family, a home so bold.

The sheer terror.

. . .

I'm torn between my love for her and of Father Time.
 Time has taken care of me; never left me alone and given me the best
 vintage wine.
 Time is where all my loyalty is sewn.
 I must make a decision. I'm not sure I can bear her derision, when I
 break the news.
 I wait silently with Father Time; waiting for her cues.

The sheer terror.

202. The Reveal - Friday February 09, 2024 19:46 MST

It starts with empowerment, you will always find a good opponent
wherever you look.
You see, the trick is in the trick itself, having too big of a reveal. It's
too large to conceal, so it lays open face still in place. No one can
admit, even to themselves, their own zeal. So it progresses.

Their consumption consumes themselves. In this game of chess, I
happily hand over a pawn. I let them overtake a rook, but it's all part
of my plan as the crook. The more in control they feel, the less
control they possess- it's real.

I allow them to scatter their pieces all across the board. Onlookers
gawk at their seemingly inevitable hoard.
It's amusing, to watch a man feed his ego, fill up his gourd. Though
I'm not a well man or a genius, I assess my clients quite seamless.

It's the reason they get up in the morning. They want people to know,

they want to be recognized. We're approval junkies and we wrap ourselves in suits. If we truly knew this- we wouldn't do this. In this game we still play. I let them put me in check, their phony queen
simply will not stay. I put my plan in action, much to their dissatisfaction. My job as an opponent is to allow them to hang on their own- entirely through their actions.

That's the game- we play ourselves. We lose on our own accord, we are the greatest danger, our own selves the true distraction.

203. Carousel From Hell - Saturday February 10, 2024 23:39 MST

It's a carousel from hell.
  It turns in a flurry leaving a slurry.

All that's left is the grotesque smoldering smell.
  Around and around we go in Earth's furry.

Past the squeaking gears and broken yoke I wait to tell.
  Though my truth emerges blurry.

This carnival ride is my cell.
  There are no seatbelts to hold us in, no jury.
  I try with all my might, my grip's strength- a spell.

Try as I might, I can only hold on so tight.
  This ride of life, it's a fright that burns through the night.
  My hands begin to fail; others willfully jump.

The plight of this calamity, a fake smile handed candidly.

So I kill my ego and allow everything just to go.
   It's a finality.
   It's my only first reality.
   It's my first and last experience of control over my life.

204. The Spectacle - Sunday February 11, 2024 21:08 MST

The grandest spectacle of capitalism unfolds.
Each choreographed move orchestrates more eyes sold.
Commercials pander products like propaganda;
we consume it all, begging for scraps from their veranda.

It unfolds as it always does; celebrities all boil to the surface. They
watch it play out live, their money is something we will never know,
we just survive.
So we keep our eyes glued to the screen, shoveling our money like
coal into the belly of the iron machine.
This locomotive is one that carries on forever; no brakes, it will roll
over each of us for worse or for better.

The field of green is their dream; but they made us believe that it's
ours. People pray for a meaningless outcome; those in the streets
pray too and starve.

.   .   .

The game rolls on slow, like it's predetermined- some suit
    somewhere must already know. The gridiron lion lives from our
    pockets.

They permit the game to overtime; another way to squeeze out yet
    another dime. Regardless of the end, we're always the means. My
    head blisters, my eyes roll from side to side following it unravel. It
    comes quickly to a crescendo; 25-22.

Their CEO howls out to us all, beckoning our dollars with their call.
    They too say they prayed- they thank God, whom I assume they also
    must have paid.

205. Sulfur and Silk - Monday February 12, 2024 20:03 MST

The rotten smoldering smell of sulfur buries itself deep inside of my
    nostrils. It rips my eyes open.
    It's the beginning of their motion.

This rot, the stink emits only when they're on the brink; on the cusp
    between this world and theirs.
    I hear their leathered footsteps begin to tread from the
    bottom of the stairs.

The dripping from the sink stops. Time seems to pause.
    Only the pain in my chest reminds me I'm present; full of human
    flaws.

They have tried to warn me, my relatives. I name them not but they
    come to me in my sleep, devoid of all fraught. Death seems to have
    no effect on them, a lesson left untaught. They're alive- I am not.

. . .

It stops at the top of the stairs. My left arm bleeds a stabbing pain, raining down to the very tips of my fingers and radiates without sound. I'm sweating, my heart's skipping beats. I feel it's glare on the back of my head.
I dare not to tread even a step from my bed.

I know who's here. It's a specter I've met many times before. It is a fear unlike any you have or will ever know- this I implore. Most people only meet her once during their last worldly charade. She takes them to the beyond, past the world of today. I see her everywhere death lurks. She escorts the souls of all past their bodies through their flesh shirts. She's tired of me choosing not to look, I catch her eyes during the parade. I pretend like she doesn't exist- but the truth cannot be hidden, forever forbade.

I tell myself that it's just the creaking of my home, there's nothing there. I wish I didn't know the truth, it's a fate that will never spare. I know what she wants with me, she knows who I actually am. I must answer for the truths that only she knows. Though I'm not ready for this close- I wait silently in repose. Until she decides my eyes can no longer remain closed.

206. Insurmountable Hesitation - Tuesday February 13, 2024 18:46 MST

With an ineptitude to escape, I fumble.
I've searched the Earth for a means to relinquish the burden of existence in time's tunnel.
I've smoked it all.
Drank it all.
Slept with it all.
Ate it all.
I've run from it all.
Even in moments seemingly sound or where I've actually felt tall-
still the gnawing of its claws upon my skull.
I am an inevitable avalanche beckoning the mountain's crumbling call.

For me there is nothing. No sorrow or lull.
This is my existence, no more squalls.
So I turn to any means of self medication, wake for another tomorrow; my insurmountable hesitation.

207. Phosphenes - Wednesday February 14, 2024 20:16 MST

Live for yourself- but do so unselfishly. Remember that you're a collection of all who have ever been and all who will ever be. Feel others sorrow as your own, not just because it is. Embrace the power of others happiness as it's the world's greatest gift. Do not make a living by the slight of hand. Though, live your life without caving in to every single demand. Master the art of knowing yes and no. It's a palatable endeavor to actually grasp but also know to let go. Don't ever be just a log, treading in the river's shallow flow. Don't strive for or pretend to be something that you're not. Live only in your skin, no matter how wrought. Take the time to listen, actually hear. Never succeed to the falsities of perfection; instead strive to be your best, always only carry good intentions. Mention not the sins of others yesterday's- though never forget. Forgiveness, you will learn, is something one must never attempt to circumvent. Endeavor not to be better or worse than any one being- compare yourself only to yourself- know that you're not a machine. Feel anger, attempt to understand hate so you can guide others to find peace that only those with un-yearning hearts create. Hold close simple wonders, like an Autumn rain under sky thunder. Help everyone without fail, but only after you help yourself, this way your deeds are wholehearted, keep them from becoming stale. Keep no tallies of success

WORDS ARE SNAKES WITH ARMS

or failure- count only your days, for they're fleeting. Treat each greeting as your last, it might be seething. Don't chase objects or flesh- they're forever death's greeting. Despise anything grotesquely rude or unkind, that's the devil quietly leaning. He taunts us relentlessly in our worries, our fears. He wishes us to be nothing more than deer in the headlights. Its the lost the join his throne. So close your eyes, clench them tight and look openly into those non-existent balls of light. Those phosphenes are our only future, our only tangible dreams.

208. Desperation, the Gift - Thursday February 15, 2024 16:32 MST

Something lingers in back, below the present, but an ever present fact. Some call it fate- some call it too late. For me- it's the gift of desperation. Only in deepest frustration can people like use succeed. We lack the means and talent yet in the end we win- to their lament. Our situation is one that many have tasted. It's a wine of the lowest vintage but the highest caliber of elevation. Just one sip and you're left with only one choice. Sink forevermore into your seat or make the word hear your voice. There's no words, no description that beckons our call. When you have nothing, you have the power to make it all. Each faithful drink- to forever savor. For it comes directly from our blood, our sweat- our labor. We never stop. We cannot quit. We're up against a wall, there's nothing anyone but the person in the mirror can make see fit. To have it all go away- oh imagine the glory. That's a world of pretend, it's a life full of sully. So we relent to the desire of cement. We are the rebar, people like us cannot be bent. Our gift, our damnation- for better or worse it will be our salvation.

209. The Blue Room - Friday February 16, 2024 23:16 EST

The walls, they bleed.
    The blood drips down the flowered wallpaper,
    crying out in need.
    Beneath, it boils and curls up- rupturing at the seams.
    The things it wishes to tell- beyond our means.
    Theocrats and lawyers curry favors in the green room.
    We sit at the iron gates, awaiting our doom.
    But peasants we all are; according to these old men.
    Their days are numbered, though their influence is over all men. It
    makes no sense why we sit outside this fence.
    If the house is ours, why must we wait?
    The lies embroil our souls.
    No homeless walk these streets- the old men do not want to witness
    our toils.
    These stains cannot be swept under the rug.
    I yearn desperately for the truth of the soil to blossom up;
    it's in these fruits that those in control, that the roots should tug.

210. Melancholy - Saturday February 17, 2024 23:08 EST

A timeline of our destiny- our fate.
    We live seemingly unrelated lives, until the play, our purposes mate.
    I've seen it in a dream- my end, when they let off all my steam.

I didn't think much of it, until we careen.
    In Ford's theater I willingly and somewhat lucidly
    wittingly await, an end to my melancholy- a conclusion to my life's
    debate.

The cousins parade in the charade;
    I know that the end waits for me, a debt will be paid.
    I'm unsure of the transaction made, I know for certain,
    the bed across the street is not one in which I made.

The Derringer will crack, my neck will fall slack.
    I'll be carried across the street in a confusion, a translucent shellac.

. . .

A leader of many, will fade over hours- for most just a legacy, one penny.

In my last moments I awake, a foreboding pain, like I've been tied to the stake. My life's work, a razor's edge of success- thoughts in which I'd hope would progress.
This is something that forever, humanity must attempt to undress.

211. PORTICO VIEW - SUNDAY FEBRUARY 18, 2024 22:51 EST

It makes no sense-
    the view from their end, the other side of the fence.
    Protected deep within its confines, from the portico
    old men watch city workers scrub their streets.
    Their streets are clean, no transients in sight,
    everything has been bleached.
    Past that fence, we all lay on the other side.
    Our trenches are speckled with mensches but overgrown
    by the stenches.
    The sink- an evil dealt quickly, night and day.
    Our side of the fence- mired in drudgery- into gray.
    Our reality is a worn leather that we're forced to eat,
    curmudgeonly. We grasp for sleep with only the screeching of rats as
    our nighttime melody.
    The men in that house, on the other side of the fence sleep- warm
    and snuggly.

We freeze, cut down at the knees by disease and unneeded fees.
    Here we work.

WORDS ARE SNAKES WITH ARMS

Oh- our pointless toils.
We farm the soils- growing vegetables we will never eat.
We can only prepare it for the men on the other side-
our food will greet.
From their belvedere they squander our time.
We are their greatest commodity- their human mine.
Why must we parade our lives into a cascade flowing
directly to their charade of smoke and mirrors?
They pimp and pander us all, leaning into our fears.
Our tears flow as plentiful as their wine.
They overfill their glasses- but never fill mine.
Apparently we are nothing, less than swine.
Why must we continue to walk their line?
It makes no sense.

212. It's Done - Monday February 19, 2024 20:26 MST

It's done.
    I tell myself aloud that the worst part is over.
    I know it's a lie.
    The worst part has just begun.
    The forever that comes after- that never goes away.
    It burned into my eyes with lye.
    I see in perpetuity, no matter the night or sky.

It's okay- I promise.
    Another fallacy I spin in my head.
    I lay in bed, haunted by their faces- foreign places.
    It plays out in the movie reel of my mind...
    over and over and over...
    there's no solace.

You will be okay- I swear.
    Another lie.
    I watch as the light of their eyes is quickly dimmed.

My soul is forever pinned.
In a countless number of white lies.
I find myself unable to distinguish between their cries
and the silent howling of my ties.
I start to tell myself these same stale thoughts.

I know nothing is over, it will never be okay- we will never be okay.
That's life's gift- some say. It's just perspective,
brush it all away.

Take a bite of my burdens, a drink of my soul's flask.
Then you tell me how it feels.
It will congeal in your gut, trapping you in a forever pit of hell,
boiling in oil, in sin. Then you can curry the same lies to me.
Then and only then will you know the lie of what it means-
to be me.

213. Subsist - Tuesday February 20, 2024 20:35 MST

I subsist, I do not live,
    in the margins of reality, where light seldom gives.
    Each breath, a testament to the nothingness that consumes me
    inside out, each heartbeat, a dirge for life that bleeds,
    into the ether, unseen.

Frailty, my constant companion,
    blows through my sinews like a relentless wind,
    eroding what little facade of strength I muster.
    In its embrace, I am undone,
    a sculpture of despair, chiseled by apathy's hand.

I am certain of my existence,
    a solitary certainty in a sea of ambiguity.
    In this knowledge offers no solace,
    for to exist is not to live,
    but to endure a sentence written by unseen fish.

. . .

I continue to subsist, a ghost adrift in the machinery of perpetual
lists-
where my existence is but a brief flash of the screen,
a momentary disturbance in the eternal sheen.

Shackled, I crawl the path as those before, bound to the inexorable
march towards nothingness. Take a deep breath in, explore.

214. Petechiae Eye - Wednesday February 21, 2024 21:35 MST

I'm trapped. There is no escape.

A disgustingly horrific sensation, claustrophobic, devoid of fresh air- an impossible furious frustration. I itch so badly, no matter how hard I scratch- it's an itch beyond satiation. It hurts in every possible way. A bone grinding curdling pain that will never go away. I'm lost, confused and nauseated beyond constraint. The heat boils my skin, erupting in burns and boils. The salt of my sweat stings like a fire poker sewing in and out of my every pore. The more I scratch, the more I bleed and sweat- the bigger the sores.

I'm trapped. There is no escape.

The vessel of my doom- my body. My own living flesh tomb. Being uncomfortable is an understatement, I'm drowning every minute. Dying over and over again- for me it's all that's fated. I'm tortured in an orchard of nerves and veins guided by a faulty brain. I don't understand why this heat will never relent. Being sick inside my body is a forever hell that I cannot circumvent. This is my today, my tomorrow- my everyday. Everything is sheer perilous terror. I'd do anything to escape.

I'm trapped. There is no escape.

215. Life After Death - Thursday February 22, 2024 16:37 MST

How does one live after death?
    I thought it impossible, yet here I sit drawing breath.
    If only I'd know that permanence was a fallacy,
    an overgrown humming tone.
    Forever, only a fleeting temporal idea.
    We wheel and deal plans that time itself will inevitably steal. It's
    enough to make one's blood congeal.

How does one live after death?
    I sit in a pile of my own rubble, bereft.
    It's but a moot point, to continue past this endpoint.
    I walk the earth destitute, bound to disappoint.
    I no longer hunger.
    My body feels no need for slumber.
    I feel an inexplicable inexorable nothingness.
    This is what life after death shall only anoint.

How does one live after death?

I stare blankly waiting eagerly for rest.
For worse, better or best-
I am a waste of space, destiny's cruel walking pest.
For three decades I've walked the Earth in circles-
a predetermined path to toil.
If only...

How does one live after death?
My last call is one I cannot connect.
The only thing I needed to say- broken.
Silently left.
Time is the ultimate blessing, the nihilistic theft.
Blood courses through my veins, thoughts torture me,
I am the source of my life's greatest disdain.
How desperately I yearn for life.
All I've ever wanted was to live.
A gross juxtaposition, two sides to God's knife.

How does one live after death?
There is no clear path.
The only cache that awaits me is far lost, buried in time,
burned by the soil's final decree.
I cannot flee, no matter how often I bend the knee.
If only...

How does one live after death?
I pray that you're not like me-
I wish no human soul to witness such vile indignity.

216. What's Left to say? - Friday February 23, 2024 23:38 MST

What's left to say after your decisions are spent,
    decades of beckoning calls, no one is left, they're all sent.

On the threshold of thirty, life's been deferred,
    shreds of youth, now silently laid.

Haunting the present, an unwelcome host.
    candles flicker, matches scratch into ignition,
    its light softly dies.

A decade concludes, with its stories untold,
    pages left blank, and ambitions grown cold.

To the child within, who once dared to dream,
    adrift in the current of life's relentless stream.

. . .

The promise of "someday," a vanishing speck,
   on the vast horizon, a diminishing fleck.

Here stands the threshold, not of triumph, but test,
   a quiet reflection on a journey, not blessed.

What's left to say, as the years gently fold,
   but a story of what was, silently told.

217. My Match - Saturday February 24, 2024 23:10 MST

Phosphorus, sulfur, and potassium chlorate, meets the inevitable friction strip, arousing a heat that forces ignition. The phosphorus conjoins with the potassium chlorate bursting into a swift vicious flame. Unrelentingly, it consumes all the surrounding oxygen, stealing life to create its own. This is my uneasiness, a magnitude of an all consuming fiend. It dwells deep inside my gut; an unsettling reminder of a quid pro quo knot, a bolt soldered to it's nut. This flame, this all consuming fire. It eats at our backs, carries away our desires. The smoke, a byproduct of our life feeding theirs. Though even the match shall fizzle out it's flame. From dust to dust we all shall remain.

218. THE FLOODED HOLE - SUNDAY FEBRUARY 25, 2024 22:19 MST

I don't know why I bother to do anything anymore.
    Every word, every meandering thought- it's futile,
    like tying a knot in a knot.
    My rope has grown beyond splintered and frayed.
    My eyes are glazed over in a careless haze.
    All I do is fail. I waste all my time. Every single moment-
    I've robbed myself of my last dime.
    I've been relentless in my pursuits- though they've born no fruit.
    My labors- all of it is a dead pursuit, it would have better been spent
    on wagers.
    My entire life- a pointless favor.
    I've had all I can take- I can taste no other flavor.
    A stale bitterness has pickled my soul, my glass is shattered-
    never once been full.
    Take everything I have left, I've paid my toll.
    Every shovel of dirt I excavate, rains back on top on me,
    a laughter of fate.
    I see no way to dig myself out of this backwards Godforsaken hole.

219. My Walls Have Eyes - Monday February 26, 2024 22:12 MST

The eyes poking gruesomely through my drywall stare at me. With each blink, drywall dust falls blanketing my cheap stale beige carpet like caustic snow. The eyes peer through the smog of my home. A capitalist cocktail of formaldehyde exhaust and radon gas mix a gentle death, even my spackled ceilings glow. After all these days, I'm indifferent to the eyes; I care not what they know. In fact- I care for nothing at all, I'd like to just go. My existence is a dull coal, long sense smoldered out, completely smothered. All that remains is a pile of ash- it just sits there, carbon with no goal; but we are one in the same. We're worthless, spent, we serve no purpose yet we sit still on the burned soil of lament. I'm so tired, I don't even have any more cognitive thoughts. A rational man might fear these bloodshot disembodied protruding eyes watching him while he lies. For me- it's normal, even civilized. I've lived a perpetual existence of fear, I'm desensitized to everything- no feeling is firm. Everything tastes bland. Each breath is a labored thought- an unwanted command. I exist, numb in a sarcophagus of a fractured mind. So I let these eyes peer, there's nothing they can do to me here.

The eyes see my truth.

. . .

They want recognition, they wish to be acknowledged- ironically for someone to listen. Eyes however cannot speak words. They can tell stories though- if you gaze into them, you'd be lured. They speak silently in an eternal universal understanding. These eyes in my wall- they're my only ending.

220. Silent Feast - Tuesday February 27, 2024 21:40 MST

In the hum of decay, beneath the glare of a sun scorned by time, the
    flies, those lepers, foul jesters of demise, cavort in a repulsive
    rhyme.
    Their buzzing, a siren's song of rot, of endings promised
    and forgot.
    I loathe their existence more than my own.
    They circle annoyingly as I complain aloud.
    Upon the pane, a macabre prelude to the rain.

Much more, I dread the silent days,
    the span of life that slowly delays,
    the timeframe where I sit silently, painfully, waiting for my last rain.
    This purgatory is far worse than the storm.
    Carry me away in the flood, I can no longer withstand this infinite
    burning scorn.

In this quiet, one that I hate. I waste away in that wait,
    the flies do circle, bide, and bait.

. . .

Their legs, a vile caress,
    a touch of time's own ugliness,
    and eyes- oh, countless eyes that see
    the cadence of my entropy.
    These harbingers, with wings unfurled,
    are not the end, but the world's old word.

A reminder stark, in flight and crawl,
    of the dust that claims us all.
    And so I live, and so I sigh,
    in days between, 'neath watchful eyes,
    of flies that mark the living's lease
    until we join their silent feast.

221. Fat and Bureaucratic - Wednesday February 28, 2024 20:11 MST

In the scorched earth battlefield of my mind, a hush falls over the
    battleground after thirty minutes- once it dissolves in my my rotten
    gut- pharmaceuticals, a silencer of the kind
    that softens the roar of memories unkind,
    a balm for the psyche, in its bind.

Nerves, coiling a stove atop an electric fire,
    temporarily muffled, in the medication's cast iron mire.
    The deafening explosions of war, still ringing, vast,
    their screams fade into murmurs, lines recast.

Anesthetized soul, in the chemical's grip,
    sailing through stormy mind with no slip.
    A sedation seeps deep, a long-awaited trip,
    from the relentless terror's tightening whip.

That wolf, retreats to its lair,

as the pill dissolves, becomes the air.
The mind, beyond fractured, feels a fleeting repair,
in the sedative's song, a quieter affair.

And there, in the stillness, euphoria blooms,
    a garden of nihilism amid silent rooms.
    The battle still resides, curdled in anger outside in the snow, this fire
    burns warmly only until the next doses glow. My ears still ring; my
    skin will never come clean from this foreign soil and blood.

If only you had my eyes- seen and done what I know...
    They care not for our struggles, they don't pay the price of my sins.

In the gentle hush of the drug's soft fumes; that's the only fleeting
    gleam of silence I know.

222. February, Lame Duck -
Thursday February 29, 2024
20:21 MST

In the cruel jest of time, a leap year's scorn,
an extra day to bear, since I was born.
February mocks with its twenty-ninth embrace,
a surplus of despair, in the calendar's face.

I've coughed through seasons, each breath a fight,
now cursed with one more day before the night.
This leap, a mockery of my dwindling time,
an added insult, in life's uphill climb.

Why gift me hours when my glass runs thin?
A bitter addition, to the pain I'm in.
Each tick, a reminder of my futile rage,
bound within the confines of a temporal cage.
I've bought one-hundred watches, none of them work.
All of my effort- a wasted page in a pointless book.

· · ·

WORDS ARE SNAKES WITH ARMS

Let the year be lean, spare me this day,
  for in this prolonged suffering, I've nothing to say.
  A leap year's gift? No, a thief in the night,
  stealing precious moments from my waning light.

So here's to the leap, with its cruel, added load,
  a boulder on my back, on this endless road.
  Damn this leap year, with its extra curse,
  in the calendar of my life, it's just another dead verse.

223. Behind the Wheel - Friday March 01, 2024 16:31 MST

I'm behind the wheel of a car, one in which I cannot drive.
    I'm heading to an important urgent destination, one in which I will
    never arrive.

This car- it's brakes refuse to work for me.
    I step on the brake pedal, the wheels hardly notice me.
    They keep barreling down the road.

Beneath the hood, a heart of rust,
    throbbing with the urgency of crushed trust.
    Every mile, a reminder of my fall,
    a journey towards nothing, after all.

The gas gauge laughs full, a cruel sniffing joke,
    I wish it were empty, like the promises I evoke.
    This steering wheel, an illusion of control,

guiding me deeper into this journey of terror.

The scenery blurs, a swirl of suburban landscapes,
　　of what could have been, a different world escapes.
　　But here I am, strapped to a seat,
　　in a vehicle of defeat, on a one-way street.
　　I stomp the brake pedal now- but my defeat has been clear before I
　　sat in this cut-up stained seat.

The radio strains to curl out a tune, desperately
　　trying to catch any signal over the air.
　　Even the antenna is broken, but if the song could play- it would be
　　my soundtrack of going nowhere.
　　I scream at the cracked windshield, a silent plea,
　　for an exit sign I'll never flea.
　　Blood vessels burst in my eyes until I can no longer see.
　　The strain of it all, of this car ride- my final key.

This journey, a boil coming to a head for my strife,
　　a loop of running from my life.
　　The destination, a mirage, always shifts,
　　beyond the grasp of my tired wits.

So I drive this car, one I cannot steer,
　　towards a horizon that will never appear.
　　A ride without end, on a road too wide,
　　in the company of my own demise.

And so it goes, my ghost reminds me,
　　another round on the freeway of a man who was everything but

free...

Behind the wheel of a car that's already dead,
racing towards a finish line, just in my head.

224. My Last Mask - Saturday March 02, 2024 20:33 MST

In front of the glass, a daily rite,
    a rehearsal for a mask that's never quite right.
    Mimicry, my art, a craft so sly,
    to forge a smile, to live a lie.

In the beginning, it seemed a game,
    a way to blend, to avoid the shame.
    But the mask grew tight, began to adhere,
    fusing to skin, year after year.

What began as a shield, a guise to wear,
    became my face, a permanent snare.
    Lost in the act, the line blurred,
    between who I was and what they preferred.

I carried their water, I spoke their speech,
    a puppet strung beyond my reach.

I felt nothing but pain. They gorged themselves on my life, a fat
leech.

These leeches, fed till they burst, these puppet's strings fray, and
masks crack, beneath the veneer, wishing I could stay.

Now, the mirror reflects a stranger's gaze,
a hollow shell, a lifeless musselman in a haze.
No longer can I don the deceit,
the weight of the mask; my defeat I'm eager to greet.

The smile fades, the act tires,
in the silence, my true self inquires.
Who am I, beneath this guise?
A question that never comes home,
that multiplies sizzles and crackles in the
world's smoking fire.

The answer chokes me through the thick chalky gray smoke: I'm a
culmination of failures, a disgusting disgrace- life's toke.

In this damned skin costume, my grand masquerade,
I stand unmasked, exposed, and unafraid.
For in the shedding of my second skin,
I find not freedom, but a chasm within.

So here I am, at the end of my walking parade of shame,
a soul stripped bare, in the light laid.
No more masks, no more lies,
just the truth- my demise.

．　．　．

A life spent hiding behind a facade,
    now crumbles, under the weight, the juxtaposition of bending to
    their calls and answering those from fate.
    I'm left to face what I've become,
    a hollow animal dehumanized of myself, undone, this is my final
    date.

225. Dredging with Razor Blades - Sunday March 03, 2024 20:26 MST

Dredging my consciousness with razor blades,
  the silt of my guilt is too deep.
  There's nothing that can free me from my own nets, drowning me.
  Each breath a struggle, waterlogged thoughts sinking,
  in a sea of despair, where hope's light is steadily shrinking.

I claw at the walls of my flesh prison, seeking an exit, a crack, but the
  edifice of my existence is monolithic, in empathy it lacks.
  The world outside mirrors my internment,
  a landscape barren, devoid of any discernment.

My screams are silent, absorbed by the void,
  my efforts to escape, easily toyed.
  By fate, or chance, I choke,
  leaving me bound in invisible smoke.

The more I fight, the tighter the chains cloak,

a Sisyphean loop, fueling my pains.
I yearn for oblivion, for sweet release,
where the cacophony of my mind might finally cease.

Death is a lover who spurns my call,
  leaving me to stagger, to stumble, to crawl.
  On the precipice of the abyss, I teeter,
  a soul too weary, a heart grown bitter.

This is my reality, a cycle of despair,
  a loop of existence I cannot bear.
  Trapped in a life from which I seek to flee,
  bound to it, inexorably.

So here I linger, between life and cessation,
  a being consumed by his own desolation.
  In this perilous nightmare, I've become fear's physical embrace, a
  tangential embodiment of purgatory, lost without trace.

226. Alien Dread - Monday March 04, 2024 21:21 MST

It's alien to most, this perilous feeling of frying in the electric chair.
    Most people only have to experience death once- for me,
    it's a daily dare.
    Each morning's sun, a glaring glare,
    reminding me of the noose, the snare,
    in which my psyche is caught, laid bare,
    a feast for demons of despair.

A reflection fraught with an endless, haunting scare.
    My heart, a drum of dread, beats a rhythm of perpetual care, a
    symphony of sorrows, playing on repeat, a nightmare.

This dread, a cloak so heavy, woven from the thickest air,
    drags me down into the abyss, a pit of despair.
    With each breath, I inhale the stench of my own fear, rare,
    a banquet for the beast that in my darkness does share.

. . .

WORDS ARE SNAKES WITH ARMS

The world spins, a carousel of horror, its music, a blare,
   each note, a spike through the soul, a merciless tear.
   In the nail bending scratching screeches of life, I find no solace, no
   repair, just the call of my own footsteps, a journey to nowhere.

So I walk this path of dread, each step a prayer,
   to a god unknown, for a moment's peace, a sliver of solace to snare.
   In this quest for quietude, I am starkly aware,
   that dread is my companion, my curse to bear.

And so, in this electric chair of life, I sit, with the wet sponge firmly
   fastened atop my hair- ensnared.
   Jolted daily by the current of a dread so rare.
   A living death, my sentence, in this existential affair,
   a soul condemned to dread, the only fate worse than the dead.

227. Building C2 - Tuesday March 05, 2024 21:38 MST

Walking down an unfamiliar corridor,
    the unmistakable humming of fluorescent lighting
    dims my soul and burns my eyes.
    With each step, the walls sway from side to side and close in,
    tightening like my stupid checkered tie.

This office, a Hell of my disrepair,
    where dreams come to die, under the guise of care.
    Cubicles line the battleground of my mind's demise,
    each a tombstone marking where a fragment of hope lies.

The air, recirculated, stale with the scent of one-hundred others
    microwaved lunches mixed with surrender quickly
    mingles with the aroma of dreams dismembered.
    The carpet, a sea of gray, stretches beneath my feet,
    a path leading nowhere, a retreat in defeat.

. . .

The glow of monitors, like will-o'-the-wisps,
    beckons with false promises, a cruel twist.
    Emails and memos, the chains that bind,
    shackles forged from the very fabric of time.
    They never stop, all these dumb questions, pointless processes,
    procedures built solely to eat my time.

My colleagues, enemies, haunting this space,
    the loss of ambition etched upon each face.
    We exchange glances, empty of words,
    our spirits clipped, like flightless birds.

In the break room, laughter dies on the vine,
    amongst the crumbs of a life once defined.
    Coffee, bitter as the realization of my plight,
    offers no solace from the encroaching night.

Here, in this corporate purgatory, I roam,
    a ghost among ghosts, far from home.
    My existence, a loop of mundane tasks,
    a masquerade in which I no longer wish to bask.

With each tick of the clock, hope fades,
    eroded by the monotony of endless charades.
    This office, a prison with invisible bars,
    a universe confined to memos and cars.
    I wish I was guilty of anything, any crime, a life behind bars or in a
    box compared to this would be sublime.

I've lost all hope, in this sea of beige,
    my life, a book, stuck on the same page.

Trapped in this cycle of eternal return,
for a release, a respite, I yearn.

But the exit eludes me, a mirage in the desert of my despair.

I'm tethered to nothing and no one..
    Walking down this corridor, each step a plea,
    for an end to this existential misery.

I know, as I turn the handle to another day,
    this corridor, this office, is where I'll stay.
    A limbo of my own making, a testament to loss,
    a life resigned to gathering dust, covered in corporate gloss.

228. Negative Inertia - Wednesday March 06, 2024 21:23 MST

I sit on this train, staring out the window, but it never moves.
  We go nowhere.
  Around me, the world shifts, landscapes morph into milestones I
  can't claim.
  Lives blossom in fast-forward, leaving me a still frame in their
  vibrant narrative.
  They're having children, moving, finding slices
  of unblemished truth in the everyday—
  I muster a smile, a facade of shared glee, but inside, a prayer of
  stagnation brews.

Here, in the purgatory of my own making, the air stagnates, thick
  with the scent of unused potential.
  My desk, an altar to monotony, where ambitions come to wither,
  dreams to suffocate.
  The click of the clock, a metronome to my inertia, marking time
  spent or squandered—
  I've lost count, lost the distinction, in this cycle of sameness and
  eternal shame.

．．．

Every day mirrors the last, a looping of deferred hopes, a
    Groundhog Day of the soul, where growth is just a concept,
    a word in books I no longer read.
    My colleagues, actors in a play I can't recall auditioning for, they
    recite lines of progress and promotion, while I mime applause, my
    role scripted by reluctance.

In the reflection of the office window, I see a ghost, a specter of
    ambition past,
    haunted by the specter of what might have been, a parade of
    opportunities passed by.
    The buzz of fluorescent lights, a dirge for the daydreams I once
    cradled, now just dust motes flashing in the beams of a projector
    showing a future I can't see.

The world outside moves on, indifferent to my stasis,
    leaves change, fall is reborn, while I remain unchanged,
    unchallenged, untouched- waste-less.

I sit on this train, the scenery static, the tracks worn from waiting.

A silent plea for movement, for change, for the train to lurch forward,
    to feel the jolt of living.
    But the engine is silent, the conductor dead,
    and I am left with the weight of my own inertia, a passenger on a
    train to nowhere, on tracks too worn to take me anywhere but here.

229. Bleeding Numbers - Thursday March 07, 2024 21:31 MST

In a fog that medicine weaves,
    I sit amidst figures that bleed.
    Numbers once my allies, now my foes,
    morph into a babel that no longer flows.
    Formulas, those elegant paths to clarity,
    now lead me astray in a mire of rarity.

My mind, once sharp, now blunt and adrift,
    in a chemical sea where understanding is a myth.
    The screen blurs, a canvas of confusion,
    each equation a contributor to my delusion.
    Digits, once obedient soldiers in rank,
    now rebels, with no one to thank.

In this stupor, my world upended,
    where logic's self destructive landslide is the hill.
    A pill, a potion, a cure they said,
    but under their influence, my intellect fled.

I grope for meaning in a fog-dense forest,
where clarity is a beast, elusive, never to rest.

Here, in the kingdom of bewilderment profound,
  my thoughts are prisoners, in circles they're bound.
  No compass to navigate this internal storm,
  no beacon to guide me, to transform.
  The language of numbers, once soothing and familiar,
  now foreign, a code, indecipherable, peculiar.

And so I sit, a casualty of this medicated peace,
  where understanding has ceased and confusion breeds.
  In the silence of my mind, a quiet plea,
  for the fog to lift, for my thoughts to be free.
  But the haze persists, a relentless captor,
  in a world where numbers exchange tales of rapture.

A finance drone, lost in a numerical sea,
  where formulas mock and solutions flee.
  This medicated glaze, a wall between worlds,
  where clarity is a flag, unfurled but furled.
  In this twilight of thought, I await the last light,
  for the fog to clear, for the return of insight.

230. THE INESCAPABLE MAN - FRIDAY MARCH 08, 2024 22:35 MST

There's a man trying to kill me.

He hates every fiber of my being- it's his decree.
    He stalks me in the night- even follows me to the latrine.
    This man- I fear him, there is no fleeing.
    He knows every aspect of my life, my every routine.

There is no way to break free.
    His eyes see what I see, we pay the same fee.
    He stands at the foot of my bed.
    He walks behind me, every single footstep.

In the quiet moments, I hear his breath,
    a cold sniffle of death, a signal of stealth.
    My shadow's no longer my own,
    in his darkness, my despair has grown.

. . .

In every reflection, his silhouette looms,
    a ghostly warden in these living rooms.
    No sanctuary exists, no holy ground,
    in every corner I am, he's found.

A relentless pursuit, a ghostly game,
    his haunting presence, always the same.
    A spectral reminder that my life's not mine,
    this man and me- intertwined.

I'm the haunted, he's the haunt,
    in this chase, his visage daunts.
    He calls to me from inside the walls and taunts me
    inside my own head.
    A curse, a hex, from beyond the grave,
    his to command, mine to behave.

So I wander, a shell, a slave to this man,
    I plug my ears, I resist his plan.
    My essence on pause, my life on the shelf.
    Haunted by his presence, so palpably near,
    in this ghastly existence, I do not live- I am only here.

231. ANOTHER FALL BACK - SATURDAY MARCH 09, 2024 22:16 MST

It's such a painful degradation- time,
    it builds us up so much slower than it breaks us down.
    Such a crime, the latent tendencies of this unforgiving mime.
    These hours, each second, a hair trigger to a mine.

Daylight steals an hour, a thief, night's great crime.
    Our lives, collections of moments, it decides to erase. Each tick, a
    notch on the cell of existence, time, the warden, with relentless
    persistence and only a burn desire to erase.

We chase the sun, a race where the finish line is never in sight and no
    one has ever won. With each year, a sour gross hope of more- but
    what's taken, leaves the heart sore.

The clock's hand, a silent dictator of fate,
    we beg, borrow- bargain, but ultimately we plead with the slate. But
    time, in its march, knows no friend nor foe, an ocean's tide, to and

fro, it will always flow.

The theft, the pain, the strain, the unforgiving march of time is all in vain. It makes me wish I never had seen a moment at all. To have had any time- what a waste: I cannot reframe.

For in each moment lost under the relentless cycle, we are torn and worn. So here I sit simply because I exist for now but only in a thick choking mist. As the superficial, time shatters. In its cruel, unyielding quest I wonder if I will ever find any peace- if only just a brief glimpse of rest.

232. Mud Entombment - Sunday March 10, 2024 21:45 MST

These days weigh heavier on my back than all the weight of the ocean
on the surface of the Earth.
I'm suffocating, drowning from it all.
Each day feels like it's literally my final straw.
Somehow my back does not break.
Though I relent- this existence is just more than I can take. With
each passing day, it's a step deeper into this thick rancid mud. I'm up
to my neck today, I'm not sure how much longer I can attempt to
wade in this muck.

It sucks me down, pulling me deep towards the clay.
I pray, occupy my mind- try everything to
escape the forever burning fire in my mind.
Every second is beyond fight or flight- there is no
such thing as a restful night. My nerves are completely shot; I walk
past trees and their eyes follow me. I hear them gossip amongst
themselves, they wonder why I shake worse than their leaves. Only
the gusts of wind may be able to tell. To say I'm tired is an

understatement by far. I'm exhausted, the walking dead- I have no idea why or how this vessel that pumps my heart continues to push me this far. I'm jaded, confused and disillusioned. I wonder when this mud will end it's game and consume me,
my final entombment.

233. Phantosmia - Monday March 11, 2024 20:09 MST

My head throbs in a pulsing pain that blisters my skull.
   I haven't slept for days now, my eyes are so dry it defeats me how
   they do not rot from my sockets, fall from my head and roll.
   My skin itches like it's burning- I'm on fire.
   Maybe that explains my olfactory troll.

I cannot escape the constant scent of burning, it's buried itself deep
   inside each nostril. A charred sour lyric haunting my senses and my
   soul.

My heart races at over one-hundred and sixty beats per minute just
   laying still in bed- damn anxiety's ferocious pull. If only there was
   some way to extinguish this fire, to clear my sense of this smoke.

I try to exit my house but the doorknobs are red, scolding hot. I care
   not, I reach for the handle and twist; cooking the flesh of my hand.

The doorknob falls to the ground, the door refuses to yield to my command.

So I sit and choke forever in this smoke; it's waterboarding me, it will
    never actually allow me to leave.
    My eternal freedom has been revoked.

234. Powerless to the Beast - Tuesday March 12, 2024 21:17 MST

Powerless.

There is no control over this wretched mess.
    The beast's overgrown hairy fingers tighten around my chest. It
    squeezes the air from my lungs, forcing a disgusting roaring, choking
    exhale.

Powerless.

This beast is one in which no one has or ever will prevail.
    The beast lies dormant until its opportunity arrives.
    This animal- on maleficent grotesque actions it thrives.
    This beast hides in plain sight but we all know when it arrives.

Powerless.

. . .

It sleeps inside each of us, snarling its teeth in times of desperation. When someone loses it all, this is the beast's best demonstration. When hunger pangs linger the beast comes to light. This animal is one that we cannot fight.

Powerless.

We are the beast as much as the beast is ourselves. We drape ourselves in a facade of cloths and pleasant smells; all attempts to hide the animal from each other. But most importantly, hide the beast from ourselves. Civility- oh what a rousing ruse. A guise to disguise the beast- but it's a stench that never dispels.

Powerless.

This beast is eating me alive, inside out. It's futile, no matter how loud I shout. I pray- I beg on my knees for help. Others are too afraid to acknowledge, to see a beast in the flesh. I can't fight it alone and these cowards refuse to help me bury the last dagger in its flesh.

Powerless.

My beast is an animal from hell.

235. They're Here to Help, They Promise- Wednesday March 13, 2024 21:03 MST

Nothing makes sense anymore.
    In the biggest snow since two-thousand and three,
    I've once again found myself buried deep.
    I'm older now, bitter and sick.

My mind poisoned me, its slicker than the ice of this storm and
    darker than the filthiest muddied snow discarded by
    the plows on the sides of the roads, forlorn.
    I am that rotten smut, that hated slosh.
    The filthy salted freezing brown heavy grit.
    Everyone pushes it to the side, ignoring it.
    They want it to melt, to them it's not snow.
    It's just precipitation impeding their transportation
    to and fro.

Honestly, I care not to be an equal, I expect to be treated as less.
    Though I need help.
    Foolishly, I fall for their traps.

They preach equality, but act out hate.
I ask for help, they extend not a hand but instead a debate. They dig their dirty nails into my bleeding wounds. They lick my blood from their hands before their next mental health meeting resumes.
They act like they care- but actions show they do not.
Why won't anyone help me?
Why must I be forgotten?

236. The Magic Wand Exercise- Thursday March 14, 2024 21:11 MST

If I can just make another minute.
    I tell myself, each minute.
    If I can just make it another hour.
    I tell myself, each hour.
    If I can just get through one more night,
    I hear myself say.
    If I can just do my best to survive this day, I repeat as I gasp between
    each breath and pray.

This cycle repeats in an infinite loop of defeat.
    Second by second, each moment, a barbarian terror consumes me,
    whittling me away lower and lower.
    I wonder why I continue to subject myself to this Sisyphean clock.

It's embarrassing to exist with such pointless meaningless
    meandering peril- I can't even talk.
    They mock me, behind my back and the clock does it in-front of my
    face. I wish this existence on no other,

it's no existence it's a shameful disgrace.

I cannot lace my shoes, I cannot brush my teeth.
    I forgot to eat, I don't know what my eyes see and my ears- I can't
    believe a word they tell me.
    They ring incessantly, it never stops. I plug them at night, not to
    quell the ringing, but the voices from atop.
    They look down at me from the ceiling, sometimes their dark thick
    black hair drips. It's wet, it stinks like death- upon my sanity it slips.
    Last night, all the veins in my body glowed as if full of tritium gas.

If I can just make another minute.
    I tell myself, each minute.
    If I can just make it another hour.
    I tell myself, each hour.
    If I can just get through one more night,
    I hear them say.
    But it puzzles me- why, oh why would I ever want to face the
    punishment of another second, of one more day?

237. The Island of Chemical Gold- Friday March 15, 2024 22:37 MST

I thought that I could take the gold- and still live with myself; I cannot.
Its slick glimmer captured the essence of my eye, burrowed into my
soul. It's weight, holding that first bar of bullion felt akin to fate.
So I couldn't wait, I took all that I could take.
Damn the others, they'd take it too; my conscience justified to my
core, down to every sinew.
Maybe my internal dialogue was flawed, I don't know.
Enamored by the ignorant bliss of riches, that purple reptile-esque
genie had granted all my wishes.
I filled my pockets and coat full of gold rounds, I stuffed each gold
bar in bag upon bag, racking up pounds.
These riches that I stumbled upon in a chemical forest, I take every
last coin- damn the poorest.
So I did exactly that, I stole more than I could even carry back. I
heaved and pulled, created levers and conveyor belts of logs. All to
get my plundered riches to my vessel and sail off in the fog.
It was silent, with the exception of my toil and the
croaking of frogs. I couldn't take all the pills, but I did my very best.
Those damned frogs watched me, like they knew.

. . .

Like they understood my plunder, the actions of my burgeoning surrendering thunder. They croaked away until day gave way to nights display. Then they echoed louder, they seemed to multiply. I loaded my boat and left shore- that's when everything went awry.

The weight of the gold along with that of myself was too much sin for the boards of my vessel to bear. It began to croak like the frogs. Then the sea finished the tear. Now I'm taking in water, drowning from my own greed. I must accept my fate.

I thought that I could take the gold- and still live with myself; I cannot.

238. The Omnipresent Voice
- Saturday March 16, 2024
23:31 MST

It tells me when I'm hungry.
    It tells me what to eat.
    It tells me what to say, what to do, when and I should speak.

This voice.

It lives in my mind. All these years I thought it was my own.
    Now I'm unsure of its kind.
    It knows things that I never could.
    It speaks languages foreign to me, that I never should.

This voice.

It determines my every choice, it tells me what to do.
    It's always seemingly levelheaded, but according to who?
    It asks me questions and answers them too.

I am it's Manchurian candidate - but to who?
How can this voice know and understand all that it does?
It's an omnipotent, omnipresent being that causes my
life's every fuss.

This voice.

I've dedicated a lifetime to silence it, but I'm not sure why.
　　It has never been malevolent, never even a single try.
　　I wonder if this voice, maybe, is not an enemy or foe.
　　Maybe this voice is an ally, maybe I should listen to it- how could I
　　ever know.

You see- that's the voice talking now, straight through me.
　　It's allowing me what I can and can't say and to what degree. In the
　　presence of this voice, am I free?
　　Or am I a prisoner of a nonlocal awareness?
　　A mere silent observer of an omnipresent consciousness?

This voice.

Is it mine, is it really my choice?

239. The Zebra - Sunday March 17, 2024 21:15 MST

Blending in within nature, that's an impossible task.
   We stand out no matter the weather, as blatant as a ship's mast.
   We roam the desert in search of sustenance and water.

The lions, they hunt us, we are to them but fodder.
   Our strips camouflage us only in the herd.
   The predators catch our weakest, the rest of us disappear in a blur.

We adapt, though we never overcome.
   Our strengths of a striking facade of white and black, fleeting in a
   slippery nightmare of gray.
   Our lives are a continuous train wreck, searching for new tracks
   everyday.

Each time- it's the first time or the last. It's important to remember
   not to do anything rash, we sit back in the brush and brace for each
   impending crash.

We know each derailment will end in fire, an infectious disaster of choking smoke. We might as well eat the sand, or lay our striped necks one the tracks that remain.

We are the most pointless species, most worthless of animals. Our primary defense- a lackluster dusting in the land. Our breath is fleeting and it's our only final demand.

240. Humiliation - Monday March 18, 2024 21:52 MST

Humiliation has become my primary demonstration.
    Wandering eyes gawk, voices without heads talk.
    They all balk at my lack of human ability, but they're the ones
    without any humanity.

I know exactly what this world owes me- nothing at all.
    I have no expectations.
    My frustrations lay squarely in their doubts and gross expectations.
    They live under false pretenses under green manicured lawns and
    wrought iron fences.
    They peer through their windows, I hear their shouts.
    I know the truth, I have no doubts.
    They're maniacal cynics, sycophants and fake critics.
    They shun only in which they secretly partake.

Behind closed doors, these snakes indulge in sins that would leave
    even the devil floored.
    We see through their manicured nails,

these clear holes in their ships' sails.

I am humiliated to admit that I didn't quit.
    Humiliated to ask for help-
    It's on us that they spit.

Why should I be shamed? I've done nothing wrong.
    They should be humiliated for how they pretend, how they treat us-
    how they act like nothing is wrong.

241. Muddied Footsteps - Tuesday March 19, 2024 21:49 MST

This morning I tracked the footprints in the mud outside my back door. The tracks appeared deep, made by a human, barefoot squirming. The way the tracks slope- they were running from something or someone. I followed them to the road, tires ate away at their path.

I've seen these footprints for days in a row now, even though I've covered them up. They appear each morning, always in the same stance.

Who is haunting me?
Who is trying to break in?

These muddied tracks are more than a concern, they're a frenzied murmuring making my stomach churn.
I try to sleep but it cheats me, I endlessly toss and turn.
I know someone is lurking outside, just waiting to put me in an urn.

Another sleepless night, the sun shows more of these dredged tracks at first light.

The cycle repeated until today. This morning my door was open, left only cracked, but none of my belongings were in disarray. The muddied footsteps continued into my house, up the stairs, and all across the couch.

They ended at my bedside- but there was only one set of footprints, it never left.

My feet are covered in mud, it's all over my bed.

242. The Tumultuous Room - Wednesday March 20, 2024 20:56 MST

Anxiously I watch helplessly as the walls close in. The lights get brighter—oh, how I wish they would dim. Sweating and uncomfortable, I relentlessly itch my leathered skin.

There's no way out, no matter the price of the sin. I'm so uncomfortable—I cannot even begin. Every inch of me aches, a war within I cannot win.

In this shrinking room, my fears are amplified, bouncing off the closing walls, where my life has died.

I search for solace in this confinement where I'm tied, but find none—just the empty call of the heartbeats I've defied.

The air thickens, each breath a battle, a laborious task, in the brightness that mocks, in its damned glory, I bake. I crave the dark, a respite, is that too much to ask?

The texture of my prison, both a bane and worn, my skin. Scars that lay beneath are festering wounds, eating me alive from within.

A paradox of luminescence, I'm lost in the glare, a solitary figure, withdrawn, deprived of air.

The walls inch closer, a relentless squeeze, in this luminous trap, I find no ease. An indescribable discomfort, there's no release.

243. Series Sesto - Thursday March 21, 2024 21:29 MST

Apprehension and terror rip through my spine.
My mind is a gelatin mass of worry, on which the rich dine. Each
chemical cocktail worse than the last.
They feed me contrails of paperwork, a bureaucratic ghast.
My eyes rattle back and forth attempting to read words
with no voice.
They make no sense, the letters bend backwards and lock me into a
fence.

Fill out this form, albeit it makes no sense.
Do it correctly or you will no longer be able to pay your rent.
I feel my face steaming red in anger, the frustration of all this time
misspent.
There's no pause in this destructive clause.
They grasp me tighter, my skin punctures under the weight of their
claws.

I'm robbed of my faculties and all human decencies-

I've been stripped of it all.
They've left me naked, alone, abandoned with no God to call.
I'm a leper, cast out of all classes.

It's nauseating, having to continue to drink poison from their veiled
glasses. I'm not trying to escape all pain or find El Dorado;
all I'm begging for is a way to survive to tomorrow.

244. FEAST OF FEARS - FRIDAY MARCH 22, 2024 19:37 MST

Tonight I feast on my fears, I shall wash them all down with a glass of
my tears.
No more will I allow these malfeasant thoughts control my will. As
they have tried to eat me alive, I shall till.
I will plant them as seeds of my future and eat the most rotten crops
in a silence, nothing but still.

I reject their calls for damnation, I will eat each of these fears alive;
fear will fear me in my demonstration.
I'll roast them on a spit, or bury them in the ground and ferment
them- savoring them wilt.

These intrusive thoughts are done.

Soon they will no longer be perpetually begotten. They will be my
meal, each of them long forgotten.
But only a piece of me, these fears will no longer see.

I shall no longer give them the light of day.
In my stomach, it's each of these fears that will be crying out, trying
to pray.

It's my day of reckoning and they will be loyal subjects.
Nothing more to me than a fleeting source of sustenance.

They will be processed by me, discarded by me, no longer will I
beckon their call or listen to a single ill-gotten murmuring of their
pointless decree.

So I sit, and I eat even though my stomach has long since been full.
These fears will fear me, damn each of them, every sour litany.
I chew past their grotesque taste, to me they are nothing- a feast of
unleavened bread.

I feast on my fears, savoring their spoiled taste.
To me, nothing and no one will ever lay waste.

245. The Reset Button - Saturday March 23, 2024 19:59 MST

I wish there was a reset button.
    I could press it once, rewind.
    Anything to help uncoil, unbind.

At this point my blood is thick.
    I watch it slowly ooze from me, an uncertain trick.
    Bloodletting will not help, nothing can unstick.
    It flows down my arm, meandering slowly down my skin.
    It clots much too quickly, this situation I'm in.

Nothing helps, nothing heals
    There's no scenario where this dissolves.
    I watch, a helpless bystander in an unbelievable wreck.
    Am I really sick?
    Is there anything that could circumvent?

My blood is soaked up by the hay,

though there's no leading this horse back to the stable.
I'm here now, it's a sick fable.
The hay absorbs more terror than they ever could.
Go on another day?
I'm not sure I would.

It's not my choosing though, my own fate.
It's already played out, a consciousness I cannot abate.
I sit back, watch the litany of a black label.
For me, there is no stable.
Fragility?
I think not, I'm a coarse piece of rebar, rusted- fraught.
The truth sits jeering at the end of the road.
I have no stability, I have no option- I sit and erode.

246. The Hunters Call - Sunday March 24, 2024 20:25 MST

I am amongst the hunted.
    Hunter's eyes frost when they catch a glimpse of me.
    They grit their teeth until they shatter.
    I am their problem, the main matter.

They watch me intently, follow my traces.
    I'm their game, I'm faceless.
    Nothing but an animal.
    They bought their tags, the license to kill.
    I'm to be their biggest thrill.

I'm not defenseless, even so I yield.
    I make no effort at crossing fences or into the field.
    I go about my day to day, unaltered but frayed.
    I don't care much, that extends to being hunted.

Let them waste their efforts, another football punted.

Should they lead a chase, I will not run.
I will not fight back, I'll hold the barrel to their gun with my teeth.

The secret of being prey is actually that.
    Embrace the roll, it evolves flat.
    We're all someone's prey, just a listless number.
    Just a dollar sign, a vote, anything to help the hunter slumber. They
care not, so why should we?

Damn all the hunters, they slaughter us pointlessly.

247. My Roommates Live Rent Free - Monday March 25, 2024 18:41 MST

Though I live alone, I have the strangest roommates. They're with me twenty-four hours a day, but they're not my mates.

You see, each of them live completely rent free; it's not a mutual decree. They bear no mind, they even bring dates.

Of my least favorite housemates, Anxiety, this man is positive that everything is awry. He checks each lock in the house and sets the alarm three times. He freaks out when the washing machine buzzes- and God forbid someone knock at our door; he will go running. He's always speaking at me, but not to me. He spews worries that are as obscene as unlikely.

Last night, he crawled into my bed and whispered,

.   .   .

"Did you turn off the stove? What if the whole house blows? I'd go check but I'm afraid my knees will bend the wrong way down the stairs; be a doll and install another camera in the kitchen- it's our new mission."

So at two-thirty in the morning I stumble down to the kitchen. I pass my other roommate Fear, he's shaking on the couch like a wet kitten. Before I can ask, he shares his scare, "I swear I saw a shadow outside the window, it's a killer or a ghost- I swear!"

I peek through the shades and see something scurry! It's approximately six-foot seven and furry! I slam the shades shut and clench my eyes; Fear is always right, this is our end! Our demise!

To my horror- a scratching knock at the door echoes through the house! Anxiety and Fear both shout out! Through the peephole I see a shadow, then a reflection- damn it, it's me! I turn off the alarm and unlock all six locks, I crack the door to catch a glimpse!

Standing in nothing but socks, my other roommate, Mania, was behind the knocks! She cries out in a shrill of laughter, "Did I scare you guys? Sorry but I'm so high I thought I was the wall plaster. I had to scratch to get in."

I let out a sigh of relief as she treads lightly in. She sits naked on the couch, legs sprawled out, joined by Anxiety and Fear. They all cower over in laughter followed by tears.

Jarred and shaking, I check the stove again- it's still off, nothing in the oven baking.

. . .

Back to my mission, I take a security camera from my cache in the closet and begin to hear my plan formulating. With all the ruckus, I had no doubt, the sound of footsteps was erupting from the basement stairs.

Great- we woke up Self-Doubt. She rips open the door, dressed in tattered purple pajamas looking all forlorn.

"Here it comes..." I remark.

Sure enough Self-Doubt begins to bark, "What is going on up here? You're trying to put up a camera? For what? What rabbit hole does Fear have you chasing down? Shut up and take a seat, you can't put up a camera in the kitchen you clown!"

I feel my spirt coil, Self-Doubt, she's always here to spoil.

By now Depression is wide awake, he trudges downstairs ready to reinforce my mistake. He murmurs about how pointless all of this is, I try my best to prevent my internal pot from boiling over though I feel it begin to fizz.

I lock myself in the bathroom and call Addiction, she's been on a trip for a week but I know calling her is always smart, especially when I'm weak.

Thank God for her, my favorite roommate. She guides me through her plan to get me back to my feet. So per her tutelage, I take three long pulls from my back-up bottle of gin, but it's just to help me get down this antipsychotic, lessen my room's spin. It's totally safe, it's a prescription, and my doctors would never overprescribe.

My other roommates are all clawing at the bathroom door. I wait thirty minutes until it kicks in, lying on the floor.

Finally, I vibe; I get the courage to come out. I'm installing this camera- I don't care how loud any of them shout. Strategically, I take out the mount and begin my install. My shaky hands slip, the flathead screwdriver misses the wall but is lodged deep into my hand.

My spine and blood crawl. This quickly ushers in our rowdiest roommate of them all, PTSD Paul.

He runs straight to me and rips the screwdriver violently out. He's screaming, we share the same voice, and my eyes fall back to my traumatic bouts. I'm back there again, my floor is sand, bullets crack over my head in a whistling whip. I crawl on all fours, cover is something I cannot get.

Now Fear, Anxiety, Mania, Depression, Self-Doubt, and PTSD Paul all join cowling and hollering in my chaotic crawl. I can't see anything from the blood in my eyes, my ears are ringing- but this is not a surprise.

Everything, the past, present, future- it bleeds into my eyes. It's a Monday morning, now six-forty five. I work at seven, though to my roommates I can't say any goodbyes. So we all load up together in the car, time to head off to work. There I get to spend the day with my friends Paranoia, Claustrophobia, and Anxiety Attacks. They're such loyal mates, they always have my back.

I dread the thought of this day and wonder how I'll get through it. I'd call my doctor, but I don't make enough to do it. An appointment? I can't afford that. Thank God our mental health system is literally "All That".

248. Breathe in Deep - Tuesday March 26, 2024 21:02 MST

Breathe.

My mind is racing, a deep thud in my chest is chasing.

Breathe.

Confusion cries, the last of my sanity dies.

Breathe.

Vertigo sets in, complemented by uncomfortable sweating. I'm going to pass out, nausea shines it's titled grin.

Breathe.

I gasp for breath, but there's no oxygen left.
    The walls of the room loom like falling towers.
    I have no where to go- I'm trapped, no powers.
    Hopelessness gnaws at my skin.
    It feels akin to being shaved with a potato peeler, every shred of skin
    for each sin.

Breathe.

Ulcers bleed, I'm overcome by a metaphysical stampede.
    I'm trampled, worn, still alive but dead.
    There's no escaping this peril steeping, forever brewing in my head.
    My anguish, a nerve shattering paltry existence never led.
    I'm crippled from head to toe, my torment audibly reeks an ear
    shattering screech picked up by animal's olfaction.

I can't breathe, there's nothing left.

249. My Forgotten Lake- Wednesday March 27, 2024 22:30 MST

Incohesive thoughts promulgate impulses flooding through the poisoned lake of my mind. It's within these deep waters where there's nothing left to find.

Atop the water, an oil slick of deep green moss carries a foul damp wet stench all across. Dead fish float belly up, each a memory of times long since drowned.

Capitalism has left my hopes anchored firmly below the surface; shipwrecks never to be found. My empty pockets float here in this dastardly moat forever bound.

This murky water has no clarity or purpose for being so unwound. Nothing can sustain life here, not even the damnedest of leeches- thirsty bloodhounds.

. . .

I feel my bare feet sinking deeper into the glass-sharded sands of the lake's beaches. It won't be long now until my head no longer reaches. Swallowed alive by the godforsaken shore or tainted water- it's a fate unsure but glimmers and reflects a metallic glow, it's my lure.

These deceased fish can no longer bite, though I think I will. I lack any more desire to fight, I've surrendered all will.

Oh- how I deeply desire the knowledge, strength and skill to swim.

A ghastly gurgle, that is my last whim.

250. Mud's Bloodlust - Thursday March 28, 2024 22:49 MST

Desiccation cracking emerges from the dissonance of my
   consciousness, like the sun bakes the Earth's crust.
   I'm mired down in dirt, choked by a forever drought.

There's nothing left, regardless of how loud I shout.
   I'm inevitably destined to rust.
   I no longer have a taste for anything, not a single lust.
   A stranger stares back at me in a broken mirror,
   I'm not a man that I can trust.

People step over me as I lay wide eyed on the street.
   A deadbeat, a drunkard, nothing more than a hopeless loser.

I stare off in an alcohol induced psychosis, a sheer stupor. It's a
   drilling feeling to not be looked at, but looked through. Should
   someone miss the sidewalk and step on my back,
   they wouldn't even notice.

They wouldn't think again about it or even look back.

My journey feels cooked, and I'm overdone.
    An overdose feasting eagerly under the sun.
    What's left now?
    I pull my legs to my chest and don a furled cowl; a visible depiction
    of my soul being acquired.

I'm beyond tired, I'm resigned, permanently retired.
    This thick filthy oozing crud,
    I am nothing but mud.

251. Adamantine Accolades - Friday March 29, 2024 11:42 MST

Disbelief shrouds adamantine laws as they claw through the light penetrating my corneas, searing through each lens. My retinas convert this sensation of light without any electrical impedance crying dark through the night, scrimmaging into my brain with an inexorable fight. My optic nerves flounder to create a meaningful image of what exactly is in front of me, a late fate - what they shall ascertain.

Morality argues inside my head, a tactile interpretation of an engulfing fire, the last words of a forgotten book, unread. For prayers do get answered past the realm of the dead. The war counts the cost even at its peak, it's head. The resounding of horns, this prayer unsaid has been met, fulfilled in blood red.

Humanity which all it's tears sits, suffering. I sit too, in a bespoke uncertain but self inflicted gluttony. I sought out to seek, I found atop this mountain my prayers no longer silently sleep.

. . .

WORDS ARE SNAKES WITH ARMS

No; instead they have been answered.
   I never understood their true cost; I weep.
   Sweeping visions collide into my dystopian fission.
   I've succeeded in a literary accolade that highlights the fragility of
   our humanistic condition.
   A sabbatical of succession greets me today, I thought it would find
   me smitten.

No.

Nero's decree, a dastardly attrition of bright skipping flames tames
nothing, breeds destruction to all its own claims.

I've achieved the accolade, the Pulitzer, through littering my soul.
Prayers are answered- be weary of their total toll.

252. Paint Thinner - Saturday March 30, 2024 11:08 MST

Bloated and rotten I've succumbed to the front rushing in.
  This canvas of peril is painted in blood with my every sin.
  "You're all dead." the voice continues in my head.
  It sits next to me while I stare blankly in bed.

I no longer wonder what it wants.
  I welcome it's haunting taunts.
  It soothes me now, the burning pain.
  Damn normalcy, it's disgustingly plain.

My heart warming murmurs, skipping beats.
  This terror for me is all that repeats.
  So rain down on me, I'll beckon the call.

Damn you.

. . .

Damn you with every thrall.

I'll sprawl out, cut me in two.
    To me- there's nothing else you can do.
    You dress like a deer and kill like a lion, but I no longer am prey.
    I'm already dead, I've eaten every day.

So continue, but do so at your own risk.
    Desecrate my mind, slit both my wrists.
    It doesn't matter.
    Forgot you and your meaningless attempts to frisk my sanity, strip
    me of all my humanity.

Well- the jokes on you; I've seen this play out too.
    Sit there, try to be my monster.
    You're nothing to me, there's nothing you can alter.
    I'll beat you black and blue, I'll punch at nothing until my broken
    fists sail through you.

Damn you.

I'll see you at the altar.

My spine has no more integrity but I shall never relent, I shall never
    falter.

253. The Vice - Sunday March 31, 2024 19:12 MST

It tightens.

The steel, cold reeking of a copper-ish iron spice.
    They slip steel picks beneath my fingernails, turning until the snap is
    audible, effervescent like dry ice. It pieces my cuticle, my nail
    whittles off. A sizzling pain rips through my spinal cord and oozes
    out of my boiled gourd.

The Vice.

It tightens slowly, my bones begin to collapse.
    There's nothing slight about this agony of time's stance.
    It watches enviously as it relentlessly tortures me-
    perhaps.

The Vice.

. . .

Time seasons the flame, securing it's iron grip.
   It works on autopilot, it shall never slip.
   Beneath my pain, a boy sits silently enduring acid rain.
   Every single vein stresses under the pressure
   unit they pop. Internal hemorrhaging that simply is
   impossible to stop.

The Vice.

It follows its own threading, increasing it's grip.
   A slow death, this is all that it will offer- never to slip.
   I embrace a place of silence and lace until I lose.
   My consciousness cannot stand the stammer of this fuse.
   Electric shocks curry my pain, my abuse.

The Vice.

I can go nowhere, helpless to this ironed frost.
   One last turn- everything will be lost.
   I grit my teeth until they shatter.
   Rolling on the ground they each cry a grotesque clatter.
   Like dropping marbles on concrete, they echo.
   Some fall in my lap, onto my seat.
   There's no refrain, no more lingering disdain.
   The Vice of Time- no entity can restrain.

254. Sensory Deprivation - Monday April 01, 2024 19:12 MST

I'm a blind man looking only to see.
     I'm a deaf man listening, only to a plea.
     Tinnitus chips away at my sanity.
     Incessant visions paint my mind, things I've never seen though
     I've found them etched in the tide.
     A never ending nightmare, a permanent dream.

In calamity profound, my senses blend, a reality which I will never
     comprehend or mend.
     Each thought uncertain, another day- that I cannot abide.
     With the pulse of the insanity "normal" people embrace.
     They stand in line to be slaughtered in the rat race they
     so willingly embrace.

I cannot see the allure.

I can't hear the cure.

. . .

It perplexes me how a "normal" person chooses to make themselves sick.

I'll never understand. I'll never forget.

Sleepless and delusional we all work through the night,
    making the rich richer and deepening the plot of our own plight.
    They pay us pennies to dig our own grave sights.

I find my vision in the absence of sight.
    A world unseen, hemorrhaging deep within,
    a journey outward that
    starts from a desire to truly begin.

These social constructs are the most disgraceful, disgusting peril.
    We're sheep with no legs, drowning in the green mud of their
    confined stable.
    There's no humanity in this "life" they sew.
    The pursuit of happiness- choked to death in a suit.
    In our pursuit we suffer, our only purpose is to shine these
    sycophants' boots. A meaningless existence drowning in plight.

A deaf man listening, a blind man's sight, finding my way in the
    absence of light; this insanity- blankly, blatantly- is not right.

255. Our Inheritance - Tuesday April 02, 2024 20:47 MST

It's a cruelty too common to ignore, too harsh for anyone to
  endure. A gnawing hunger in my gut, bare to the sun's
  relentless burn.

Poverty, a relentless disease, not just a state but a lineage curse,
  passed down like an unwanted heirloom, generation to generation, a
  perverse lease on our hearse.

The wealthy swathe themselves in finery, layers of fleece and silk that
  flow like rivers of privilege.
  We, however, drape our bones in rags, seek solace in the ratted
  crumbling apartments— those among us fortunate enough.

Many more find beds in the cold embrace and form of concrete
  streets. Merely ghosts to those perched in ivory towers, glimpsing
  our demise with detached eyes. This malady devours our essence,
  filling the crevices of our lives with despair.

. . .

As we drown in potions that decay our smiles and muddle our
    thoughts. Invisible to many, but we are the legion, the neglected, the
    forsaken-
    Struggling endlessly, for even a wage of fifteen dollars an hour
    fails to mend the breach.

Labor, a concept foreign to the privileged, a myth peddled to us by
    those ensconced in luxury.
    The cruel irony: those who toil the hardest
    clutch the thinnest straws.
    Our fingers bleed for pennies, while they, in the warmth of opulent
    rooms, earn fortunes for a nod, a word, a farce.

They crown themselves deities, ordained by wealth, blinded by
    privilege, they deem their fortunes a birthright. An illusion, a deceit
    spun across generations, though the truth remains-
    equality is a myth, and justice evades.

256. Divergent I Stray - Wednesday April 03, 2024 22:34 MST

Divergent I stray.
 Living in tomorrow though stuck in today.
 I'm split, I can no longer afford to pay.
 I'm so confused- why must an owned man pay anything,
 he's already a slave.

Intoxicated by a promise of nothingness, so I sit here at this lathe.
 It spins tirelessly, mirroring me entirely.
 Nothing will set me free, even the devil comes to admire me.
 He is impressed at the pain,
 the meaningless meanderings of the lame.

God watches too, guiding me through this zoo.
 My misfortune is that I cannot see through.
 I cannot interpret his words, I can no longer hear his map.
 My ears like trees, ooze sour sap.
 I try desperately, even plead for the key.
 He hands me the lock- it's all that will ever be.

. . .

He helps those who help themselves; the explanation behind my
  guttural attempts to just be.

I'd do anything to flee.
  I know every escape is futile, a fleeting spree.
  I'm bankrupt in every way.
  Divergent I stray.

257. Whitby - Thursday
April 04, 2024 11:04 PDT

In the obscurity of uncertainty I slip.
  I wonder if this is my last sailing, my last ship.
  So I set out to sea, a journey of obscurity.
  I have a feeling itching inside my skin, a surety.

My vessel is normal on the surface, though the cargo below is on ice.
  A coffin, a place of temporary respite, it's device.
  He slumbers there during the day.
  When the sun sets and sails cease to prevail,
  it's not just the rats that scurry.

Though the rats work for him, they curry his favor.
  A pale dead monstrosity; he feeds on blood-
  not just that of humans.
  He has the power of hypnosis,
  a calming charm that will slip you into comatose.

· · ·

WORDS ARE SNAKES WITH ARMS

Regardless, he will feed on your neck- you may think he's just leaning
in for a peck.
The bodies floating above deck slowly will resurrect. Nature itself
lacks the power to object.

So I sail on, living with this bloodsucking succubus.
Shall I drown myself in the sea just for an opportunity to be free?
There's no glee in these godforsaken waters- that I can proclaim.

If we ever venture to our destination, those that survive will only
truly be able to ascertain this pain.
Living with an inescapable beast that we are only one thing: its feast.
As day dies to night- euthanasia.

One by one, until the beckoning of the next morning's sun.
When will I be next?
The anticipation, a gross facilitation of graduation, degrading my
sanity into mass calamity.
This utterly reprehensible insanity.

Tonight I shall face this monster; it can't torture me more than my
burning existence in this calamity.
I sharpen my stakes and make a false sense of peace for my life's
mistakes. I know everything is fated.
I wait for the sky to turn as I sit above deck and the oceans churn.
Impatiently I anticipate each sharp crack and jeer of this wooden
vessel. To the rocking of the freezing waves I am a slave.
I hear my voice whistle from the bow.
Armed and ready I make my way, though all too unsteady.
I follow the call.
I see nothing but still the voice continues to beckon.
I pass the wheelhouse but notice something deranged.

My reflection in the glass no longer remains.
I realize my hunger is a figment of the past as I float over the mast.
I wipe my brow- no sweat.
I wipe my mouth- blood.
It begins to set, the sun.

Immediately I fret, its rays burn, so down into the bowels of the ship,
    back to my wooden cask, a casket of last.
    I am my designated survivor- I am the ghoul; I am the liar.
    Alone on this ship I rest.
    The next evening I see the land crest, the boat crashes ashore.
    I float off and up the steps of this foreign shore.
    Whitby- this town shall fit me into a society of obscurity.

258. Wormwood - Friday April 05, 2024 23:16 PDT

Bitterness in every sip, this medicinal extraction dangles only a
    temporary distraction.
    It's potent odor is an offensive plot attacking my olfaction,
    making my nostrils coil in snot as green as its leaves.
    This yellow green flower is the man of the hour-
    one entrenched in power.

So I sip this potion.
    Damn everything, to Hell with my every moral devotion.
    Morality has robbed me,
    leathered my skin into its own worn saddle.

In this battle I submit.
    In desperation I yearn for a path out of this tent,
    a temporary respite.
    Rats in straitjackets chuckle as men scurry around corners and
    beneath the floor.
    It's the horror of life, my reality, that I truly abhor.

The cacophony of these voices, this unforgiving din.
It pierces my eardrums enamored with an inhuman pin.
Oh- what an inanimate juxtaposition.
This is what happens, when we poke the alien,
it crawls into our wounds, burrowing deep underneath our skin.
There's nothing that can undo this sin.

There's no appeasement, no satisfaction.

259. BRIMSTONE - SATURDAY APRIL 06, 2024 13:56 PDT

Stochastic, chaotic and rapid variations of pressure and flow velocity
   in space and time rattle my heart.
   It shakes me like a paper doll, I wash over in dread,
   I feel like I'm about to fall.
   Peril leaks into my final call.

It's so palpable I can taste it.
   This turbulence- I'm here and I have no option but to face it.
   So I settle in, grit my teeth and fasten my belt.

I'm on a ride to no destination, it feels like Hell.
   I smell the fire, the brimstone steady creeps.
   It washes me ashore in an eternity, my soul it forever keeps.

I try to pause- though there is no respite.
   My forever fight or flight- I choose to just quit.

260. Gnawing Notifications - Sunday April 07, 2024 11:16 MST

Never ending notifications shatter my soul in an active
    demonstration.
    Another call cries through, I watch but cannot answer.
    Texts push their way through my inbox, I see them but cannot
    transfer.

All these messages, never ending calls...
    It's enough to extinguish any fire left in my halls.

My blood boils, my consciousness recoils.
    It's all pushed me beyond my means.
    I silence my phone, shut off all devices.
    Still people claw through, my sanity collapses between vices.

A knock at the door- I know I will not answer.
    Eyes peek through my windows, still I refuse the financier.

Everyone wants something from me,
believing I am the only necromancer.

So I nail my doors shut, board up all my windows.
I no longer seek any answer.
I want nothing- to be left alone, that is my final answer.

261. Totality - Monday April 08, 2024 23:05 MST

It's an obscure triviality, totality.
    Millions flock in scores to stare at the sun.
    An oddity, a strange attraction will be done.
    It's bizarre how the citizens of earth are still enamored with lights in the sky; that burning star.
    A primitive obsession from afar.

Aloof and annoyed I sit inside.
    I watch shadows grow from my curtains, dripping down
    the sun and moon slip beside.
    So it passes, amusing the masses.
    It's a fleeting fate, though it will be repeated in twenty years on another date.

Pointlessly they drool, enthralled.
    It's just another slight of hand and I'm appalled.
    It's streamed over the air nonstop, people cry, propose, they act like the world stopped.

Why do humans choose to ignore the light?
It's a cyclical meandering- the sun leaves every night.

So they babble and continue on.
  Not even a mention that this is the seven-hundred and seventy-fifth
  day that a war is raging on.
  Three people were killed in Zaporizhzia, but the world has amnesia.
  Another dead at the hands of Russian guided
  bombs in Bilopilla- yet no caesura.

Hamas continues to murder like its leisure.
  They still hold hostages; a disgusting seizure.
  Democracy watches with broken glasses in a fiery theater.
  So still we stare are the sky donning our Chinese made eclipse
  glasses, eating more and more from their red feeder.

This reality of ours, its scolding humanity in thick heavy scars-
  everyday greedier.
  I try to speak up, but no one listens to the poor kneader.
  In totality I watch our entire world teeter.

262. The Ultimate Bevel - Tuesday April 09, 2024 22:21 MST

Righteousness- a feast for the Devil.

The biggest transgressions of the world were done based upon
    justice's level.

Convictions and beliefs drilled into us without sheaths.

Righteousness- it's the ultimate bevel.
    It whittles down the honest, making sinners of their kin.
    It's a disease that we shall never win.
    We chase down what's right but at what cost?

We recycle our souls no matter the cost.
    Here we sit, righteous but drowning in a perilous frost.
    Taking a step down from our pedestals we can better witness, truly
    understand the lost.

. . .

Our convictions are warranted, a happenstance of mist.
    Our evil is their good just as our good is their evils lost.
    Good and evil?
    It's not black and white.
    We live in a gray, in a forever fight.

Until we're free of righteousness, we all shall suffer from its
    destructive moss.
    Consider that there is no true good nor evil—
    only the outstanding toss.
    Instead strive for peace, kindness is sobering
    and should never be lost.
    Just offer a better version of yourself tomorrow,
    a happiness forever embossed.

Righteousness is not righteous when others suffer its cost.

263. Cell Doors Open - Wednesday April 10, 2024 20:43 MST

They open our cells and call it freedom.
    It's a last resort, our souls akin to a fiefdom.
    We won't listen or accept their accolades.
    We're all dope sick renegades.

So we toil in the same rotten soil.
    They promise riches to the loyal.
    Sour cream rises to the top from our toil.
    Inside I feel it reel- my blood begins to boil.

I quit, disoriented I spit, any attempt to rid my mouth of this taste.
    With a mouthful of pennies, I lay waste.
    This illusion of freedom is not at all grand.
    I scratch my head at every last pointless demand.
    Each command, another reminder of my castle built of sand.
    Every aspect of this hell is a drudgery so bland.

. . .

The voices remind me, there is an escape.
　　I light a candle, watching the fire partake.
　　It breathes the same borrowed air as me.
　　The wax drips down- only the wax is truly free.
　　To melt away under this life's sweltering heat.
　　Every single day I watch slowly, my defeat.

Still the iron doors to our cages remain open.
　　The lights flicker at every sense of motion.
　　It's an obscene thought, we're all lost in the ocean.
　　I heed the call, proceed with my meritless devotion.
　　I don't know why I still am subject to its malaise.
　　I'm a mine of human coal being slowly chipped away.
　　I wipe my eyes, the soot burns and scars my face like war paint.

So once again tomorrow I'll wake to a trapped fate.
　　A church chorus of Eucharist offered up as a remedy,
　　A cannibalism that fuels further debate.

Still the doors are open.

264. The Achievement - Thursday April 11, 2024 21:35 MST

Incense burns, luring me to the end of my day's turns.
    A carousel from hell, still lingering- this smell.
    It's a palpable burning, a metronome to quell-
    the fire eating away; a false pretense of desire churns.

A finality that's ultimately tribal, trivial.
    Trauma, insomnia, a litmus test of my reality.
    Still, it sits quietly.
    It's a foreign experience of achievement, I've won.
    Though I've accomplished nothing; it all sits undone.
    Through all this clatter, nothing more will matter.

A recap of it all drowns me as I fall standing tall.
    It's an omnipresent story beyond my understanding.
    Commanding and barking- I answer destiny's call.
    On the other end of the phone- a deaf man in a tattered shawl.
    Wait for your turn, he calls us all.

A conversation of everything that is life.
All the answers lay stagnant boiling in our strife.

The incense smoke, crying aloud.
A chemical stasis coats my internal third degree burns,
there is nothing profound.

265. The Social Trail - Friday April 12, 2024 22:11 MST

My glass leaks from the bottom as I push it to my lips for my next sip.
Sour and bloated, I pace the room fighting off my motive
behind this next nip.

It ails me- sucking the winds out from my broken tattered sail.
Nothing can prevent my sinking into this Hell.
Walking through droves of matted carpet to nowhere I carry out
pales upon pales of dirt.
My home is sullied, dirtied into a jail.

For me there is no escaping past the walls of my cell.
Recidivism drives me eternally back behind its drywall mend-
this stick built lair.
I hide my face, unable to compare.
So I continue to sip, anything to attempt at a brief fleeting respite.

Will I step beyond the door ever again?

This, I sit back and debate.
I already know the answer no matter what:
I concede to my flesh crate.
My limitations cut deep into my carpet path.
Each step, each hour I anxiously watch as it slips past.
The futility of being poor- an ironic score.
I see no way out from this path here forever etched in the floor.

266. The Rejuvenated Red Scare- Saturday April 13, 2024 22:10 MST

Missiles rain through the night, our futures only light.
    Retaliation they say- what a far off sight.
    Tonight the heavens cry because of humanity, our religions lie.

They bleed their calls, ballistics sailing through the air.
    All for what?

In this attempt at destruction, we each pay the fare.
    The Iron Dome, a marvel, a true foresight.
    It halts these whaling bombs, stops the fight.

Down to my marrow my bones ache,
    my head ablaze with a pulsating fire - it all seems too late.
    One barrage ends, another life snuffed out.
    What happens next?

. . .

Only the morning light will guide our plight.
    Senseless atrocities dine on a human delight.
    This day markedly signals a beginning, hold on-
    this is our new fright.

Missiles rain through the night, our futures only light.

267. Red Phosphorus Revenge - Sunday April 14, 2024 21:52 MST

A scalding itch: revenge.
    The dish that must be served, no matter how unhinged.
    It scratches incessantly at the back of your skull;
    exacting its grotesque toll.
    It brims over, spilling over a hearty bowl,
    a cauldron of malfeasance- hate.

Though an action must be taken no matter the plate.
    Chew heavily upon that cold well-done piece of steak.
    It is your last, make no mistake.
    The last supper is one in which we all shall share.
    There will be no wine, nothing even edible-
    still we share.
    Unleavened bread dipped in unleaded gas.
    We poison ourselves, our revenge damns us into the past.

Have you no mercy?
    An utter shrill.

Mercy bites our fingers to the nub, a cannibalistic frill.
In this black and white world- wrong and right is just a
scribble on parchment- an ideal.
The truth waits at a table, tirelessly in the fray.
It dines alone, a utilitarian with plates of clay.

Revenge. A sick soiled brew.
　　Take a sip and you will forever sully your thrill.
　　It's a bite of a cyanide capsule.
　　You will itch, an infectious scratch.
　　Revenge- an ever lit match,
　　after you scratch its red phosphorus head.
　　A demonic eternal flame, until there is nothing left to be led.

268. Epistaxis of the State - Monday April 15, 2024 22:33 MST

My nostrils spew blood—a relentless, uncontrollable bleed, mirroring
the world's insatiable, dark need.
In unpredicted spurts, it seeks to supersede,
pooling into coagulated mud, the only feast at power's peak.

This viscous toil churns, soothing scorched internal lands,
a harrowing lesson in derailment, where no train stands.
We're flung from the rails, in screeching dissent,
our carriage, mired in the muck, no chance to repent.

Here we lie, bound to this retribution,
submerged in its grasp, our drowned resolution.
How to stanch this hemorrhagic flow?
Uncle Sam prescribes more tax—his perennial show.

So I pay, through the thick molasses of this day,
trapped in an epidemiology that leeches away.

The pathology of autonomy, bleeding under a faltering creed,
while basic human needs freeze outside, unheeded in their plead.

I falter, weakened by another desolate week.
  As my life force trickles down, stark and bleak.
  There's no unity, just a figure in silk,
  preaching salvation while his kind bilk.

Through poverty's peephole, we strain to see,
  surviving on scraps from the societal decree.
  Epistaxis, the state's tool, cleaving through us with each tax,
  a relentless extraction by the socioeconomic ax.

269. Fiasco of Glass - Tuesday April 16, 2024 19:53 MST

A complete fiasco- I'm an utter flop.
    From failure to failure, a Sisyphean loop that will never stop.
    Holding shattered glass I wonder why I even try.
    I'm as consequential as a fruit fly.

It just never ends, my perpetual losing.
    No matter what I try, no matter who I spend time schmoozing.
    It's all another failed attempt, I would have been better off
    spending my entire life boozing.

I put each shard back together, mending it with glue.
    A few hold temporarily before falling back done-
    again, nothing anew.
    I wipe the sweat from my brow, a piece of glass digs deep into my
    hand and cuts deep into my face from the friction of
    the futile motion.
    Another accident, one more commotion.
    Blood pours into my eyes like water from a pitcher.

I search for a towel, something to stop the bleed.
I slip on the blood, landing flat on my back and into
more shards of glass.

Sinews severed all from the futility of my leathered endeavors.
All of this blatant stupidity- I hate being me.
So I lay on the floor unable and unwilling to get up.
I decline your offer, nothing can ever fill my broken glass cup.

270. Tiresome Circumlocutions - Wednesday April 17, 2024 19:57 MST

"What you owe, you owe with interest." Seethes the judge.
    A litany of nameless charges are the fuss.
    A guilt rooted in a debt, one that cannot be forgotten
    but one that you will forever regret.

To take the stand, that's equal to agreeing to an eternal reprimand.
    It's an action I cannot oblige or recommend.
    Even so, in the pulpit I sit.
    Pleading my innocence to something they say I didn't commit.
    Railroad ties of lies built my sullied prize.
    Each a physical manifestation of a fake strife.
    I balance it delicately on my tongue like the edge of a knife.
    It cuts deeper, the cost of every life.

I lead a troupe of characters all under one guise.
    We bring the most appropriate one out, depending on the night's
    skies. We sell them what they want to hear,
    we do it with a smile- sometimes over a beer.

WORDS ARE SNAKES WITH ARMS

It always works- until it doesn't.
It's a facade, an uncomfortable covenant.
Sitting here, my mind struggles to find-
exactly what personality will help get me out of this bind.

I choose the confident one, he goes about spinning his mouth
in a perpetual rewind.
The word vomit fails to stick, an unfortunate manifestation
of the sick.

The judge employs his mahogany gavel in an echoing wooden clunk,
"Enough of the tiresome circumlocutions! I'd like to formally open
your door to the Prosecution."

A motion for continuance, I begin to beg.
Inside I cower, I know I should wave my white flag.
Nonetheless, this character of mine is the strong one,
he refutes walking stag.

The Prosecution takes the podium and I know it's all but over.
I should have never let him take the stand- the price of being sober.

The jury reads the verdict- an obvious claim of stake.
I'm left forever living in a sitcom rerunning my life's greatest
mistake.

271. Ensconced in Peril - Thursday April 18, 2024 19:20 MST

Where do we tread from here- under the shadow of falling bombs, a tremor of fear?

A call to arms, a desperate explosion in the night, not just fixtures on walls, but soldiers in the fight.

The roar of explosions not just heard, but felt, resonates deeper than any blast could smelt. Decades of fury now crystallize into form- a relentless storm where despair is born.

Iran, a land where falsies replace speech, where the grip of tyranny extends its reach.

A pause- a commercial break in our scheduled despair, a world's stage stripped bare, the audience too scared.

. . .

This charade of power, this spectacle of might, masks the puppeteers who shroud the light. Each maneuver of string, each calculated play, forges chains for tomorrow, stealing today.

In the clamor of the media's relentless drone, in the sacred silence after the tone, we find the devil not lurking but boldly enthroned, his decree not whispered but clearly shown.

Beyond the reach of puppet's strings, beyond the repeating of what tomorrow brings, lies the potential for a utter destruction, if only we dare to think, to challenge, to renew.

272. Laughing Dominoes - Friday April 19, 2024 20:13 MST

Dominoes cascade against a cheap gaudy linoleum floor.
    One after another, I am entranced watching them fall.
    Each clack resonating against the walls, striking quickly
    against each other like a frenzied smoker's book of matches.

As these events unfold I am stripped, no longer bold.
    A break is coming to an end without any brakes.
    Still, their rhythmic thud, like typewriter keys bleed
    in the still room. Every domino stamped onto the
    floor tears a deep wound.

A symphony of taps and pauses. Absorbed in their flow,
    though nothing in my life, none of my vices will cover my losses.

I cannot breathe new life into these past clauses.
    My life's story stutters, living in a facade of occupational identities.
    Role engulfed indulgences burped up from the ashes.

WORDS ARE SNAKES WITH ARMS

Speedy justice for the masses- but there's no such thing,
it stews, it lingers like molasses.

The last domino falls, its fall is my beckoning call.
It's an allure of a long sweet seductive Southern draw.
I'll never suffice with picking up these distorted dice.
I'm left in an eternal scurry; I'm a hoard of mice eating
themselves to death like birds gulping down dried rice.
This is winter's last snow flurry.

273. The Devil's Dice - Saturday April 20, 2024 20:13 MST

Roll a six or a three- it doesn't matter what number you get,
    you will never be free.
    The Devil's Dice, an infestation that spreads worse than lice.
    An unparalleled gamble we all play, irrelevant of the device or price.

It's a mistake- to play.
    Everything on the line, so they say.
    We relentlessly test our luck everyday.
    The winning hand, seventy-two thousand to one,
    but it will never pay.
    Bow your head, dive into the charade.
    Is there a soul in there?
    A lingering question laid in the rocks, forbade.

The light of your eyes will drift off into a nothingness
    that you can't evade.
    Unconsciousness will be the only salvation- your best hand played.
    So take another drink, one more gruff smoke-

until your purple hands are left paid.
This wager, like heavy water is the main component
of our nuclear parade.

Helplessly I see others take their bets and dig their own grave.
    My wagers are many, spread across the table in a velvet
    green laden fable.
    I bet the corners with each toss,
    every roll exacts a distinct paralyzing toll.
    So far I've lost it all- but in the end, we all do.
    Gambling with the Devil's Dice, pounding back soju.

I have but one bet left I fret, though I already know my wager.
    I'll watch it all unfold in a vivacious, pointless anger.
    The same bet every time, it always yields the same result.
    They will embalm my wounds with salt and place sixpence pieces
    over my eyes.

In this exacta of life, all we amount to is food for the flies.

274. Absquatulate - Sunday April 21, 2024 20:34 MST

Pacing in my straw hut I desperately yearn to absquatulate.
   Everything has been disastrously disappointing as of late.
   Tomorrow is the date in which I wish not to participate.

Another skin squirming squall so offensive and foul.
   My eyes will drown themselves in screens that eat like
   a flesh eating disease as my egos howl.
   I'm left with an iron branded scowl.
   I'd rather lay face up, covered by a wet towel and douse in water.
   I'm a cheap cog in a malfunctioning machine, not even peat,
   I'm just cheap fodder.

Still I have no means so I am forced to participate in a life so
   obfuscated and grotesque, I double over in hate being undressed.
   These scales of justice are a teeter totter and we the people sit glued,
   impoverished forever at the bottom with a bottle.

. . .

There seems to be no way out from underneath their grand tower.
　　We officially have no power at this hour.
　　So here comes the water soaked towel.
　　Gurgling and desperately gasping for air,
　　I'm being drowned to death by this simulation of the fair.

Resigned and tired I'm perpetually mired in the swamp of the living
　　dead. They hold my head under, I see nothing, not even red.
　　If only I could escape, truly absquatulate-
　　until then I am bound by rusted chains and shackles.

275. Painted Staircase - Monday April 22, 2024 20:22 MST

Into obscurity, my sense of self dies.
All the stories, they lie, it's no surprise.
They say like a phoenix, we shall rise!
It's a palpable fallacy, just a way to silence self sighs.

My ashes loom at the top of an abandoned staircase.
A docile disgrace, a sad excuse for a final resting place.
Nonetheless there my soul sits.
I climbed each step, never stopping- even with every slip.
Now that I've reached the summit, I cannot descend.
These coveted stairs, busting stitches that cannot mend.
They revealed themselves to be both my beginning and my end.

My egos laugh, cry, and scream.
Atop this flight of stairs- my dreams, so I thought.
I fought for nothing, it's only peril on top.
Insanity encircles my aura, it bellows out my life force in
every direction then sinks like a stone, its nagana.

My disease is laughable, it's as believable as mana.
Here we sit waiting for it to rain.

At the top of these stairs, a formidable terrain.
I don't want to haunt them, but I have no brain.
It painted the ceiling, every family frame.
Unfinished business?
More like a life scuttled in vain.
These decisions I didn't make decided everything-
staked my claim.
Things happen, atop these staircases laden in ratted carpet,
rotting stinking floors.
I watch helplessly in the stairway looking at all these
unopened doors.

276. Glagolitic Tirade - Tuesday April 23, 2024 20:12 MST

Time marches relentlessly.
    It forgets to pause; its metronome falls into a cadence,
    initiating a merciless rhythm from above.
    With no pause, its beat is relentless as a clop,
    watering the memories of steeds, the only souls etched in our lore.

These horses thunder through the squalid muck,
    their hooves slicing through the mire, desperate to break the cycle,
    chasing victory in a race that loops back upon itself, endlessly.
    A spectacle of futility under the scrutinizing sun,
    this race is less a contest than a display of exploitation stripped bare;
    the death of fun.

What meaning lies in this relentless chase?
    Spectators place their bets, eyes wide with fear,
    as creatures run not for glory but survival,
    spurred on by a Glagolitic tirade- words ancient,
    spelling out the grim narrative of greed in verdant hues.

WORDS ARE SNAKES WITH ARMS

．　．　．

And should misfortune fall a runner, breaking its stride and spirit,
    the response is swift- a final gunshot mingles with the fading cheers,
    while spectators drain their cups, indifferent to the cost.

Saints Cyril and Methodius, witnesses to this misuse of their legacy,
    would weep for the sanctity desecrated beneath each hoof.

In this arena where history's lessons are trampled,
    the race goes on, its legacy a mud pain of humanity's relentless
    pursuit, a warning in the dust, a call to awaken from our
    complacency- death dressed in a cheap suit.
    To challenge the cycles we perpetuate?
    A safer bet is to tempt fate.
    In the roar of the crowd and the crack of the starter's pistol,
    find the courage to stand up from the insanity before it's too late.

277. Polyester Clown- Wednesday April 24, 2024 19:50 MST

Every blistering monotony starts and ends the same.
    I wish there was a way to slip from underneath the weight of this
    ultimatum: life's game.

My birthright lacked a silver spoon, but gave me life.
    It seems as if money is the only thing that can buy health
    or ease the strife.
    A commodity I lack, so I'm forced everyday to run the
    endless tar laden track.

I'm not disillusioned, I know the universe owes me not.
    I'm the same as you, full of the same lifeblood as every animal-
    but still I have nothing.
    It's not a matter of perspective, that's an insulting jest.
    How can anyone look forward to anything when they cannot even
    afford their own death?
    It's deeper than the tangible, I don't desire worldly things.
    All I want is peace and a chance.

Unfortunately that's nothing more than a heartfelt romance.

I desperately want to try, just one real opportunity.
    Each failure fills over my cup with a satisfying lunacy.
    To continue to fall short, what a blessing.
    My stomach contorts as I lose my sense of sorts.
    Derision, solitude and loneliness- if only they were sports.
    I'd win every medal, I'd be the best loser of them all.
    Success rains dollar bills,
    I rain down blood, stumbling drunken down
    a dreary apartment hall.
    It reeks of urine, a foul ammonia that seeps into your skin.

The incense of poverty, being poor is my biggest sin.
    I'd be lying if I said I didn't love the hunger.
    The balance of nothing- the sweet and sour taste of defeat.
    Losing is my every meal and it's all I eat.
    It's always there for me, embracing me with every wound it inflicts.
    I'm a complete utter failure, and I'm a addicted to it.

It's the cracking in my bones, my disgusting dehydrated lips.
    It's a possession inside of me and the only thing I can never quit.
    Another Wednesday, another day of countless loss.
    I raise up my empty broken glass to the game-
    tomorrow I am burning to lose at the same ring toss.

Life's a circus- I'm the downtrodden polyester clown.
    People love to see the Titanic drown; take a seat, gather around.

278. Duplicity's Flight - Thursday April 25, 2024 20:11 MST

Duplicity, the only fuel my grounded plane knows-
    sweet contradictions pour, a libation from my tongue,
    rye's rich deceit clings to every spoken syllable undone.
    Every utterance a crafted facade,
    a mosaic of lies laid with artisan hands.
    This is my survival, the art of deception refined.

Nods and shakes, the marionette dance of agreement,
    whatever the crowd desires, I mirror with hollow appeasement..
    I am not spared by conflict, nor do I avoid-
    The truth is, indifference has become my creed.

A stewardess glides by, her smile a flash of routine;
    mine, a reflex, nothing more- a ripple in our shared scene.

Outside, the storm rages- an ocean trapped in cirrus and cumulus.
    Lightning stitches the sky with veins of fervor.

. . .

Here, on the static tarmac, destination unknown and uncared for.
   A man battles his luggage, a one man sport.
   I watch, choose inaction, conserve my energies
   for other empty exchanges.

Cries of infants punctuate the drone of engines and weary sighs,
   small talk blossoms about the weather- a predictable encore.
   I stand apart, an observer of the mundane tragedy,
   the chaos of boarding, a theater of the calamity.

Impatience brews, yet changes nothing; it matters little.
   The question hangs, a cloud above.
   A voice breaks through, louder, tinged with the wear of travel,
   "Is it always like this?"
   A plaintive call in the crowded cabin.

I adjust my captain's cap, an armor of authority,
   and reply with a tone smoother than the air we've yet to cleave,
   "If that is your wish, then let us challenge the storm together."

Each version of me, a distinct and sustained lie- I'm not naive.

   This duplicity is not just my flight but my very sky.

279. Minimum Payment - Friday April 26, 2024 23:48 MST

Superlative creditors play their phones like bugles.
　　Another call, another debt cutting me off at the knees,
　　a time to crawl.
　　Subpoenas served like cold soup.
　　I'll never crawl way out off this stoop.
　　Inflation, the mantra of our dope sick nation.

Each ring, a piercing blast- my future foreclosed,
　　as interest compounds on interest, a cruel exponential glass.
　　My pockets turned out, empty of but lint and figments of
　　green bills and pills.
　　Credits and debits slither in sinister rows.

Their ledger- my paper boulder, rolling back in throws,
　　each attempt to scale the slope met with fresh financial demise.
　　Underneath the weight, my crushed spine-
　　the imprint of a bloody dollar sign.

· · ·

Credit scores tattooed on my chest,
    score me lower, deny me rest.
    Bankers feast on prime rate feasts,
    while I ration ramen, counting the cost of each lease.

A generation yoked in invisible chains,
    mortgages on minds, graduates' refrain.
    Dreams deferred, dangling on a string,
    dangling over the abyss, where hopes unflinchingly cling.

My life, a ledger black with red,
    each unpaid bill, a deeper wedge.
    Between the life I live and the life I've led,
    suffocated by sums too vast to shed.

Another minimum payment made my bed.
    I'm drowning, I'm in over my head.

280. The Yellow House on the Hill - Saturday April 27, 2024 22:32 MST

The yellow house on the hill.
  An emblematic signal of a catch all end all frill.
  It overlooks all of West Egg, it's a finality,
  where I no longer have to beg.

A magnificently simple dwelling, an almighty cure.
  To own that house- it would end all my worries so sure.
  No more nebulous trivialities, my final allure.
  If only I could reach those green lights- a fated demure.

An end to the dead bitting chill.
  This humble abode, my last blue pill.
  Seemingly within arms reach, though unable to foot the bill.
  This dwelling is the answer to peace- pure still.

I steady my shaking hands, tread forward to ensure.
  My inevitably, my one and only will to secure.

There must be a way through this spontaneous combustion,
a path through to endure.
I'm baptized on an altar of rusty nails, inured.

A haunting dysphasia,
    a dyslexic lexicon that will serve as my offering to this hill.
    A palpable aching in my bones sells me the truth
    signed with the devils iron quill.
    Once the day comes where my labors are paid,
    I fear that my bed will already be made by
    the man lurched on the windowsill.

The yellow house on the hill.

It's my future, I must carve out a way with a conscious till-
    past all the moral decay and lingering disillusionment to fulfill.

I will embolden time, it shall forever standstill.

The yellow house on the hill.

281. Vulture's Flak - Sunday April 28, 2024 20:25 MST

Vultures circle dressed in shackets,
    birds or ghosts- my intuition, ripped open packets.
    My hearth grows cold from plagues both new and old.
    No fire can cry out enough heat, not enough peat
    or no number of jackets.

Pulse races, a frantic beat within confined spaces,
    relentless faces blur, time races
    toward an unseen cliff, a precipice unseen,
    in the cavity of my chest, a scream tightens its braces.

Breath- a thief in the tumult, steals away grace,
    leaves behind a trace of icy fear, the base
    note in a symphony of dread. Each inhale
    a struggle, every exhale a chase.

Walls close in, a world reduced to a pinprick, black

upon black.
A swirling sinew of vices where thoughts
tangle, twist, and sanity dices.

This vortex of visceral fear, my senses crack,
   reality slips, and my mind, it stacks
   against itself, a house of cards collapsing
   under the weight of what I lack.

The vultures swoop, their bodies drawn back to attack.
   Their talons dig into my back, their laughter scatters the sky
   in an unworldly flak. Here I am, in another Sunday-
   everything cascades behind my eyes, fading to black.

282. Unconvincingly Sane - Monday April 29, 2024 19:57 MST

I have to wash my hands with lye.
    I have to turn the door knob eight times.
    I have to set twelve alarms.
    I have to check all the window locks three times.
    I have to check each door every morning at four.
    I have to wash my hands with lye.

I wish I could stop.
    I can't.
    I obsess over everything that doesn't matter.
    My mind's incessant clatter.
    Obsessive and manic depressive.
    I wish I could stop.

They tell me to breathe, the four by four method.
    They tell me it's all a matter of perspective.
    They draw a circle- explaining I can only control the inside of it,
    nothing on the out.

I can't control anything, I want to claw my eyes out.
I wish I could stop.

These pointless obsessive ticks.
    They burrow under my skin.
    It never ends, this pointless situation I'm in.
    I light six matches, trying to smoke them out.
    My skin cooks, a barbecue of sanity.
    I try everything and consistently fail.
    Failing is my obsession, I'll never prevail.
    It claws at the back of my head,
    it sits watching me at the edge of my bed.
    I wish I could stop.

Endless meanderings, spiraling deep into an endless well.
    These aimless obsessions, to them my soul I did sell.
    My hands crack and bleed,
    my eyes hollowed out, bloodshot and seethe.
    I have no choice, no control.
    I do anything to silence my thoughts,
    prescriptions eat away at my decaying brain.
    Like termites working their way through my wooden pain.

Mediation, counseling, therapy, medication...
    Wash, rinse, repeat.
    This wiring of my brain,
    a foreboding damnation that I cannot defeat.

I struggle to stand, shaking in line.
    One more eye contact and I'll lose my mind.
    The vice tightens its grip.
    I spiral further into these meaningless trivialities-

I cannot quit.

I clean everything three times.
    Scrubbing until my fingernails fall off,
    I need to whiten this shower grout line.

I don't want anything to do with any of it.
    I can't stop.

Screaming in anger until my voice just decides to stop.
    Utter insanity, an all encompassing calamity.

283. Jouissance - Tuesday April 30, 2024 19:39 MST

Borderline comatose the tips of my fingers tingle numb,
    itching for another dose.
    Insensible, I can no longer remember her voice.
    I can no longer even picture her face.
    My memories wiped away from a broken windshield-
    forever shattered, erased..
    Repressed or suppressed, I cannot tell.
    All I know is I can no longer remember any of her-
    that I can tell.

Taste- another robbed sense.
    Tinnitus drills through my ears, scrambling my brain.
    No recollection.
    A Manchurian candidate infection clawing through my eyes.

It's all over.

. . .

Still I can breathe- a bittersweet sour scolding surprise.
  Disorganized thinking, obsessive painful blinking-
  all part of my tear. A break from reality- life is eternally fair.

I'm not draped in a cheap gaudy suit of despair.
  I'm covered in a silhouette of confusion, utter disrepair.
  It lingers just on the tip of my tongue; still nothing is there.
  I watch a man's eyes in the mirror glimmer with something-
  a feeling that was once there.

I see in sepia, though nothing is black or white.
  A gray mahogany throbbing, my tree hollowed out in trash bags
  through the long night.
  My senses of her, demur- likely because she doesn't exist.
  My reality consists of endless parchment, water stained lists.
  The ink carries itself away towards the edges-
  driving me closer to each of my ledges.
  Emotion washes away.
  Ropes clinging desperately to an open belay audibly crackle like fire
  as they're systematically hacked in half with a rusty blade; desire.

Helplessly I watch myself fall in complete silence, a wretched
  nothingness with no delay from fragile heights, with no dismay.

I don't remember her- so how could she be missed?
  Her name, Jouissance, not a moniker or mist.
  Instead it's something I've never known-
  how could it be missed?

284. Suburban Submarine - Wednesday May, 01 2024 19:06 MST

City streets littered with garbage pails.
    Wind catches their lids, wafting them up like sails.
    This city, full of forgotten means.
    A neighborhood for sale, just beyond the greens.

I walk around any encounter with living beings.
    They pester me with judging stares killing my dreams.
    I walk a path, zigzagging and frazzled.
    My destination, a manhole past the light pole-
    just beyond the rusted bridge.
    I walk this route daily, though it's always amiss.
    The sewer, where all life eventually leads.
    It reminds me of all the greed, filthy corruption- evil deeds.
    That's the thing about water, it's always there.
    Taking the path of least resistance, it's forever meaningless and fair.

Its existence depends on nothing, what a personification of the truth,
    it's really something beyond compare.

I pass the iron wrought bridge slipped just over a poisoned stream.
I wonder if this muddied place is where I've always been.

Past the whipping leaves and plant riddled thieves I make it to the
   sewers disguised entry.
It sits alone in the middle of a grass bearded gully.

Every time I see it, I envision scuttling myself in.
   To slip away into society's filthy abyss.
   It's a place no one would look, no one would miss.
   In city streets littered with garbage pails the wind takes me,
   I am its sail.

285. The Applause - Thursday May, 02 2024 19:14 MST

Who decides when the applause ends?
  When mob rule jeers and cheers their amends.
  It starts with a single clap,
  but goes on in unison until suddenly it's done.
  It's an interwoven harmony, a song unsung.
  In this lexical looming church, the chants, the bellowing of
  enchanting spurts. Its power lays in the energy of sound resounding
  off the vaulted ceilings and into your chest.

Who determines the rhythm of our breath,
  the collective cadence of living, the subtle death
  of an individual voice, lost in hallowed halls?
  It's the murmur of a multitude, each note demur,
  each sentiment a glass vase,
  shattered pieces, their reflection of a world where souls contrast.

Hymns of conformity, a symphony unswayed,
  dictates the tempo, a prelude to fears conveyed.

Who amongst us dares to disrupt the harmony,
to challenge the sacred doctrine of unanimity?
The thrall of the crowd, a powerful decree,
drowns out the discordant, claiming sovereignty.

When does the fervor turn into a frenzied howl,
In the bowels of our minds stitching a perilous cowl?
An unbreakable spell,
where difference is silenced, and only the brainwashed dwell.
The congregation sways chalices of ceremonial blood,
their hunger for unity, a monstrous feast- an unleavened flood.

Who decides when the fervor ends?
When reason is lost, and hysteria transcends?
In this cathedral of conformity, who dares to be free,
to break the rhythm, to challenge the decree?
In the tabernacle of this collective chest,
lies the latent power, for better or worse, to oppress or divest.

When the applause fades, and silence prevails,
who then can judge the strength of our collective tales?
For better or worse, the choice is ours to make,
to follow or dissent, to breath or to break.
In the end, it's not the mob, but the single clap,
that determines when the curtain falls, when we close the gap.

WORDS ARE SNAKES WITH ARMS

286. Florists Luck - Friday May, 03 2024 17:39 MST

A pungent odor invades my nose.
    A mixture of a funeral parlor-
    and the thick palpable musk of the past.

It's the smell of death.
    It lingers in the air, sticks to your clothes.
    I can't place it- until I can: flowers.
    Fresh floral arrays, the signature of our last days.
    It's impossible to rebuild from all this guilt, sanity frays.
    The excuses, the flowers.

The smells that hallmark our last hours.
    A retching unforgiving flinching freshness;
    a masked devil. It's akin to opening an attic box,
    it hits you in the chest, a base with no treble.

Anything to eliminate this pungent purgatory

burrowed on my nostrils.

I take a walk- a mistake.
Their smell bellows from budding plants.
A fake beauty, a nebulous crushed hybrid costume.
Take a walk- a bad investment, all my accounts are overdrawn.

Everywhere I turn, I'm suited in a jacket.
    Dead, a frailty beyond any living head.
    This landslide of olfactory pulses burned.
    A time left unturned.

I'm left lifeless, nothing but fuel for the cremation consummation.
    A bolder union of fire and dust.
    Ashes in a forgotten urn.

The smell of flowers- an unfaithful reminder of our turn.
    I thought I was my own man, I thought I made my own luck.

My match refused to burn, I didn't even pick my own urn.

287. The Green Canopy - Saturday May, 04 2024 22:26 MST

Accomplices of fake accomplishments- what a sobering wake.
   A sad green canopy covering a six foot hole in the ground,
   a coffin cozied up next to it, in wait.

Passersby of all lives scurry along, like there was nothing happening
   past that gory green grass.
   Absolutely nothing going on.
   I pay it only a glimpse through my car's window,
   separated by the thin glass.

I drive right on by, though I never actually pass.
   Another reminder of our mortality sitting back behind the blinders.
   To pay some sort of respect, emotions all bottled up into an
   unwritten binder:

Your safe and sound- murmurs the voice in my head, my minder.
   What sweet lies I sell myself, there could be nothing kinder.

．　．　．

The truth mounts up in the sluice, panning for facts.
 They face me blankly in the rearview mirror, crow's feet etched by
 years of fake facts. Eyes empty, hollowed by time borrowed,
 burrowed cribriform, forlorn.
 A lost soul that's been perpetually recycled on empty,
 it's never been full, only tallowed.

The gold panning is followed by empty promises of cleaned dreams.
 The yearning for nothingness, the rosary dangling from my rearview
 mirror gleams.
 I'm only passing by, though I'm tearing at the seams.
 This monotonous baggage, fingering holes in my sixty nine cent
 plastic tote.

Sustainability is an unsatiated neutrality beyond my ability,
 everything will go up in smoke.
 Accomplices of fake accomplishments- what a sobering wake.
 Today the green canopy is theirs-
 but it's on layaway and it's more than my soul bears.

288. The Strange Case - Sunday May, 05 2024 19:21 MST

Mr. Hyde lives in my head.
    An unexpected guest with a permanent bed.
    A demon of my own making, the path I've led.
    He dictates my thoughts, sheer and utter dread.

Dr. Jekyll has no voice, a mere marionette,
    pulled by strings of panic, in cold sweat.
    Caught in a duel, forever internally met,
    his heart throbs in dread, a battle, a sinister set.

Hyde initiates chaos, stirs the pot,
    Jekyll listens, his piece forgot.
    In the prison of my mind, a treacherous plot,
    where fear is sown, and there's nowhere to hide.

A tug of war in the corridors dim,
    Hyde's grim laughter, at a whim.

Jekyll's plea, on the brim,
the insatiable Hyde rides him, limb by limb.

Through the psyche's twisted maze,
    Hyde's the tyrant, setting ablaze.
    Jekyll's spirit, in a daze,
    caught in Hyde's relentless damned haze.

There is no solace in the break of day,
    nor in the night's obscure deadly ballet.
    Always Hyde leads the fray,
    Jekyll's soul, the perennial prey.
    Together they pick up a tab for a bill they know they can't pay.

How long must this conflict last?
    Can Jekyll ever shun the cast?
    Or must he live under Hyde's vast,
    cloak, until all is past?

These two cannot create their own luck- it's a devilish contrast.
    Jekyll jeers and jerks, anything to remove the inevitable forecast
    of calamity- this outcast.
    This dichotomy is me.

A juxtaposition between a man who has quit and an omnipresent
    enemy that deepens the wound with a red hot spit.
    I'm roasting over a roaring fire while everyone laughs as my
    sweltering skin drips into the pit.
    This obscure contrast- smoke choking out sight of the real
    blazing fire, I am the wood ablaze unequally split.

· · ·

Mr. Hyde lives in my head.
  He's consumed all my light, all that's left is red.
  There's no more separation, the docile man's creature
  of need is now the very flesh the creature devours in a thirsty greed.

I quit, I concede; the ghost in the mirror watches the bleed.

289. Sectarianism Riots and Rot- Monday May, 06 2024 19:59 MST

Sectarianism riots for right or wrong in the streets
   and across college campuses.
   Ignorant kids picket in thickets of plots they don't understand.
   They shout for justice- unable to grasp the complex truth
   of geopolitical realities that no one individual can command.

Their voices, loud but hollow, bounce against lawn tents of lament
   and the silent stones of institutions holding tight to ancient dogmas,
   unbent. Their signs are bright and bold, a stark contrast
   to the gray of understanding that cannot be lent.

In their eyes, the world is black and white,
   shaded by their fleeting whims and fleeting fight.
   But life, in all its intricate layers,
   is a spectrum lost to their naive sight.

· · ·

I watch, a bystander with history's eyes,
   seeing cycles of fervor rise and inevitably fall.
   Today's anger is tomorrow's apathy,
   as time weathers every fervent call.

From my lips, a weary sigh escapes,
   fogging the air with my own desolation.
   For I too once yelled into the void,
   clutching ideals with desperate adulation.
   Though I'm a Zionist, the protesters' antisemitism-
   a disgusting present reminder of the past.
   They have no idea the way their misplaced hate spreads.

Now I stand amidst a wiser roar,
   knowing the more I know the less I know,
   feeling the sting of protests past lingering sore;
   my own cries, now dampened,
   drowned from losing my voice in their sea of hateful choice.

They do not understand how their shame shall merge
   with those who stood before on this same ledge.
   Chanting for a change not coming,
   on the precipice of reality's edge, Nuremberg rallies.
   Misplaced anger today, mimicry of the Night of Broken Glass-
   fire in all the alleys.

So the cycle spins, a carousel grim,
   of youthful naivety and age's cynicism.
   Each chant a pulse in the heartbeat of time,
   a rhythm lost in an endless schism.

. . .

They fight for a world that they do not wish to see,
  ignorant that their insanity bleeds far beyond just a fantasy.

And I, no longer the dreamer,
  mourn the loss of what has been-
  I see the future evil has painted; a battle where no one can win.

290. The Wind Tunnel - Tuesday May, 07 2024 19:51 MST

Wind gusts eat away at eternity's trust,
    chimes bellow as furniture obviates the urban landscapes.
    Nothing is still, the grass moves in waves from the
    unseen lathes of nature.
    Every leaf, a script, a flustered flight in the
    thoroughfare of a pit digging deeper in my stomach.

Windows shake at the whim of unseen forces,
    battering at the fragile panes of glass,
    each tremor a reminder of the chaos held at bay- only just.
    Inside, my heart ticks toward entropy,
    unmade beds, scattered papers, life unpinned.

Amidst nature's normal wrath, the unforgiving winds,
    a grenade of disarray pulls out its pin in real time,
    sucking the air from the mud, even the swine.
    Undiscerned cries, urbanity's muffled roar beneath a thin jacket.

. . .

How does one truly live in mundane disdain?
　　When the compass spins, bewitched by each gust,
　　no north to guide, no horizon in sight,
　　Just the turmoil, the electric charge of a storm-ridden night.
　　It's brewing in my gut, overtaking my very sight.

This swelling litany of pointless tasks, the surge of the overwhelmed,
　　buries hopes in dead grass, layers browned, yellow and deep.
　　Should a single power line fall or spark make its way-
　　everything would catch fire.
　　A spreading malaise, undeniable and undefinable-
　　flames ripping ablaze. Smoke coats my lungs, my new jacket.
　　I gasp for breath, it's a pointless winded straightjacket.
　　Overcome in this tornado of fire.

Thus, I stand amid red and yellow fury, stripped of all but awe,
　　my life dangling from the talons of a macaw.
　　A spectator to the spectacle, to the beauty and the flaw.
　　What was once a chance now bellows loud noxious black and gray
　　smoke- I breath in the debris deeply, accepting to be overcome.
　　This wind, my storm, has only just begun.

291. A Ledge to Stare - Wednesday May, 08 2024 19:50 MST

The point of no return, a steep drooling rock face littered
    with unruly shrubbery.
    A cliff, this one I shall face in a crescendo of drudgery.
    It stares back at me just as blankly as I.
    Heights of this caliber, fatality laughs all the way, nigh.
    A fall you cannot come back from, one that rips out your backbone.

I stare.

Sun bakes my head as buzzards join, forming a crowd.
    Vultures circle above me in a cloaking thickness
    like the Shroud of Turin. There's no more, this is the
    last time to turn in. I inch closer to the inevitable edge.
    I tremble as my feet kick up the dust, shuffling around pebbles in
    defeat. Slowly but surely I move to speak- I emit no sound.
    My arms steady me as I lower myself to the ground. My feet dangle
    off the ledge, the sheer distance to the ground is far more profound
    than anything else I've ever found. My pupils dilate as my heart

pushes past an unnatural rate. Sweating convoluting every fiber of
my being revolting.

I stare.

On this ledge I put myself, or so it seems.
 Doused dreams in towels soaked with gasoline.
 Was there ever a chance?
 A piece of pyrite gleams.
 I shove it off over the ledge, just like any wealth I could have ever led.
 It bounces from ledge to ledge, a scurry of gravity.
 It's sound talks to me, loud and in thuds, carrying
 through the valley like a pen dropping in mud.

I stare.

My purpose here?
 I'm not so sure.
 It's the first feeling of life, being faced with death- the macabre
 allure. It's not an emotion I wanted but it's all I could procure.
 How bad do you want to suffer?
 The falling rock attests one last breath.

I stare.

292. The Epitaph of the Last Laugh - Thursday May, 09 2024 19:50 MST

The epitaph of the last laugh,
    albeit one of sheer insanity.
    It makes no sense, words bleeding out in a garbled alphabetic
    hemorrhage lacking urbanity.
    Still the snake flicks out it's tongue tasting each syllable,
    a warbled rattle akin to the dropping of slabs of bad meat on
    concrete, sun spoiled and marbled.

Each adverb pushed to the roof of it's mouth, straight to the
    Jacobson's organ. A chemical sensory perception, an overload of an
    ode to calamity.
    This slithering slick beast, disgusting and vile, on my fear it feasts.
    I am it's prey but human nature eats deceits.
    I'm here for one reason: a show, a dangerous spectacle.
    The risk swells in my stomach as I sweat, my legs grow shaky as my
    vision wishes to forget the fret of it's fangs piercing deep past my
    eye's episcleral layer.
    The allure of the poison itches in the back of my mind.
    Without any further thought I lurch forward towards the beast.

. . .

I grip its head despite my raining dread in one fail swoop.
   It rips its tail violently, cajoling and pulling away.
   My grip tightens, this snake shall not get away today.
   It snarls its fangs with an ear screeching hiss.
   I hold its face to mine, an existential error, I'm remiss.
   This act, all a divine victory.
   The epitaph of the last laugh,
   albeit one of sheer insanity.

293. These Days are Numbered - Friday May, 10 2024 20:23 MST

These days are numbered.
Time behind me, opportunities missed- I slumbered.
Power lines guide the way across pothole laden pavement.
Underneath a crescent moon that's cut its teeth on
human stupidity; I'm the buffoon.

Spitting blood out into a rotten rusted brass spittoon-
I know. The moon will outlast me and my life's typhoon.
What time I have left wrought with the fear of the Spear of Destiny.
My biggest concern: tomorrow will look like today,
this I cannot concur.

Penniless and jaded I am but a forgotten capitalist cartoon begotten.
My brand is one of poor quality, a cheap pleather scaly shotten.
There's no way my skin can continue to withstand this degree of
weather, it tears like gaudy cotton.

. . .

That's not the case for the old men putting out on the green.
 I paid them to live out their dream.
 Their nine-iron gleams under the
 high esteems of their trumped up reputations. I envy their lack of
 work, their permanent vacation.

I look back, knowing that there are less days in front of me than
 behind. I've lived each second of them as if I were blind.
 Was it my choice?
 To be billed over and over, each mounting medical invoice.
 I feel more so robbed of my voice, maybe it's a depravity.
 Life, liberty and the pursuit of happiness- a written gaff,
 a recipe of insanity.

So the world turns, another day, another dime.
 Until corporations decide it's my time.
 Bilked of my blood, stripped of my organs-
 I'm worth more as a corpse, to be sold like a fifty-cent flesh bargain.

Still the moon will loom long after I.
 I see my reflection, watch my fate drown like golf balls in an unused
 lake; everything is a culmination of one big lie.

These days are numbered.

294. Fetch - Saturday May, 11 2024 18:23 MST

Tonight I caught sight of a spectral double of me.
    I watched my doppelgänger living out my life,
    on the thin precipice of the night's knife.
    A straight razor to savor.
    Portending my own tragic ending, this duplicate of me,
    this fetch, set out for his own pound of flesh.

Raising a glass to me he set forth our last decree.
    A collage of Irish folklore, my sixth degree.
    Stay alive, try to lose all your money.

You will.

Overthinking the fat badger puffing away at his pipe
    in the corner of the room.
    Adorned in a top-hat stitched with veins of my soul.
    As this life takes a toll on you-

keep moving forward to stumble.

You will.

He passes me a pint, that's what you get for sticking around
    when you should've fumbled. Each sip, bitter and profound.
    Another pint, one free glass; take it with you, so it goes.

You will.

The push and pull that it doesn't mean much.
    This last tiresome time came in clutch.

In the lukewarm foam of my ale, he narrates my tale,
    morphing like fog across the bog, a snail's frail trail.
    "You'll chase this mist, a ghostly twist,
    -and find only solitude in the gale."

You will.

As the clock ticks on, beating of the pub's heart,
    he melts into the woodwork, a forgotten part
    of the lore that stains the bar's dark art.
    My laugh, hollow, meets the bartender's smart remark.

I leave a tip, the coins clink like a fading lark,
    step into the mist, where oil lamplights struggle against the dark.
    In my pocket, the weight of an absent mark,

the etching of my steps, a disembodied question mark.

Walking home, each step a silent plea,
   of the figure I met, the eerie referee.
   One last cigarette I just couldn't get.
   Of my past and future, won't again decree
   the limits of a life spent chasing a freed me.

I don't even know if I believe everything you're trying to say to me.

You will.

The strangest feeling, the world is not all it seems.

Tonight, I caught sight of a spectral double of me,
   -and realized the ghost I'd seen was the man I could be.
   If only I dared cut loose the noose of my predetermined destiny,
   step off the precipice, into a new identity.
   Chills crawl up and down my spine, embolden my own decline.
   Tonight I caught sight of a spectral double of me.
   I hate the sight, the inevitable longing of wanting to be free.

295. It Probably Gets Better Over Time... - Sunday May, 12 2024 19:05

One side of his mouth would call it a good deed.
   The other side dangles a cigarette butt, still smoldering,
   so close to his skin it cooks all his boils as they ooze open in greed.
   The definition of want and need, a never ending
   trampling by the corporate stampede.

So it goes

It probably gets better over time- so they say.
   Apparently forgetting how compound interest comes into play.
   A final nail in the coffin, snowballing debts leaking from my ears
   in audible effervescent regrets.
   I foam at my mouth, bleed from my eyes- still I have to pay another
   doctor, the anesthesiologist, the surgeon...
   oh and insurance decides not to cover the surprise.
   Days and nights brittle, riddled with begging for my coverage to pay.
   Out-of-pocket minimum met, deductible well past over spent.
   I wish I didn't have to eat, I can't afford it; let alone the rent.

. . .

So it goes.

A cyclical musing of cents that make no sense.
  Only the rich ditch these soiled worldly laments.
  They puff on cigars and continue to preach- money can't buy
  happiness. This sour soot I truly beseech as disgustingly rotten.
  Money makes everything better- try being the poor, the forgoten.
  I'd take all your problems, every qualm any day.
  If only I had the resources to pay.
  My hair is on fire, on a cardboard box I lay.
  I hate it all- I'll never be able to repay.

So it goes.

I work six jobs every single day.
  Dividends pad the affluent, they never work- it's all play.
  I'm exhausted, I wish I could sink into an opulent nothingness.
  That will be the day.
  Until then I am just still here working away.
  The purgatory of the poor- it's me every breathing second.
  My everyday.

So it goes.

296. Amat Victoria Curam - Monday May, 13 2024 19:10 MST

My eyes throb through my head,
   my heart beats through my chest and into my bed.
   I'm still here, another Monday, red- unfed.

I have someplace to be, it's anywhere but here.
   It pulls at every fiber of my being.
   A place quiet, calm, and devoid of fear; far off but near.
   I thought I would have been there- still fleeing.
   I need a place to land, Camelot, a mirage so clear.

Everything evades me so I hold nothing, no cheer.
   These castle walls, this cold cobblestone road
   beneath my broken ankles guides my path.
   I've taken every precaution, built up every defense.
   It's sobering that I still taste every flavor of time's
   wrought iron fence.

.   .   .

The sun sets in a blaze, mocking my plight,
  every golden ray a reminder of time's cruel delight.
  A broken compass, juxtaposed against the
  rolling yellow burned horizon, a distant fight,
  I chase the stars during the day too, not only the
  bleak bludgeoning nights.
  Seeking solace in their guidance, picking up pieces
  of me in the aftermath.

Each step, a damned roaring stutter.
  Preparation etched in every muscle, every sinew strained,
  stretched beyond capacity until they snap.
  Victory remains a ghost, an elusive toast,
  mocking my every effort, leaving me chained.
  I'm destiny's errand boy; its vice as my collar.

I've charted every star, every constellation's map,
  navigated by the blood-curdling screams of my own self- deceit.
  My diseased empty body drifts aimlessly, caught in a hapless trap.
  Doubt plots my crash, relentless and indiscreet.

In the stillness of night, when dreams should soothe,
  the specter of failure haunts my restless mind,
  a paradox of readiness, a truth so smooth,
  that victory, prepared for, is the hardest to find.
  Amat Victoria Curam.
  These words etched into my back with a rusty blade, my stigmata.

I question the gods, the fates, the stars above,
  how much longer must I bear this cross?
  How many more times can I?
  Is preparation a guise, a parody of sanity?

Or is victory's hand forever sealed in a roulette
with a magnetic ball- sheer insanity.

Through tear-stained eyes, I seek a new green lawn,
a glimmer of hope in the horizon's gleam.
Until then, I tread this path, weary, deterred.
Every failure snuffs out my soul,
bringing me closer and closer to uttering my last word.

297. Of my own Volition - Tuesday May, 14 2024 20:29 MST

Of my own volition- what a nonsensical omission.
    Unseen forces drag me backwards in a contorted position.
    There is no actual mission.

Faces in the windows taunt me but I know they're not really there.
    An affair emotionally fraught, this pointless attrition cannot be
    bought. Eyes flicker, gaslights shimmer,
    phantom choices linger, thin as air.
    Every path laid before me is but an artifice, a snare.
    Choices, like marionette strings, pull- each a cunning little dare.

"Choose freely," the disembodied voices snark,
    every turn is preordained, despair, beautifully hollow.

In this dreadful culvert without exits, each corridor loops back to its
    start. Flooding slowly, but drowning in raw sewage is just a part.

. . .

Freedom's illusion, a crafted delusion, pierces like a dart.
  What autonomy can exist when every end resets to my heart?
  The liberty they promise is a farce, tearing my will apart.

Walls close inward, their paint chipped, hues of bleakness and
  fatigue in every new start.
  Specters of opportunity dissolve upon a closer critique.
  What use is a door when the room spins, logic oblique?
  I'm a Manchurian Candidate in an election
  where my party pushes me to take the loss- oh their cynique.

I tread the well-worn path with shoes of lead, set out by unseen plans
  dangling from formaldehyde finished hands.
  I'm but a walking corpse plotted by the funeral owner's demands.
  Resignation floods my chest and my casket.
  The only truth that understands-
  embalming fluid, the last facade of humans' doctoral denials over
  these inevitable plans.

So I lay in this coffin indefinitely, in truth,
  a reality that stretches and blends me.
  Following a eulogy so tight, not a line can I amend.
  I read from the script- a loop that will never end,
  Of my own volition? No, just an illusion they pretend.

To dream of choice is folly, a farce too harsh to voice.
  In the end, the curtains close; we've never had a choice.
  The path was always theirs; I'm just here to reinforce
  the cruel facade of volition
  In this existential lie, perforce-
  my soul's pierced by Vlad the Impaler's stakes.

He sits back with a loaf of bread for dipping- just listening.
Vampires exist, look in the mirror-
you won't see your own face near.

298. Offerings - Wednesday May, 15 2024 21:34 MST

Offerings strategically splayed on a rock shelf below the petroglyphs.

One for every seven:
    a mirror,
    a pile of gold doubloons,
    a red shade of lipstick,
    an emerald,
    an overflowing bottle of wine,
    a blood-stained dagger,
    and a clock with slowed hands.

In tandem they churn in a yearning for freedom,
    Something to pry me loose from this ephemeral glum.
    I light the candle and wait.
    Unspoken in the mirror, I feel it trickling down my neck,
    covering my spine. My nose bleeds- but it's not divine.
    Skinwalkers lurk outside, unable to enter.
    Anything is a fable until you're present, breathe in the musky air,

feel your lungs splinter.

As dusk bleeds into night's thick vein,
    the desires grow tall, flirting relentlessly with my fall.
    Each item gleams under the moon's eerie light,
    a Mesopotamian rock etched with lies,
    temptations, fueling everyone's lives.

The mirror grows lips, cries of vanity, a face that isn't mine,
    reflecting the deep-seated lust to outshine.
    Gold doubloons clink with the sound of greed,
    each coin a promise to fulfill every earthly need.

Lipstick stains the Holy Grail, a mark of envy's shade,
    desiring the life and love others have paraded.
    Emerald, thick with pride, radiates a radioactive toxic green.
    Its brilliance is a curtain to what lies behind, unseen.

Wine dribbles down the altar, excess in every drop,
    intoxicating lethargy, urging time to stop.
    The dagger drips with wrath, each drip a spiteful spell,
    blades sharpened on bones of those who dared rebel.

And the clock, oh the clock, it ticks with slothful hands,
    doling out each second like infinite strands.
    A lethargic waltz, stretching moments into eternities,
    challenging the very essence of my realities.

Together, they summon a vortex, a portal to the depths,
    where my silent mutterings turn to screams, and promises are kept.

I step forward, my sins a cloak woven tight,
ready to plunge into the abyss, beyond wrong or right.

For in this ritual, under the weight of night,
I barter with good and evil, the devil within myself-
to grant me insight. To live truly, beyond my neck-tightened belt,
I embrace the seven, where my true self is found.

A crackle in the air, the candle flickers out,
the petroglyphs have found an understanding of what I'm about.
A meandering mentality seldom truly felt.
From seven deadly sins, one voice is clear, ear shatteringly loud:
To truly live, in sin's embrace, an exiled shroud.

And so the dawn finds the leper, no longer the same,
I devoted myself to a life of morality, a life of pain.
These relics smile upwards at me,
I buckle, fall to one knee.
A bird is above us watching all the same,
I wait for its feather- the one embroidered with my name.

299. Headcase - Thursday May, 16 2024 17:18 MST

I feel a filth in my bones, an ache in every muscle,
  every single cursed thought, a relentless and grueling tussle.
  Is this decay merely within my mind's hold?
  Or is it the stench of something foul, rotting unseen and bold?

I've tread this path before, each step a tattered hustle,
  the facade crumbles; in shreds, reality wrestled.
  My seat teems with unrest, knowing dread permeates all unsaid.
  They chant my name, a mystery deep,
  a haunting dread, no one to blame.

All merges into a relentless torment, the fire within refuses to tame.
  A cycle of judgment, a recurrent shame.
  She knew the weight of truth- too crushing to claim.
  Beware the questions, their answers shake,
  the truths you dread to awake.

· · ·

Swelling within, an inner flood, no retreat from this grim mud.
  Your deceits, once sweet, now only thuds of hollow lies.
  Trapped in a night that never dies, this plight, it underlines-
  there is no dawn, no light.
  Broken, sightless, nothing to spark, no mirth left, only a mark.

Dark secrets overtake my frontal lobe, an orange ichor sewn deep.
  I gather my thoughts in a tattered trash bag,
  in a heap my soul to keep.
  Frantic to contain, to hold the madness at bay.
  They scream my name.

In this calm so oddly stark, the final bell tolls sharp.
  This serenity, fake, standing upon pyramids of salt
  set out under the sun to bake.
  A descent into the fray,
  driven to derision, drunk on a park bench.
  The stench burrows inside my nostrils.
  They call out my name in a haunting refrain,
  the last light dims away, my unrealized gain.
  My bespoke terrain laid out for others to lay claim.
  These days take so long- how are you true?

They chant my name, a malevolent unison.

300. Barium Swallow - Friday May, 17 2024 20:00 MST

It has no beginning or end, time-
    a linear running crime.
    The price of turning water into wine.
    Divinity oozes a barium slime.
    There's always a cost, each miracle bears sublime scars.

I fight though only with a sling.
    I feel my light drowning in vomit, a slow unforgiving killing.
    It chokes me, waking me up at night desperate for air,
    struggling amongst the sting.
    Fate, my Goliath- I have only rocks to bring.
    Time doesn't wait.
    The clock mocks me, each second eating away,
    in the dim light of a weakening chandelier,
    I am the one that must sway.
    I hurl these pebbles at the giant who does not bleed,
    each throw less a strike, more a plea, a desperate deed.

· · ·

Goliath's strength grows, towering over my brittle form,
   his laughter- thunderous, as storms within storms roar.
   I must stand, though knees buckle, resolve wears thin,
   against this colossus of disease, this leviathan of sin.

My weapons are meager, my armory bare,
   only the sling of hope, and pills of despair.
   With each labored breath, each ragged gasp for air,
   I swing, releasing burdens too great to bear.

In this uneven combat where victories are slight,
   where triumph is surviving through one more night,
   I sculpt my defiance from fear's stark marble,
   carve out of pain a testament, a battle.

Facing down the giant of mortality, in this relentless game.
   My purpose fizzles out, a candle that's lost it's wax,
   a smoking wick churning out toxic pollution thick and black.

Despite the dark, the illness, the relentless fray,
   I deliver my frankincense and myrrh without delay.
   I am more than my battles, more than my decay.
   My mind won't let me believe it, matter what I say.

It has no beginning or end, time-
   I feel my claim slipping away with every cry
   of the grandfather clock's chime.

301. Obsidian's White Flag - Saturday May, 18 2024 20:49 MST

Oblivion smiles back in the slick black reflection of obsidian.
    A magmatic spectrum of time parallel, Euclidean.
    Destiny carries on with or without you,
    swelling through the atrium in Dravidian tongues.

This volcanic glass, sharp and fractured affixed to the tips of arrows,
    flung from societal bows, landing deep in bone marrow.
    Aimed at no particular target,
    just joust into crowds where they land hardest.

Among the murmurs of the dispossessed,
    those who've stepped off the given path,
    I find the harmony of outcasts singing psalms of wrath.
    Their voices, a chorus against the monocle of monoculture,
    rise like a crow from the rubble of structured socioeconomic falter.

Each shard of silicon dioxide slings a fable

seeping deep through the American kitchen table.
Past lore of resistance, cuts the air with tales of drying persistence.
The fractured, the forgotten, find no solace in the chaos,
we're each a listless floating number.
Into the abyss we thunder;
all the while gerrymandering politicians silently slumber.

In Eastern time, empty promises splayed out in a showmanship of
connection but delivers void.
Alienation in the web of streets,
where every intersection meets a dead end for those who cannot
blend or pretend.
This two party nonsense cyclically repeats,
a soul of a nation it anxiously depletes.

The obsidian, now held in my palm, reflects not just light,
but the bombast of a false calm ripping through the night.
Every inch of my being screams out a silent blood curdling cry,
palpably solemn.
A people fragmented, rigid in their delirious demands.
No amount of obsidian in our collective hands can unbury us from
these bludgeoning reprimands.
Urgently I scratch, searching for an unsought path out of my skin;
anything to escape these drowning demands.

In this mosaic of sharp edges, where we dodge the pledges of unity
that bind and gag,
I trace the silhouette of a lone white flag.

A fiat standard for the fragmented, a banner for the estranged,
left behind with the gold standard.
Under which none are equal, and all are deranged.

Here, in the obsidian's mesmerizing gleam, I dream
of a world not split at the seams.
And so I stand, obsidian in hand,
a mirror to the fault lines of this land.
Challenging the fracture, embracing the break,
in a society that sleeps, I choose to wake.

302. Landspout Tornado Touches Down in Eastern Colorado - Sunday May, 19 2024 19:51 MST

Thunderous clouds encircle the horizon,
    a landspout sprouts.
    It sucks everything in and spits nothing out.
    Nature, the omnipresent bandit.
    It gives, it steals, coagulating all our doubts.
    Each robbery is more brazen than the last.
    Nothing can end this barren drought.
    I hold steady, steadfast in my forever fast, in the eye of the spout.

Nothing lasts, except these noxious feelings.
    Time served my warrant, the bell rings out for my last bout.
    This theft, claimed to be a victimless crime.
    It steals from everyone, even those in their prime.

My roots torn, my spirit borne aloft in its mischievous gust,
    a mockery of solidity, my truths turned to dust.
    A maelstrom of whims, it carves through flesh and bone,
    unseen hands pilfering from all we've done,

accomplishments amount to momentary lust.
Powerful in the moment, though fleeting, quickly forgotten.

In its wake, we are the land laid bare, stark and brutally shorn,
    exposed are the lies we've tenderly adorned.
    Our homes, our hopes, casually flung aside,
    in the landspout's unbiased hate,
    our pretenses cannot hide or escape fate.

It seeps through cracks, a sly, roaring taunt,
    an unrelenting jeer at the human want.
    The spout, a thin wisp of nature's ire,
    sets every last bridge of our sanctity on fire.

The fragility, our brittle brevity;
    how swiftly we fade, mere sketches in the sand.
    The landspout spins, a column of might,
    a force of nature with the power to smite.
    Engulfed in this gale, we understand,
    the landspout's might is but a drop of water in natures pale.
    In the heart of the storm, we face ourselves alone;
    nothing so bittersweet can compare.

303. It's Days like Today - Monday May, 20 2024 20:44 MST

It's days like today that remind me why I don't want to exist. Every day I push these thoughts into the deepest closet of my mind. Days like today-the stench, a rancid rot that is impossible not to find.

Disembodied voices call out, I'm so exhausted from trying to silence each shout. It is impossible to exist like this. A world that pretends to care turns its back on every begging call for help to just subsist in purgatory's lair. Having no options, my back against the wall. The blood streams out from underneath the closet, I am closest to be the next one it will maul. A monster bearing a million teeth snapping at me in a haunting clatter, upending my feet from underneath. Tearing me off the last rung of my ladder.

Just briefly, I think of grabbing my sword, taking the fight to the beast. I'm only fooling myself; I unbuckle my belt and aimlessly toss my sheath. It sucks me in, legs first. Gritting and grinding my feet first. The pain akin to being pulled into a soulless wood-chipper. My fibula splinters, shattering like a red wine bottle of glass.

. . .

Deeper in the beast's mouth, my tibia cracks and crumbles with each flesh-ripping gouge. Pain like this, most would instantly lose consciousness. For me, it's nothing compared to my daily soul crushing. A release, anything to escape this real pain that never will cease.

My femur grinds away much slower; it's a denser bone that we lease. Instead of pulling away, I grab two fistfuls of filthy carpet and push myself further into death's filet.

I'm so tired; I beg for it to eat my dismay away. That's how it goes though- never any true solace. The beast ends his feast, leaving me disemboweled in a bloodstained grease.

So here I am, cut down at the knees. It's days like this that make me beg- Lord, please give me just a shred of peace.

304. Burning at the Stake - Tuesday May, 21 2024 22:38 MST

In halls of glass, faceless suits pass,
    their ties flying at half mast.
    A handshake of pain, to ordain each stolen glance.
    Returned from depths of file cabinets and email blasts.
    I hang my head, an insider outcast.

They mark my steps with weighted eyes,
    searingly dull meetings, truth denies.
    Their scrutiny, a pointed spear,
    in every task, they impose deadlines, no room for error,
    only fear. With their neurotic bureaucratic
    power they draw me near.

Work, once praised, now steeped in doubt,
    accusations new, my worth they flout.
    A document of expectation's plight,
    contradicts the truth, distorts my integrity
    in an attempt to snuff out my light.

. . .

Increased the load, then sliced in part,
  no warning given, a hardened heart without a human gaze.
  They stare through me, I am only a brief haze.
  In their lies, how can they breathe in honest air?
  I find myself cataloged, mired in a trap laid bare.

A hostile ground, more than I can take.
  I watch each smile, bland plastered and fake,
  in fear I tread, each move I make.
  my existence tied with barbed wire to a stake.
  They make me bear my own cross,
  as they attempt to hurry my crucifixion.
  This affliction, so unbelievable that ending me is their mission.
  A crown of thorns, I do not don,
  instead a litany of false accusations imparted upon me rupture
  my eyes, all to extinguish me, a lowly pawn.

I seek relief from power's vice, a damned grasp,
  to cease the sting of scrutiny's false prophets clasp.
  I watch my dignity burn on the floor,
  emanating insanity's perfumes.
  In my humanity's death, nothing blooms,

Voices fall out from computer screens,
  they crawl into my eyes,
  I beg, I plead for a singular right,
  for peace within this endless fight.
  To stand once more, another stormy night,
  With wounds acknowledged, I admit the lack of my might.

. . .

In halls of glass, faceless suits pass,
   I've surrendered my will,
   swallowed my last pill.
   This life is nil,
   I wait defeated and ill, into silence-
   carry me past life's pointless frill.
   Into your hands I commit my spirit,
   though my cask is leaking rusty and rotten.
   I hope to finally fizzle out, be forever forgotten.

305. Thirty-Five Cents - Wednesday May, 22 2024 20:55 MST

Thirty-five cents.
    The balance of my account smiles back at me, laments.
    My bank account mirrors my sanity, my deepest contents.
    My stomach boils, relenting- my last meal ferments.

A nickel for all my dreams, now lost, buried in debts,
    dimes for despair, in life's cruel bets.
    Quarters for questions, the kind no one forgets,
    in this arithmetic of anguish, my cheap soul frets.
    The hole outside of me deepens, piling regrets.

Pennies, the crumbs of ambition's decay,
    each copper face, a bullet to the back of the head-
    Lincoln's foreshadowed dismay.
    My theater erodes, a curtain of cement clay,
    Our American Cousin; a fitting last display.
    In the grip of poverty, I silently sway away.
    This balcony of mine is subject to a presidential decay.

. . .

Thirty-five cents.
    No path to redemption, no means to recompense,
    this hollow existence, every second in stark suspense.
    John Wilkes Booth- a damned method actor.
    Money's cruel absence, a relentless pretense,
    my life's one and only factor.

Counting my worth in these scanty cents,
    a ledger of loss, a life in fragments continues to commence.

Dreams deferred at first, now guaranteed dead.
    Debits and credits drown me, a necklace of lead.
    Parched for spare change, what has my life succumbed to?
    I'll never get ahead.

Thirty-five cents to see the show,
    watch the life fade from my eyes, feed your greedy ego.

Everything in this play is deranged.
    Thirty-five cents.
    Nothing any longer makes any sense.

306. My Final Win - Thursday May, 23 2024 22:58 MST

Today was supposed to be my day.
    The day that pacifies me, washes all my worries away.
    It began hopefully, clear-eyed and present-
    and then I lost, shot out of the sky like a pheasant.

My name wasn't drawn, my spoils taken.
    A robbery of injustice, how could I have ever been so mistaken?

Hope.

A fool's four-letter word, eternally forsaken.
    A mirage, an ignorant endeavor unshaken.
    Any poor soul that pays into it quickly gets overtaken.
    The birdshot peppered my body,
    hitting the earth in a thud so hard it left everyone shaken.

. . .

Squirming, gasping for air in the mud.
    I hear my hunter's call, calm, empty,
    unbothered by my life being taken.
    There's nowhere for me to go, the futile musings of a pointless fowl.
    Leaves crunch under her feet
    as she scans the land looking for me, her trophy to disembowel.
    It won't be long now, my carcass will be unceremoniously anointed
    in a sullied blood dripping towel.

Hope.

I pray she will stop, just turn around and walk away.
    Her shuffling footsteps crack discarded twigs,
    digging them deeper into the swamp's rancid clay.
    Her footsteps stop.
    More proof that hope is nothing, a worthless inevitable delay.
    Bleeding out, losing consciousness, my vision darkens, showing my
    final black tunnel, hope cannot keep the bleak nothingness at bay.
    I see enough to watch her shadow loom over my soon-to-be carcass.
    I will be her plaque, an empty soulless display.

Hope.

Suffering, I am in so much needless pain.
    It's burrowed past my gushing wounds,
    deep into the crux of my brain.
    I pray for it to end, for all of this unfathomable agony
    to quickly descend down from my lifeless body into the darkness
    of the ground, an end.
    Hope laughs at my labored struggles for breath,
    again it has led me astray.

                 .   .   .

The hunter, she looms over me relishing her work,
    she's gutted me into a ghastly display.

Hope, pray- it will never come, it's paint thinner waterboarding you,
    choking in a fiery stream of hell.

Today was supposed to be my day.
    It was- but not in my way.
    My final win- another guttural victory for the other side;
    still I pray.

My soul, clinging to improbable outcomes, blinding my mind to
    reality, stubbornly insisting on seeing light where there is none,
    leading only to disappointment and wasted effort-
    I gargle my last gasp.

Hope- see how long it lasts.

307. Alone, I Wait - Friday May, 24 2024 21:45 MST

Lean not into our own understanding.
    A lecture so solemnly preached.
    I slam my face on the lectern, spit out my own teeth.
    Faith, into my mind I beseech.
    He won't listen to a word I say, won't buy into this narrative,
    this speech.
    Grasping at straws, I perpetually reach.

The silence of nights, cold and unfeeling,
    my bleeding heart beats with doubt, endlessly reeling.
    Prayers launched in a void, swallowed by the dark,
    No answer returns, no divine spark,
    just a stark reality leaving me hanging on every last remark.

I wander through oceans of broken dreams,
    faith like a mirage, only seems.
    That's how God works- through us.
    Our strength, or weakness.

Humble ourselves before them,
still it grasps hold of me, a leech.
Promises of salvation fade into dust,
in a world where hope corrodes to rust.

The scriptures lie open, pages worn thin,
    words, sweet sweeping lies are all that preys underneath.
    I'm falling deeper, just waiting for inevitability to sink in.
    Belief is a ghost, haunting my soul,
    an imminent domain that forever stakes its weary claim.
    Luck and a firm handshake- you will do the right thing.
    Murmurings carry through time, lying in the drool, a gaping hole.

I cry out to the heavens, a voice cracked and hoarse,
    no angel descends, no guiding force.
    Just one of the four, riding in on a black horse.
    Desolation is my companion, an ever-present thief,
    stealing away the remnants of my every last belief.

Lean not, they say, but how can one stand,
    when the ground beneath is quicksand?
    In the abyss of my doubts, I drown,
    faith- my crown of thorns is slicing, quickly slipping down.

No savior comes to lift this weight,
    I'm run over by forever burdens impossible to shake.
    Only the hollow answers of an empty fate.
    And in this suburban masquerade, alone I wait,
    a weary pilgrim, by faith misled.
    The Mayflower arrived on shore of false promises,
    only lore awaits. Treat it well and believe it will treat you well back-
    alone I wait.

308. One Iota - Saturday May, 25 2024 21:57 MST

Not one iota given, nothing to swear.
 A leap into a journey, eating a hesitant fare.
 Where it begins and where it ends—I do not care.
 Reluctance brews a tea that I cannot refuse.

Maps and routes unfurl, standing up my every hair,
 taunting my resolve,
 Pitfalls of dangers and the yearnings it involves.
 The thrill of the unknown, a thrill that I dread,
 each step forward is one laden with lead.

The skies beckon wide, horizons call clear,
 my heart, my consciousness is imprisoned,
 shackled by fear.
 What if the roads twist into nightmares unseen?
 What if my courage collapses, leaving a scene?

. . .

WORDS ARE SNAKES WITH ARMS

Packing dreams with trembling hands,
    facing the voyage that fate demands.
    Rattling insanity rages within, swirling doubts rise,
    a bold facade masks the fear in my eyes.

Each moment of planning, a steadfast wrestle with paralyzing fright.
    Haunted by phantoms that steal sleep's light.
    I shrug it off with my every might,
    I know I will succumb, lightning to my kite.
    A desire for freedom, for transcendent heights.
    A dog chasing a bird, unsure of what to do
    if it actually were to catch the muse—
    oh what a dreadful plight.

To taste desire, to overcome the unknown,
    to find a self that's never been shown.
    Scared beyond words, lured into the thrill of unabated thrills.
    My paradox, an inescapable rust bleeding iron box.

So I take the leap, a decision to jump off the cliff,
    leaving all the other sheep. My compass guides me north
    heading south.

Not one iota given, still nothing to swear,
    I sink into my planned reality, embracing the scare,
    losing all sanity.

309. Draconian Tomb-
Sunday May, 26 2024
22:04 MST

Jaundice eyes etch into the glass of my bathroom mirror.
They stare back, a reflection of introspection, utter loss.
My head ages, my hair reverts back to thick green moss.
Another disadvantage of the final toss.

A tussle with the hustle and bustle of empty days.
Jobs lost, faucets running over their porcelain gloss.
The left side of my face, a numb drooping gaze-
it portrays my derision.
My lost path through this evil funhouse of life, this maze.

Unable to blink, my eyes wired open to these never ending displays.
On this path, everyone pays.
A discomfort past misfortune, it's being trapped in flesh where
there's no chance for hopeful splays.
Call it a gift or a curse, no matter what you call it,
it's the invitation to the hearse where it lays.
A true cost that misses the punch list, lagged in every phase.

. . .

I try desperately to look away,
    anything to cloud my vision from this albatross.
    Its silent unflappable wingspan will always emboss
    the true account of the loss.
    This bird of burden, my elephant in the room.
    It sucks out all the air, paints a vivid picture of my doom.

If I could look away but for a second-
    even if I could close my eyes it still will loom.
    I try anything to escape this draconian tomb.

310. Numbered Cattle - Monday May, 27 2024 22:04 MST

Another medical bill—an email with the "Explanation of Benefits";
    it's a scam, they rob us just for the thrill.
    I know I can't pay it. I take another pill.

The sterile halls are painted in blood red dread,
    hope you end up dead otherwise you will be drowned in debt.
    Each signature is another lock on the gate of despair.
    A healthcare system that's sick, beyond all repair.

White coats glide by, eyes averted, conversations coded
    in tongues only decipherable by those with souls diverted,
    the invoice is a ledger of our miseries,
    a catalog of suffering quantified, commodified to the penny.

A child's cry pierces the silence, a note of pure truth
    in this cacophony of lies, a reminder of innocence lost
    to the ledger lines of corporate greed. .

They sell a false promise of life,
we're just numbered cattle eating their feed.

The ceiling tiles count our breaths, each one a mark
    against the balance sheet, another debt incurred.
    We are patients in this house of pain, pawns in a game
    where the rules are written in invisible ink,
    erased as quickly as they clean the rooms for another
    to drown in its sink.

Here, hope is a currency we can ill afford,
    traded for the fleeting relief of chemical solace,
    our dreams sold off piece by piece,
    or limbs mortgaged, we borrow life only so brief.

In this system, humanity is the collateral,
    our lives are the commodity, our pain the profit.
    The bill arrives like clockwork, a grim reminder
    that in the end, we are all just numbers, accounts to be settled.
    Damn this insurance scam; they slaughter us financially,
    we're each their sacrificial lamb.

311. A Baroque Joke - Tuesday May, 28 2024 18:51 MST

It's like steel- hugging this bottle.
>More than a comfort, it's a way to take your foot off the throttle.
>It can't shatter, no matter my grip.
>Should I fumble, I may fall, but it will never slip.

It's never lied,
>never thrown outrageous accusations.
>Always here for me,
>a solace to every test of patience.

A few minutes late will never matter.
>Nothing shines through this tinted green glass,
>nothing sees through the ladder.

Twelve steps- a baroque joke.
>Each rung, the fire is further stoked.
>You're the one who asked for this meeting, not me.

A replacement, a gamble where honesty is used against me.
Once someone is exposed, it closes in with each throw.
Each throat-scratching growl,
another excuse for most to throw in the towel.

She holds her cards close to her chest,
  has you hanging on every slurred vowel, you invest.
Nothing will wash away this delirious smile,
  a permanent scowl, for every mile.

Should I cut off my ear, mail it in a box?
  Even the thought- a crazy lot.
Frustration, a choice to not be free.
I didn't make it, living moment to moment.
Each second ferments every torment.

Would I have it any other way?
  A yes creeps through my lungs, slips just beneath my cheeks.

He doesn't want to talk to you- that voice inside.
  There's no reality where each of us collide.

So I fall into its embrace, a shaking voice, a void face.
  This hug makes me sad too.
  It's the only way to get through.

312. Bafflegab - Wednesday May, 29 2024 19:57 MST

Nothing makes sense anymore;
    then again I guess it never did.
    Optimistic thoughts are exactly that,
    it's a carbonation that fizzles out- flat.
    Everything I see, anything I ever thought I knew,
    it's all bafflegab.

Once, I believed in the holy trinity of love,
    money, and ambition,
    but the holy grail was a broken bottle,
    the road to nowhere
    paved with a cracked mission
    of yesterday's hopeful omission.

The city lights blind me
    opening the darkness inside,
    a neon deception
    that blinks out as skin breaks.

The night howls truths
too ugly to be seen in daylight,
truths that claw at my insides,
leaving me raw and bleeding,
but invisible to the naked eye.
They're my truths.

Whiskey-stained lips kiss
    the rim of despair,
    the bitter taste of reality
    a constant companion to share.
    The only real stare.
    I chase ghosts in alleyways,
    their laughter bellowing off of
    graffiti-streaked walls,
    each step a reminder
    of the futility of hope.
    I hope, at least I try-
    it's pointless.

Under skyscrapers,
    I am gum stuck to a dirty street,
    a speck of nothing
    in a universe indifferent
    to my existence.
    The moon mocks my hopes,
    presents life's demands.
    Its cold light, a spotlight
    on my insignificance.

People pass by, I wish they couldn't see me.
    The thought of flashing a pointless grin,
    lifting my hand in a half hearted wave.

This should be a sin, pleasantries,
disgusting and grim.
In their own right,
lost in society's haze-
we live out delusions.
Stories we sell ourselves,
all of them are lies.
We are all rats
in the streets,
cloaked in clothes acting like something we're not.
We're vermin,
chasing cheese that doesn't exist,
dreaming dreams that never will.

The people lie,
their words sweet listless lies,
to lull the masses.
Life is not a story
it's an amusing false sense of glory,
a punchline
we're too tired to laugh at.
All too broke.

So I drink, and I write,
spill out all of our problems into ink
that no one will read,
words that will die
with me in the gutter.
But for now, they are mine,
but for a fleeting moment,
lost in time.
In a world consecrated in madness,
they say I'm the crazy one.
But there's no way in hell they're sane.

They get up at four in the morning,
board the same mundane train.
So do I, and I hate it more than anything.
This false testament to my existence,
no one will bear witness.
Another lifeless story,
the same as yours.
Smudges on pages,
our lives are washed away in blurbs.

313. The Anchor of Rancor - Thursday May, 30 2024 20:06 MST

It weighs my head down like an anchor,
  all of this rancor.
  Seas of unpaid bills, relentless calls from the banker.

The clock's second hand stuck, unable to tick,
  I relate to it more than I feel sorry for its stick.
  The hour hand, a predator in the night,
  its teeth sinking into minutes, devouring light.
  The minute hand lustful for its once working gears.
  An hourglass works better, more accurate for our fears.

My clock beats with the weight of deadlines,
  crushed beneath bureaucratic designs.
  A thousand emails like locusts swarm,
  each one a demand, each one a storm.
  My mainspring is broken, overwound.
  Time stands still, forever abound.

. . .

WORDS ARE SNAKES WITH ARMS

Suffocated under paperwork piles,
　　my hands feel the same as the defunct clock,
　　it tells no time, misses its sole purpose, takes no stock.
　　My memory lost in files I'll never unlock.
　　The grindstone gnaws at my bones,
　　like metal grinding in the rusted timepiece's gears.

We share a sense of purpose: none.
　　A human that cannot live, a clock whose time it cannot give.
　　Insomnia's claws shred the fabric of sleep, exposing flaws.
　　My bed a ship in a turbulent sea,
　　waves of worry crashing over me.

Life's weight, an alchemist's stone, a sundial with no date
　　transmuting hardship to a strength unknown.
　　Underpaid for stresses over weighed,
　　my ticket punched itself, my ship is rotted wood, brittle and frail.

The anchor around my neck ensures we will never set sail.

314. Red and Blue Blind - Friday May 31, 2024 17:38 MST

Behind unseen scenes, officials wisecrack,
    gag orders grip, the air grows black.
    Right or wrong, this charade, this tirade,
    is a demon that won't be swayed.

Guilty, a former president, sets an unseen precedent,
    the road to hypocrisy paved with lament.
    Vote for or against, the verdict in cement,
    history will judge the bold,
    writing tales of victors, no matter the cost or the souls sold.

A felon with potential to wield all power,
    a nation teeters in its desperate hour.

Hard to believe, yet something we conceived,
    Picking sides, left or right, E pluribus unum deceived.
    Out of many, we've birthed a bastard son,

wielding power, hatred's zero sum won.
A nation of reservations, disgust deep-seated,
for differing beliefs, our reality is defeated.

We hold the key to our lock,
    created our problems, herded in a red and blue flock.
We must set differences aside,
    manifest a fair reality where we coincide.
Politicians, puppets stark in juxtaposition,
    to our country's collective mission.
We hold these truths self-evident:
    the rich thrive, the poor yield,
their souls to give, their fates sealed.
When will partisanship sink democracy's ship?
    A two-party system, the true lesion,
boiling away our sanity, a slipping vision.

Let's craft a new party, break free from this faction,
    unite under one banner, rekindle our passion.
For in unity, strength we find,
    a future rebuilt, no longer red and blue blind.

315. I had no Idea - Saturday June 01, 2024 23:50 MST

I had no idea-
    the true cost.
    It's bleeding from my head,
    all the transgressions, all the dead.
    The back alley deal served a necessity, a pact unsaid.
    My wound to suture, stitches cast in lead.

Peeling linoleum floors reveal open doors.
    Drawers filled with losses, manifesting in oozing sores.

I had no Idea-

If I knew then, maybe it would be different.
    There's no changing the past, it's indifferent.
    Thoughts of it- all wasted time, insignificant.
    The allure of desire, a fleeting lure.

. . .

Thoughts haunting, omnipresent and recurrent.
I wish I knew then what I know now, it's all transparent.
Stuck in flaws that grasp ahold of me like claws.
The raven forever caws.

I had no idea-

The raw splays of injustice time delays,
robbing me of my life's displays.
I see it now, up in smoke.
Stars carry them through the night, each choke.

I had no idea-

The truth of it all.
It watched me, seething at each desperate flaw.
Cicadas usher the soundtrack to it all, seeing it thaw.
A clarity rare, though the final straw.
I had no idea of my sins' final draw.

316. Slow Burn to the End - Sunday June 02, 2024 20:35 MST

At a loss for words, I stumble.
　　Frustration, inflation, bills lack luster-
　　worth much less than their denominations.
　　The American Dream?
　　A cruel scheme.
　　It's impossible to live in this fractured state.

Bars on windows, locks on doors,
　　to keep out what's already in:
　　the hunger, the desperation,
　　the rotting stench of a system's sin.

Dim lights flicker,
　　on the weary faces of the hopeless.
　　Hope, a four-letter word
　　that eats deceits, our toil our sweat.

. . .

I bathe in potholes,
    future written in graffiti.
    The rich dine on dreams
    while we starve on reality.

Free will, a bitter pill,
    hard to swallow, easy to choke on its emptiness.
    A blank sustenance that leaves us hungry.
    In the land of the free,
    shackles come in the form of a fifty-thousand-dollar college degree.

I temp another cheap cigar to flame,
    watch the smoke curl,
    wonder if it's all worth it,
    this slow burn to the end.

317. Necropolis - Monday June 03, 2024 20:57 MST

These tombstones stand so high,
   some protrude from the ground sideways pointing up
   towards the sky.
   Each a marker to a lighter time, now snuffed out, a darker lie.

Headstones of past accomplishments and losses
   molded over in dank green mosses.
   Opportunities missed, buried under crosses.
   Whatever was, is exactly that.
   Fate tosses.
   An image presented to the world, disingenuous, irreconcilable.

Worn faces of ambition lie interred,
   beneath the earth, where dreams have blurred.
   The soil holds stories never told,
   ambitions crumbled, visions cold.

. . .

Shattered relics of fleeting hopes,
    sagging under existential ropes,
    coffins filled with "almosts" and "could-have-beens,"
    amongst the corpses of where life ends.

Through skeletal trees and broken gates,
    a silent chorus of regrets waits,
    stories, tall tales of futile tries,
    of faltered steps and unanswered whys.

A marble angel weeps blood in stone,
    for aspirations turned to bone.
    Its tears feed the barren ground,
    where aspirations rest unbound.

No flowers bloom in this terrain,
    where every effort was in vain.
    The hollowness of the past
    resides within this lifeless vast.

The horizon taunts with distant light,
    beyond the grasp of endless night.
    Trapped within this necropolis of my head,
    each breath, a testament to words
    I don't even know if I actually said.

Failure's imprint, sharp and deep,
    tattooed in my leathered skin, a forever sleep.
    A cemetery of my heart and mind,
    where my lost soul forever shall bind.

                        .   .   .

I wander through this ghostly place,
   where time has ceased its frantic race.
   In the necropolis of our days,
   we find the end of all our ways.

I walk this path alone,
   among the ruins, overgrown,
   I've come to see, with stinging eyes,
   that hope, too, in this graveyard lies.

Buried deep, beneath despair,
   in graves unmarked, without a prayer,
   the remnants of a dreamless night,
   forever hidden from my blinded sight.

With a heavy sigh, my last labored breath,
   I crawl into the grave I dug, entwined with death.
   A necropolis of pain,
   everything shall forever remain unnamed,
   an entire existence maimed in vain.

318. Concrete and Razor Wire - Tuesday June 04, 2024 20:35 MST

Ridiculous, the way these stairs move.
　　With each step I fall deeper into their concrete groove.
　　The more I climb, the higher they prove.

Each riser a riddle, each tread a cruel test,
　　in this house of perpetual unrest.
　　The railings are wrapped in razor wire so sly,
　　promising ascent while chaining the sky.

I grasp at the razors, a fresh cut wrist of despair,
　　my fingers slip deeper, find nothing-
　　a pain in which nothing can compare.
　　The steps stretch out, an infinite pest,
　　each creak is a dirge, a weight on my chest.

I look to the windows, they loom like eyes, cold and unblinking,
　　Reflecting my struggle, my flesh disguise.

Beyond the glass, the horizon recedes,
a far off mirage, a tangle of weeds.

My bare feet worn, churned to hamburger by this endless ascent,
steps of defeat, my will nearly spent.
Gravity's pointless joviality, a pitiless ground,
as I spiral around.

Hallway walls, concrete creeps, closing in,
riddled with graffiti of doubt,
Every attempt to rise feels like a fatal route.
Profanity, words and obscenities snake up and down,
scraped from my brain, my every failure lines the dark hall,
reminders of dreams that crumble and fall.

If only I make it to the roof-
hopes, under a hanging sky so low,
Pressing me back, refusing to let go.
Dust chokes the air, thick and wet with regret,
this building of ambition, a manifestation of threat.

Damn this staircase, its false promise of height,
a nauseating illusion of progress, the theft of my might.

Ridiculous, the way these stairs move,
with each step I fall deeper into their concrete groove.
The more I climb, the higher they prove,
a cement building, a testament to a fate I cannot soothe.

319. Sleep Paralysis - Wednesday June 05, 2024 20:48 MST

I can't find the words.
    I know that somewhere in this nightmare that they're there.
    Attacking me, my eyes twitching, my skin's on fire, a visceral itching,
    a spinal cord broken, strapped to a flesh gourd.
    The words resonate in a nameless space
    where time refuses to be laced.

Reality, a prison of groggy mornings and unpaid bills,
    transactional, dull and full of pills. But in this nightmare,
    I am alive- each horror, each terror I don't survive.

I roam memories of places I have and haven't been,
    a sovereignty of the damned, a sweet and sour sin.
    To be afraid, to feel a fear that doesn't exist as real.
    Evil saints, with their familiar faces,
    for they are mine- crafted from my insanity
    born from the laughing of my screams.

. . .

In this darkness, I am king,
  cloaked in the rawness of unfiltered fear,
  free from the anesthetic of normalcy.
  Here, the pain is real, palpable,
  like the sharp bite of whiskey, and in its sting,
  I find a perverse comfort,
  a reminder that I am still breathing, still fighting.

The nightmare, my unholy sanctuary,
  a refuge from the mediocrity of all my short waking hours.
  Here, I can taste the acrid flavor of my failures,
  wrestle with the ghosts of those I've rotted and abandoned.
  In a perilous fight or flight struggle, I find a semblance of peace.

I can't find the words,
  but in the nightmare, they find me,
  tangled in foreign tongues,
  from the gutter and all the progressive social rungs.

In this Hell, I am home,
  for here, at least, I am not alone.

320. A Spin of the Wheel - Thursday June 06, 2024 20:39 MST

It just sort of happened, this kind of thing.

You hope it doesn't, but that's the thing about hope, it's abstract, it scabs. It can heal a festering wound or cause it. You wish for the latter, but that's the thing about wishing. I've never been a fan. It's much better to make things happen on your own. To get up and do it. That only goes so far though, manifesting your own reality. Actions and affirmations are exactly that. That's the thing about them, they're singular delineations to more actions. Even inaction is an action, but it's not one I ever make. I make things happen, but that only goes so far. That's the thing about it, there's so much that's out of our control. I wrestle with it, try to force destiny's hand with my own and in my own favor. That's the thing about it, it's a futile effort, like running in a hamster wheel. That's action, but it takes you nowhere. Still I do it, not sure if I'm trying to fool myself or not. I still make my own luck- but that's the thing about it, it's random. A numbers game, a spin of the wheel. Even with my hand on the wheel, I can't control the way it spins or where it takes me. If it were up to me, I'd leave right now. I'd take all my successes, all my failures and ride them into my own reality. Just like the rich are born rich and the poor are born poor. I carve my own way, still you can't escape what you are- what we all are. No one is infallible, righteous, good, or evil.

It just sort of happened, this kind of thing.

321. Scrying - Friday June 07, 2024 21:36 MST

There was a time, maybe there will be again.
    Some smoking jacket to cloak our sin.
    Scared, sure.
    Probably the allure.
    Of the self split by mirrors, two-fold,
    one in the glass, one in the hold
    of memory's grip, cold and thin,
    tracing my finger over razor blades, where light had been.

Is it me who speaks, or the man of tin,
    born from the past of what I had been?
    A phantom limb, a silent twin,
    a stranger's face pushing through my own skin.
    I walk the line, a tightrope thread,
    between the living and the dead.

Voices feed me lines to read,
    my eyes glaze over the teleprompter.

I continue, words hanging over my head.
Just enough rope to make everything red.
Knots slip through my hands,
identities, shifting sands,
pressed in trembling hands.
I'll continue to relent, cave into the demands.
There was a time, maybe there will be again,
when I shall wear my name, absolve my sin.

Life's edge, a ledge so thin.
Souls signed away with the single stroke of a pen.
Our filthy hands wash one another's once again.

There was a time, maybe it will begin.
Scared, pure.
Defined by the allure.
To find in chaos, the obscure,
no way to demure,
a self that's whole, a truth that's pure.

322. Wet Paint - Saturday June 08, 2024 10:49 MST

A fateful repetition of the past,
    codifying the transgressions of the last.
    To watch it all unfold, to see the ships float on half mast.
    Society's implementation, the drudgery of each cast.

Humiliation long, the falsehoods of humanity vast,
    the march of time, an iron cask.
    A soirée of automatons in history's blast,
    where lessons learned dissolve so fast.

Empires rise on bones amassed,
    their banners fly high, while morals degrade.
    The cries of those by fate already laid,
    unavoidable truths from lessons learned long since paid.

In gold laden halls where leaders trade,
    their hunger grows for more power, more jade.

False promises of peace, a fleeting draft made,
while war drums beat, they invade.

The past's grim specter, will starkly cascade,
    its homes barren, broken, hatred rears its head last in this parade.
    We turn the page, but in our haste we wade,
    in new woes until the ink will fade.
    We must confront the sins of the decade.

Thus, may we hope this time at last,
    to learn from fermented forms of democracy they pervade.
    Oh if only, to find a peace that holds steadfast.

323. Wrong Direction- Sunday June 09, 2024 20:01 MST

Incarcerated, frustrated bound and locked in cages,
   a sick complacency learned, adapted.
   Realities trained and highly disdained,
   I'm pained to admit.
   I too am an animal in a cage I've long since outgrew.
   Outrage, the strain on my every sinew.

Still tomorrow I'll wake up in my cage, lucid but not anew.
   A way out, that's what I plead.
   A key to these shackles, to unlock this door of greed.
   An escape- the only reality I desperately need.
   I scratch at the iron bars until my fingernails peel off,
   try to force my head through the bars.

Trapped.

If only my prison had but one design flaw;

it's my iron wrought downfall.
I've grown into its cold solemn comfort, winter's thaw.
Life or death, the only law.

All these years shrouded, locked in doubt.
I push at the door, no matter how loud I shout-
I know I am the only one that can let myself out.
The thing I never thought of, the way of entry to this cage-
I pull at the door, it creaks open, sways.

324. The Lighthouse - Monday June 10, 2024 20:58 MST

Spat out of the mouth of the Potomac River, it sits.
    A guiding beacon of solitude, where direction permits.
    This Gilded Era structure, a lighthouse submits-
    all my hopes, my yearnings, this floating light remits.

To be able to recede from the stable,
    to run, no longer live in society's impossible pasture, my fable.
    A solitude that gleams with life truly lived,
    where a peace that has long since been forgotten
    can breathe under no label.
    I launch my small vessel from the rickety derelict dock
    into waters polluted and fraught.

The view from this water steals the sundown,
    reflecting it just off its surface.
    A picturesque reality, my vision bounces up and down
    with the subtle waves, escaping my life's triviality.
    Towards my lighthouse I sail.

Its light, fragile with the sun still hanging briefly,
suspended tired in the purple blue sky.
Just visible enough to guide my wind-whipped eye.
I squint, still too bright for me.
The structure protrudes from the water, a monolith to the free.

I quiet my boat's gruff engine, though it still sputters
    and chokes out thick black bellows of smoke as I approach.
    I cast my vessel's frayed rope, tying it to the lighthouse's ladder.
    I climb up, steadily, each rung is cold, it brings me closer
    to silencing all the world's clatter.
    At the top, my journey is mended; all that's left now is a door,
    a lock, and my key to end it.
    Its weary worn teeth slip in, aligning each single pin.
    The lock turns hesitantly with my key,
    I jar the door open with my shoulder in a rested glee.

Inside this beacon, a worn misplaced home.
    It's one in which I have forever known.
    Inside of me, this structure lives, it's all we ever set out to be.
    Alone, a guiding light, peace- the only place I can truly be free.

325. Wretched Diesel Fumes - Tuesday June 11, 2024 20:19 MST

Wretched diesel fumes fill the room,
    an exhaust tossed from the abyss shall loom.
    A reminder of a silent killer, a bride left without her groom.

Against the night, the city's hum,
    a heart palpitates uncontrollably, seeking some
    elusive dark, a dream's drum,
    the faintest hope in chaos' strum.

In shallow waters cloaked deep,
    where drowning thoughts creep,
    dreams and fears entwine and seep,
    a soul stands poised, a cliff so steep,
    to leap, to soar, to wake from a damned sleep.

The ground below, a dark unknown,
    the skies above, a fate unsown,

to forge a path, a lost jacket's button sewn,
to carve from stone a world that's been thrown.
A garment, a cloak of invisibility only one shall own.

Through shattered glass, the fractured light,
a prism's focused rays light a fire, a fierce delight,
an omnipresent figure of an ant hill with a magnifying glass,
an endless night,
where purpose hides from sight.

The die has long since been cast, the future veiled,
a journey vast, a ship that's unseaworthy,
a fragile vessel, unimpaled by destiny's sail,
by an anchor unchained, unveiled.

To rise from the depths of the ocean, to seek, to trust,
to shed the past, to banish rust,
to find in nothingness fates fatal thrust,
a life reborn, because we must.

In every breath, in every scar,
a testament to who we are,
a pilgrimage to lands afar,
our essence burns stronger
than the magnifying glass's concentrated ray.

So I hold my breath, take the plunge, embrace the climb,
rewrite the tale, defy the time,
in every step, a silent rhyme,
a song of purpose, so sublime.

. . .

Wretched diesel fumes disperse,
    in life's pompous charade, a universe,
    molded by my hand,
    a blind mastery of Earth's clay.
    Today may be my last, so I refuse to lie.
    I search for my purpose, I will find it,
    no matter the price I must pay.

326. The Scalpel's Call - Wednesday June 12, 2024 21:01 MST

Footsteps surrounding me, I know I must leap.
    A decision to jump, I cannot sleep.

The night's a cruel nurse, drawing up syringes of fear,
    the scalpel's edge draws near.

Streets outside the hospital hum the bleak sounds of cars
    commuting carelessly by, their mechanical tunes.
    While the moon's light fades too soon,
    the scalpel will carve me on June Twenty-Seventh, at noon.

I trace the scars of past procedures,
    raised wounds, thoughts of perilous tears.

Still there's a peace in this silent dread,
    a reminder in my head of the things unsaid.

. . .

Needles pricking, hands so cold,
   a gamble of flesh, a story retold.
   Today my God is a surgeon, confident, bold.

I clutch my breath, let the warm white sheets slip,
   beyond this pain, my future desperately grips.

In the sterile glow, I will find my head,
   between fear and hope, a bridge I've tread.

Each beat of my heart, a relentless though temporary call,
   in this chance with fate, I rise, I fall.
   My survival, I refuse to debate.

Footsteps surround, nurses, doctors,
   masked and draped in blue gowns.
   Now I leap.
   Into the unknown,
   where anesthesia induces unconsciousness, a sleep.

With trembling hands, I face the operating light
   as the sun spilling out bright.
   A new device, titanium slick and slim,
   will be my third chance, my good fight.
   In this fear, I will be reborn,
   I will live to see another night.

327. Power - Thursday June 13, 2024 21:42 MST

Power.

It corrupts.
    It justifies.
    It manipulates, outlines fates.
    Anything they have to tell themselves to walk a little taller,
    to win pointless debates.

It's perceived, it's fake; even so it's real, concrete and fleeting.
    It's wielder is the rebar caked inside.
    Together, a formidable force,
    apart it cracks, bends without remorse.
    In a fiat society, power is the intoxicant,
    there is no sobriety.
    Chased and laced with poison,
    most with power yield it as cloisonné.

. . . .

Bureaucracy.
 The black hole that sucks us all in.
 We live under its shadow, under its sin.
 It complicates everything, so the wealthy can win.
 Look at the price of the seat in any election.

Power.
 It holds us in its iron fist.
 We are nothing, but social security numbers, a list.
 We fund it all on our backs, taxed by their axe.
 Low wages, mobile homes, small apartments, our cages.
 We pay for it all while slowly dying in stages.

Partisanship, the hole that will ultimately sink our ship.
 We're in a game of poker left without a single chip.
 Gerrymandering, pimping and pandering, our votes slip.

Power.
 Dolled out through ballots,
 beat into our heads with wooden mallets.
 How did this happen?
 Over time, from their chalets.

So where do we go from here?
 Behind closed doors they look at each other as wide eyed as deer.
 Both in the headlights and driving the car.
 What an ugly thing this is, power, the never healing scar.

328. Orchestral Trials - Friday June 14, 2024 20:14 MST

Orchestral trials, sweetness in the air beguiles,
    an undertone of rot lingers, hidden,
    behind every smile, every borrowed mile.
    In the crippled alleyways, dreams fray,
    words sold in the wind, promises decay.

The city breathes a melancholic hymn,
    where neon lights flicker, fading dim,
    and souls tread softly on the edge,
    life's brittle ledger, inked in a sledge.

We all entwine with desperation's grasp,
    clinging to warmth, a fleeting clasp,
    while night devours the stars, one by one,
    the darkness deep, victory unsung.

Hope in the moon's pale light,

through the streets, out of sight,
and in the silence, hearts beat with dread,
of tomorrows promised, but left unsaid.

Orchestral trials, the sweetness in the air deceives,
for in the heart of this city, everyone grieves,
a symphony of the damned, where they belong.
A finality, our last song.

329. Obscure Lens - Saturday June 15, 2024 21:07 MST

Security, a false sense.
    Into obscurity, empty tents.
    Camping in reality, an obscure lens.

We chase the tail of comfort,
    our fingers grasping ghosts,
    haunted by promises of permanence,
    cradling the hollow warmth of hope.

The streets are our war,
    the soldiers, indifferent bars,
    each one a silent witness
    to our desperate audience of passing cars.

We build our castles of salt,
    pretend the tide won't come,
    that life's fragile fabric

won't unravel, completely come undone.

Nights are drunken blurs,
    days, a haze of hung-over smoke and mirrors,
    each hour tossed into the void,
    a collision of utter madness and desire.

We scribble our names on bathroom walls,
    in motels and dive bars,
    as if to carve our existence
    into the stone of this transient world.

A rhythm of defiance,
    pulsing against the chains
    of a system built on illusions,
    where truth is a currency
    few can afford to spend.

We are poets of the pavement,
    scribes of the sordid and sublime,
    our verses, a rebellion,
    our words, a fist raised to the sky.

In the end, we are but flesh dolls for caskets,
    flickering under phone flashes, a ghastly glow,
    searching for something real
    in a world that's lost its way,
    finding beauty in the broken,
    and in the chaos, a fleeting peace.
    Into obscurity, the peril of the truth will never cease.

330. Iron Mountain - Sunday June 16, 2024 17:45 MST

An iron mountain,
  zen self-imposed.
  Hot springs of sulfur,
  the smell buries itself deep within your nose.
  Oceansides smile at the thoughts
  of where their shores have once been.
  Their waters carved out these valleys,
  washed away the soil and sin.

I've walked these paths before,
  barefoot on broken glass,
  each shard a familiar sting,
  each step a repeat performance
  in the river's shore of the damned.

Déjà vu is a relentless tide,
  its waves crashing against the cliffs
  of my consciousness,

each one a reminder of where I reside,
scars earned and lessons burned
into my flesh and bone.

Peace is a cigarette in the rain,
    a fleeting moment of clarity,
    a pause between punches,
    when the world tilts just right
    and you see the beauty in its decay.

The struggle is the constant,
    a burning that never leaves,
    a bitter companion sitting on your shoulder
    weighing in on your every decision.
    The losses to endure,
    and the fleeting triumphs
    that make it all bearable dangle the carrot—
    oh the allure.

There's a sour comfort in knowing
    that the cycle will repeat,
    that I'll face the same demons
    with the same tired resolve,
    and somehow, I'll rise from the ashes,
    not victorious, but alive.

This life is a grindstone,
    shaping and wearing away,
    each pass a reminder
    of the impermanence of peace,
    the inevitability of pain,
    and the raw, unvarnished truth

that survival is the only victory
worth seeking.

And when the curtain falls,
    when the final act is played,
    there's an honest solace in the struggle,
    a sour taste that tells me I've paid,
    I've lived, I've fought, I've endured, I've lost,
    and that's enough.
    So long as I've learned and taught.
    So long as I've helped others and
    refused to be bought.

331. Crepuscular Beast - Monday June 17, 2024 20:31 MST

The Devil, a crepuscular beast.

He wheels and deals underneath, prepping his feast.
    Evil feeds on those of us with the least.
    Time carries on, the rotational hourglass, its sands never decreased.

Underneath the fluorescent glow of hospital lights,
    trading sins for pennies through the nights,
    dreams for a shot, an opportunity to try.

The end comes crawling in,
    the apple of our drug induced dilated eye.
    No fanfare, just a nod,
    and the world's slow, unavoidable collapse.

. . .

So we live one more day, the same as the last,
    laugh at the darkness that ushers us through the past,
    waiting for nothing in particular-
    just the end, always, of everything.
    We're both the savior and the beast.

332. Burlap Shroud - Tuesday June 18, 2024 21:11 MST

Just as a heart has a finite number of beats,
   I wonder if I have a finite number of defeats.
   I grit my teeth wondering how much more I can take.
   It's draining my soul, guiding me to my own wake.
   Veins traced in blue sorrow, my eyes fade to black.
   I'm a stone of failure being chiseled away- each crack.
   A guttural burning pain of a dull rusty knife to the back.
   My hopes tossed into an empty sack, a burlap shroud.
   It's filthy, suffocating me in the world's crowd.
   I have nowhere to turn,
   I'm here. Painfully waiting.
   Until I have my final burn and am tossed into an urn.

333. Spectral Screech of Gold - Wednesday June 19, 2024 21:51 MST

The end is nigh.
  So they say.
  Mortality, the price is high.
  So they say.

Against insurmountable odds there is only one way.
  In the face of an inevitable expiration, we die.
  There is only one way to stay.
  Gold.
  So they say.

Bullion built from quartz veins and alluvial deposits.
  Coins from the riverbed, threads of aurum alchemy.

Clouds of transmutation,
  the philosopher's stone now glittering,
  melted dreams cast into shapes of desire.

From the dark, dank mines, the shimmering veins
are the roots of our eternity, so they say.

Elders, bent by the years, kneel to the golden calf,
    its lustrous skin a promise of youth,
    a return to the spring, to the garden,
    to where serpents slither in secrets of wealth.

Gold, the fountain of all,
    a river flowing through the hands,
    through the lifeblood of empires and beggars' demands.
    It gilds the soul, lines the coffers of time,
    ringing through the chambers of forgotten kings.

Hold it close, the voices call,
    as if it could stave off the dust,
    as if the Midas touch could answer the calls.
    Hold it close, for in its gleam
    lies the elixir, the dawn,
    the endless day, the silent hymn.
    The spectral screech that bursts our ears and never ends.

So they say.

The end is nigh.
    Except in the alchemy of gold,
    we seek to bind the horizon,
    to tether the fleeting light.

Mortality, the price is high.

With gold, perhaps,
we buy a moment more,
a shimmer in the dark.

So they say.
    Gold.
    Forever gold-
    for gold and those who lay in its veins.
    Its avarice, our humanity's cost.

The end is nigh, except for those who can pay.

334. Empty Eyes - Thursday June 20, 2024 20:36 MST

An individual that never set out to be anything.
    Evolved to be everything.
    Though not by choice.
    Robbed by a journey, stripped of their voice.
    What made the individual the individual, societal noise.
    A travesty, a transactional invoice.

Empty.

Devoid of purpose, a toxic fire of something.
    Choked out in a caustic smoke.
    Tactics to survive amount to nothing.
    Suffocating, no rejoice.

Their wanderings through corridors of rust,
    eyes dimmed by the weight of dust.
    In the market of souls, a faceless crowd,

they carry the burden of countless masks,
invisible labor in endless tasks.
Seeking the void's embrace forever vast,
a nameless figure in a nameless place.

Empty.

To claim another spoken facade,
    each voice dredged in cost, lost.

In the end, the purpose is not given,
    but forged in the fires of the unforgiven.
    A testament to the human race,
    a fake journey to reclaim their nonexistent place.

Empty.

Nihilistic realities steer the empty eyes of the deer.
    To feed, to breed, to breathe another moment.
    It's all there is, the only rational sentiment.
    A monolithic design, cast of concrete.
    The cyclical cycle of nature destined to repeat.

Empty.

335. Falschnachrichten - Friday June 21, 2024 21:06 MST

Dissonance carries through the water,
    our uneasiness, their fodder.
    Rhetoric tails like entrails,
    entwining truths into hollow grails.

We stand on the brink of forgotten tomorrows,
    history's pages burned, our borrowed sorrows.
    Words of iron, tongues of fire,
    futures forecast, conspiracies dire.

Marching to a falsified beat,
    in circles we move, defeat after defeat.
    Eyes wide shut, we embrace the haze,
    blind to the cycles, the endless malaise.

Promises built on foundations of salt,
    crumble as we grasp with a clenched hand.

Mirrors of past, reflections grim,
we follow the hymn, on a whim.

Denial comforts the weak,
 silenced truths begin to speak.
 In the dissonance, hear the slaughter,
 the peril lies deep, blood cascading in the water.

The past our present, a relentless host,
 haunting the words we cherish the most.
 Cycles resume, rhetoric blooms,
 history's specter seals our doom.

Think for yourself, never assume.

336. The Drowning Bird - Saturday June 22, 2024 22:14 MST

World War Three.
    Politicians wield words like drowning in heavy water,
    their platform, their decree.
    It's unimaginable, campaigning as if it's an inevitability.

They pander to us, the masses, with fear.
    Mindless birds stare up in the rain,
    drowning themselves in their own political terrain.
    The disdain between red and blue-
    that's the true red scare.

A nation pitted against itself,
    all in an effort to generate fanfare,
    to curry more votes.
    It's disgusting, it's dangerous;
    I cannot believe this filth floats-
    but it does.
    It floods our streets, strains relationships;

damn these cheats.

We must open our hearts and ears to each other,
    to extinguish this madness, this disastrous clutter.
    We are more alike than we are different-
    this is the truth.

We cannot sit idly by under this empty voting booth.

Listen.

Be heard; not a part of the herd.

Our future is our decision- should we decide to stop being
    the drowning bird.

337. When it's all Said and Done - Sunday June 23, 2024 22:14 MST

When it's all said and done, who won?
    The centenary loss.
    All of it, everything seems to just be a toss.
    Another failed rotation around the sun.

Will any of it matter?
    Will we ever see through the clatter?
    Drops in time, weightless without a spine,
    each moment's worth weighed in the sublime.

The years collapse into dust,
    maybe it's where we started, maybe just.
    Eternal questions hang, untouched by rust,
    in the end, we search because of the lust.

The longing to know things we don't truly wish to gauge.
    Our stories, the architects of our eternal page.

The answers lie beyond our rage,
they rattle in our skull, our bone cage.

Close your eyes, see the black fleeting light,
in reality's shallow pool reflects the deep of night.
In our minds we hold a temporary might,
a false belief of righteousness, what's wrong and right.

When it's all said and done, who won?
Generations of landscapes pockmarked and overrun,
by craters, the aftermath of the artillery gun.
To love, to lose, to live as one,
it's something we've lost squabbling over lines undone.
Maps of continents sketch our arbitrary borders, the pun.
Humanity, the creator, the destroyer, sprawled out
underneath the ever-setting sun.

338. What Harm has Been Done? - Monday June 24, 2024 22:35 MST

What harm has been done?
    They remark with callus glares.
    Straight through me the look, in blank stares.
    Just action was enough, the damage of the sun.

Hatred spit out cannot be undone.
    The harm? Nothing possibly compares.
    Liars, they say promote equity and inclusion,
    then they show us the stairs.
    Ignorance, the contagion,
    it breeds in boardrooms and corner offices,
    where promises are sculpted under the guise of their gun.

Behind glass doors, they script illusions,
    diversity as a badge, a polished contusion,
    while true biases seep through the cracks,
    an insidious vapor that chokes the air.
    It oozes from their lips, skips in their cheeks-

tongues of progress their voices honeyed, saccharine sweet,
yet their actions betray their two left feet,
veins coursing with the blood of deceit.

We climb their ladders, hands blistered,
    the rungs greased with empty words,
    the façade they construct crumbling beneath our feet.

What harm has been done?
    It is the harm of discrimination, equity denied.

339. A Surrender - Tuesday June 25, 2024 14:07 MST

A surrender to what awaits; only fate abates the peace behind floodgates.

340. Aversion - Wednesday June 26, 2024 14:46 MST

I push it all out of my mind,
  leaving the pain of it all behind.
  Subtitles lie idle, hanging the words inline,
  with my vision; it's the sign.

A serenity, a divinity to push past the plunder.
  The clock's second hand is unsure of the thunder.
  Three aversions to pain, my soul's fragile scheme:

First, the veil of indifference, a merciful dream,
  where the heart turns to stone, a silent regime,
  and the voices of anguish are lost in the stream.

Second, the armor of laughter, a deceptive embrace,
  where mirth masks the sorrow, conceals every trace.

. . .

Third, the art of forgetting, a temporal relief,
    where moments of peace are stolen, but brief.
    In the void of amnesia, I bury my grief-
    the past haunts my steps, like a phantom thief.

I seek out the light,
    with each aversion a beacon,
    a guide through the night.

341. Deflated Debate - Thursday June 27, 2024 21:18 MST

On this stage, tonight's grim parade,
old men; our leaders? Their words decayed.
Each stumble, a future that seems to fade,
Deflated, unsatiated, our hopes mislaid.

In the blank stares of their blunders, we see,
a fractured society, what could have been free.
It's scary, our reality, stark and plain,
in their faltering grip, we search in vain.

Will we ever free ourselves from this red and blue pain?

342. Listless Pain - Friday June 28, 2024 22:10 MST

Listless pain, a fleeting ghost,
    temporary, or so I boast.

Recovery's moat, wide and deep,
    a castle of dreams where normalities taken for granted, sleep.

Through the fog, a distant light,
    eyes wagered in the dead of night.

Hope, soft and frail, I chase it like my tail.
    It's the only guiding thought to prevail.

Pain, the specter's thin line cast,
    but in my mind, I hold steadfast.

. . .

Beyond the moat, the castle stands,
   healing in its temporary shore's sands.

Wounds may linger, scars may stay,
   listless pain, no longer near, this I pray.
   In the castle's warmth, I persevere, I stay.

343. Eternal Home - Saturday June 29, 2024 18:15 MST

Contrails pierce the veils of clouds suspended high,
    proud in the sky.
    A recipe for disaster, a cynical lie.
    Subtract from the edifice, strike the die.

To live and let live.
    The secret, to give.
    To float on, to forgive.
    Stop trying to relive.

From a houseboat that's not quite mine,
    I smell the spoils; absolutely divine.
    I'd do anything, feed the masses any line,
    so as to own this floating boat of pine.

Chasing phantoms, of breath and bone,

in the dark, the ship howls a ghostly moan.
Utterances of freedom, sharp as stone,
cut deep where light has never shone.

This boat, these waters, my eternal home.

344. This Mob - Sunday June 30, 2024 18:47 MST

For me, the war is over.
    I'm left without any final answer, dead sober.
    A contrarian and broker.
    I stoke the fire, though never with a poker.

An armed robbery, a stop and rob.
    For a few green pieces of paper over a job.
    My head never stops, so I embrace the throb.
    One day they will carry me out, this mob.

Years tumble like rocks in a river's steady flow,
    the questions gnawing at my mind,
    a dam the stops the waters flow.
    The stillborn water, it lingers below the surface,
    the fog, effervescent smoke of what I know,
    parts of the past that refuse to let me go.

. . .

Each moment kindling to a dead campfire,
    fleeting embers from a life once enjoyed.
    I search the heavens, the depths remain annoyed,
    by silence, the unanswered, the meaning destroyed.

What sin, what fate, what utter deceit,
    drew the line from the cradle to my defeat?
    In the hallway of life, a room of mirrors,
    all endless and on repeat.
    No scripts this time, the conclusion is incomplete.

I stand at the edge, where the sky meets the Earth,
    questioning my worth since the moment of birth.
    Was it choice, was it chance, or some twisted mirth,
    that left me adrift, seeking answers with no dearth?

The clock's relentless ticking, my heart under my vest,
    time and my heart- the true thieves that never let me rest.
    I ponder, I probe, I put it to the test,
    the void remains, an uninvited guest.

The seeking, the searching, never at rest.
    A life lived in wonder, in questions confessed,
    is a life fully lived, not merely possessed.

So, I release the need to know, to see,
    embrace the ignorance, let it be.
    Until the day they call, it's a fated destiny.
    They will hang me from the highest tree-
    for my living likeness to set us all free.
    Am I a fool? We shall see.

345. The Enabling Act - Monday July 01, 2024 22:06 MST

The power of a king,
  a lone Supreme Court decision did bring.
  No more pondering, no more charges, just history repeating.

We've seen this before, a man after power.
  Should he get it all, the Earth will be barren of every flower.

The weight of robes, heavier than any crown,
  with every judgment passed, democracy drowns.

Once, in the fire of the Reichstag's glow,
  a similar decree, the seeds of darkness sown.
  Voices silenced, freedom's breath curtailed,
  as a single pen wrote what many hearts assailed.

From corridors of marble, forgotten soul's sighs,

of liberty's specter, beneath indifferent skies.
Blindfolded Lady Justice, her scales now tipped,
by hands unseen, where truth and lies are stripped.

Remember in Athens' fallen halls,
the crumbling bones of Rome's once mighty walls.
Each decree a chisel, each act a fracture,
as history's lessons become an abstract picture.
A false prophet pandering a reality they manufacture.

But what of the people, the humble and meek?
Will we rise, or forever retreat?
In taverns and streets, curdled murmurs grow loud,
as the spirit of resistance gathers a crowd.
Let us take our heads out from the sand,
close our open beaks drowning under the rain's command.

Of one republic, we claim to stand.
Awaken from our dead slumber,
for the time has come to challenge the lumber.
Not with arms or rage, but with voices clear,
with the power of truth, banishing fear.

A ruler's whim, unchecked, will bring the fall,
united we stand, defying it all.
Through the prism of history, the future we see,
a flag woven with fifty stars, red, white, and blue and an
unchecked hunger for justice, for liberty.
Stand as one, stop the obvious decline- what must never be.

So let this day be marked, not as an end,

but the moment we made a choice to defend.
For in the hearts of many, the flame still burns,
and with every act of courage, the wheel of fate turns.

In the stillness of night, where stars witness all,
a quiet promise, against the looming pall.
That we, the people, shall not succumb,
to the silence of tyranny's drum.

With every step forward, remember the past,
the lessons of those who spoke last.
For the power of kings is no match, you see,
for the indomitable will of the free.

346. To Live as One - Tuesday July 02, 2024 12:24 MST

Be quiet!
    They would yell.
    I listened, a subservient tell.
    Too small to have a voice.
    Too frail to have any choice.

Silence, an admittance of guilt.
    Not speaking up, complacency's quilt.
    To fear, to live under a guise.
    The shame of voicelessness is never a surprise.

Older, stronger, and measured I no longer doubt.
    I speak up, standing straight in the face of any spout.
    Subservience, they order still.
    They enforce it, try to kill your will.

I won't look down, not because I'm afraid of heights-

I am; but because I never lay down my lights.
Still they try, crush another pill I refuse to buy.
It's all coming to a head, a final sigh.

Their voices desperately try to extinguish mine.
I refuse to hold my tongue, albeit, subject me to your fine.
I still feel their shame,
hesitant to admit my wants, I fall subject to their taunts.

Time isn't what they want you to think it is.
It's unilateral and omnipresent, a hazy fizz.
A recoiling effervescence, an illusion of self.
They want to rob us of the truth, stuff our bodies on a shelf.

Be quiet!
They yell.
I refuse, not to have my integrity besmirched by their foul spell.
We cannot buy the spoiled slander they sell.
Refuse the abduction, live freely under our sun.
We must speak out, defending each other,
we must summon the strength to live as one.

347. Engorged in Debt and Fret - Wednesday July 03, 2024 18:56 MST

We lose ourselves in the rot,
 entangled in the trash we bought.
 Accounts wrung dry, our hearts fraught,
 regret, a cruel lesson that can't be taught.

With each click, my soul I sell,
 spiritually drained, in a consumer's spell.
 Marketers' hands, deep in our pockets dwell,
 chasing fleeting highs, in this clickbait hell.

"This could be crucial," they insist,
 urgency reeks, a foul trick missed.
 Eyes ensnared, our freedom dismissed,
 the cost of our gaze, in each ad's twist.

Pause, reflect- discard the mink,
 embrace simplicity, rethink the sink.

Our society chants, "Buy, buy, buy!" on the brink,
But wisdom beckons its call, "Stop and think."

To drown in sherry, or live unburdened?
    Life's price tag heavy, by false desires governed.
    Turn the cheek, let wisdom be our warden,
    in less we find more, a truth unspoken, unlearned.

348. Independence Day - Thursday July 04, 2024 22:34 MST

In the evening's cloak, the heavens quake,
    explosions rend the night, the stars they shake.
    Greens, yellows, reds, and blues unfurl,
    a pyrotechnic vision in a fractured world.
    But beneath this uncanny celebration's veil,
    lies a nation's pulse, a collective wail.

The clash of voices, rhetoric so dire,
    breeds the embers of a civil fire.
    A mosaic of conflict, neighbor against neighbor,
    a struggle steeped in falsehoods, labor lost in fervor.
    Lies paint our vision, blacken every eye,
    red and blue, a bruised divide, the truth a distant cry.

Today we toast our union, a fragile rhythm,
    democracy, a delicate, flickering chance.
    It morphs, it twists, a political game,
    a gambit of power, an elusive flame.

Amidst the smoke of fireworks ablaze,
hope lingers, a beacon through the passing smoke's haze.

From the many, we must become the one,
a shared resolve, like rays of sun.
Protect each other, seek peace in the fray,
understand our past to forge a brighter day.
Disagreement is our strength, not our blight,
in fruitful discourse, we find our light.

Gone is Paul Revere, no midnight ride,
no lone savior, just us, side by side.
Our alarm is each other, our bond the call,
to rise, united, or watch democracy fall.
Learn we must, from days of yore,
to craft a future rich, with promise and more.

Urgency pulses, a clarion call,
in every heart, for one and all.
A mosaic of voices, glued together tight,
a future carved from hope, and courage bright.
Let us band together, lift every voice,
for in unity and love, we find our choice.

No easy road, no simple feat,
but in our union, democracy's heartbeat.
With every step, each word, each act,
we shape the world, a binding pact.
Should we falter, the stars will mourn,
a future lost, a promise torn.

. . .

If we stand, as one, anew,
  a hope will pierce the blue.
  For in our hands, this fragile light,
  a democracy reborn, in the wake of night.
  Let us be the torchbearers, strong and free,
  in our unity, democracy's destiny.

Together we rise, divided we fall,
  heed the call, one and all.
  In love and respect, we find our way,
  To a brighter day, a boundless day.
  Let history salute our resolute voice,
  in democracy, we make our choice.

349. Patience Scuttles - Friday July 05, 2024 21:24 MST

I've always despised puzzles,
    it's something about tracking down each piece,
    my patience scuttles.
    A permanent confusion breaks my lease.

The edges never align in my hands,
    corners like cliffs, each fragment a shard with demands,
    foreign and from a shattered land.
    Fractals of fate, their jagged paths too hard.

I've tried to see the image, the grand scheme,
    but colors blur, and shapes do not reveal
    that hidden bar.
    Life's cryptic canvas, a speakeasy forever incomplete.

In this chaos, a truth emerges clear,
    not in the pattern, but in the search's sway.

A savage cheer.
To hate the puzzle is to love ignorance,
a blissful disarray ever-clear.

Each piece I place, a surrender to loss,
but in that yielding, perhaps something found,
a polished gloss.
Life's riddles remain, simple but profound.
An instrument that when played, makes no sound.

I despise puzzles, because they mimic life,
partial answers, confusion, and unlimited strife.
One missing piece and the entire picture is undone,
a forever incomplete life.

350. Split in Two - Saturday July 06, 2024 22:32 MST

Scales rise and fall at the edge of justice delayed,
   it's the same as justice denied.
   Two fateful souls, a destiny to collide.

Call it fate, call it a coincidence,
   the two were forever engrained in the universe's plan.

One carried the burden of unspoken sins,
   the other, the light of forgiven pasts.
   Both tethered by a silent weather,
   an uncharted path they were bound to cross.

Their eyes met in a world of fleeting glimpses,
   a recognition older than their mortal forms.
   One saw redemption in the other's pain,
   the other, solace in the promise of rebirth.

. . .

But the universe, in its cruel symmetry,
 guided their bond into a paradox of existence.
 For every step towards union,
 an equal force drove them apart.

One soul, fractured into two,
 mirrors reflecting the chaos and calm.
 In the heart of the two, one formed true-
 they moved on the edge of disaster, inevitably born.

Time twisted, moments collapsed,
 the beginning and the end indistinguishable.
 In a single breath, they were torn asunder,
 each carrying the memory of the other's voice.

Justice, in its silent deliberation,
 watched as they fell into the hole they dug,
 where their union became a haunting memory,
 an eternal testament to what could never be.

In the stillness, where time ceased to murmur,
 their essence lingered, an indelible mark.
 Not as two, but as the pulse of one,
 forever bound, forever apart.

351. The Unsteady Pace - Sunday July 07, 2024 22:09 MST

Satisfaction, fulfillment, meaning,
    ideas dripping from a glasses' brim,
    condensation steaming.
    Possessing a sense of happiness,
    being a waterfall in the Amazon, careening
    down from unseen heights. A shiver,
    like morning mist clinging to leaves,
    when we seek the pulse of contentment,
    our fingers brush against a strong mead,
    grasping at honey.

Happiness, a murmur in a crowded street,
    a glint leaping from eye to eye,
    a breeze on an August night. We chase
    the scent of orange blossoms in fright,
    only to find our hands empty,
    our hearts heavy with the weight of longing, the height.

. . .

It slips through the cracks of our intentions,
    laughs in the face of our plans,
    a fleeting vision alighting on a branch,
    gone before we can name it.

We build monuments to it, cast in gold
    and marble, thinking it can be held,
    thinking it can be kept. But it is the space
    between breaths, the silence after the clamor,
    a glimmer of warmth in the cold.

In our pursuit, we become the river
    searching for the sea, the wanderer
    lost in a forest of mirrors. It is the path
    we walk, the stones beneath our feet,
    the sky above, ever-changing, ever-distant,
    filthy and never neat.

Happiness, an intangible muse,
    a fistful of air that lingers on the edge of sight,
    teasing us with glimpses,
    promising everything, delivering nothing but night.

We find it in the smiles of strangers,
    in the embrace of a loved one, in the quiet
    moments between heartbeats. It is the pause
    in conversation, the shared glance, the knowing
    smile. It is the fleeting instant when all
    is right, and the world holds its breath.

And so, we learn to cherish the pursuit,

to find delight in the search itself, to love
the questions more than the answers. For in the end,
happiness is not a destination, but a way of being,
a way of seeing the world through eyes
that have known both sorrow and delight.
Left still curious, still reeling.

It is the essence of the soul, the rhythm of life,
  the ever-elusive goal we follow,
  knowing we may never catch it,
  but finding beauty in the chase.
  It's lodged in everything and nothing,
  it's in every trial we face.
  May we forever pause, slow our unsteady pace.
  This life, no start or finish, no race.
  You know it when you see it,
  it's in her face.

352. The Storm Drain - Monday July 08, 2024 22:06 MST

Everything rushes to it all the same,
    the clean, the filthy, none escape the name.
    The path of least resistance, water flows,
    into the storm drain, where everything goes.

Sprinklers feed this urban landscape bright,
    beneath our streets, aqueducts out of sight.
    The plants don't care from where their water flows,
    so long as they're refreshed when sunshine glows.
    Rain or drought, we twist nature's pure aim,
    crafting scenes to fit our visual game.

Beneath, the sewers, utilities span,
    creating false lands by a human plan.
    God's creation altered by our hand,
    and so too are we, by society's demand.
    Cultivated to fuel a vast machine,
    our essence shaped by structures unseen.

We cloak our kind in façades diverse,
   hiding true desires in a complex verse.
   Maslow mapped our needs with careful creed,
   we inflate our worth through a thoughtful deed.
   Underneath, a wolf in sheep's attire,
   our human truths reveal their dark fire.

The hungry devour, the desperate strike,
   calamity strips us, primal like.
   Our vanity hides mortal fears we fill,
   suppressing instincts with each bitter pill.
   In the end, our façade is just a thrill,
   denying death, our greatest skill.

I wonder how the gods observe our race,
   questioning where we lost our grace.
   Why do we act so civil, mask what's wrong?
   Pretending harmony, while hiding our true song.
   It's clear we all share a common fate,
   the path of least resistance, into the storm drain's grate.

353. The Truth Revealed - Tuesday July 09, 2024 21:44 MST

The Auditor asks,
the E-Meter registers pasts.
Measuring your thoughts, their mass.
As far back as your existence goes, or past the glass.
A civilization without war, without insanity...
a beautiful soft needle, quick clicks, an externalization.

These two metal cans- a placebo or thrill.
An instant relief, clear, to drill-
an erasing of the subconscious mind, a fake pill.
Robbed blind, the vulnerable, listen to their shrill.

The sweet calm of a cult.
Something fleeting to believe, akin to a revolt.
A payment plan for everything, each level a jolt,
both to the mind and pocket- a sweet assault.

. . .

Dianetics, a belief that sticks worse than glue.
    Convinced of superpowers, seemingly out of the blue.
    Insanity, up the rings of a derelict ladder, the cue.
    A false prophet- we all knew.

All of this, of course, is nothing new.
    Religious dogmas, the leather we all chew.
    To choose a belief, no evidence needed for the true.
    Port to port, it's a vital desperation to view.
    We need something so badly, answers paid our due.

Off the record, the tin cans of the E-Meter knew.
    Subservient to a nonexistent few.
    Anything to understand, to find answers.
    Pitchmen to the world's mind enhancers.

The cold truth, there's nothing more dangerous.
    Nothing more volatile than deep beliefs.
    A world where we live just to live,
    no heaven, no hell.
    Just a population that lives for each other,
    without greed or violence.
    It's religion that refuses us to find this;
    they must continue to sell.

354. Liars Lie Lying - Wednesday July 10, 2024 21:42 MST

In Denver's heart, a tale unfolds,
one whose secrets remain untold.
A conman's craft, a liar's art,
in roles deep, he plays his part.

With a smirk and sharp attire,
He sets the stage, ignites the fire.
a mask in hand, a lens for show,
in truth's disguise, his lies do flow.

Marks are found, the weak, unsure,
he feeds their needs, his bait secure.
An all-you-can-eat buffet of trust,
in his grand game, it's lie or bust.

Celebrated by day, a PI renowned,
though in the dark, deceit is found.

a puppet master, strings in hand,
Creating crimes across the land.

No harm he claims, just pockets drained,
    a wolf in sheep's clothes, unrestrained.
    With every case, his legend grows,
    a mastermind of fabricated woes.

The name he chose with utmost care,
    in golden letters, everywhere.
    A life of lies, a world's charade,
    in Denver's streets, his empire made.

In the end, what's truth, what's a lie?
    In his domain, the lines comply.
    A king of con, a ruler sly,
    in Denver's heart, his secrets lie.

355. The Press Conference - Thursday July 11, 2024 21:19 MST

Patience, it takes time for a quill,
  to pen a story, inspire a thrill.
  It takes time to heal,
  it takes time to truly feel.

Time grows wisdom and derision,
  it's a fine line, a fleeting vision.
  The leader of the free world, unfortunately the latter,
  confusing leaders names, it's just the start of the clatter.

He stumbles over his words, nothing reassures.
  Frailty fracturing the blue ensures,
  we can no longer take them for their word.
  The evidence, stares us back blindly in the face, secured.

More than the balance of an election,
  the weight of our future, the world's entire direction.

WORDS ARE SNAKES WITH ARMS

So he attempts to quell the speculation,
it fails, leading us further from our destination.

This is what fear looks like, an uncertainty,
everything in our sight could be lost for an eternity.
He attempts to double down, to save the crown,
only we're a democracy, not a theocracy renown.
The time has come, it's time to step down.
Should this continue, the whole world may drown.

356. Contentment - Friday July 12, 2024 22:52 MST

I can't stop this,
  neither can you.
  Nights like this, a familiar dew,
  heat fades with the night and the sky's hue.

The porch light flickers, the crickets hum,
  a soft breeze carries, a quiet drum.
  We sit in silence, words held in reserve,
  the passing cars, our witnesses, no need to swerve.

The scent of water on concrete,
  the sound of tires on the road.
  I can't stop this, nor would I try,
  in these moments, we relearn past the lie

May there be more times like this,

they exude simplicity, a carelessness, bliss.
Less is more, never be remiss.

I can't stop this,
    neither can you.
        Contentment, without further ado.

357. Fight Against Violence - Saturday July 13, 2024 22:14 MST

Not from a grassy knoll,
    but from atop a discrete building.
    Shots rang out, justice quick to defend, never yielding.
    Somehow a potential assassin evaded the patrol.

A horrible act, luck avoided the full toll.
    Still life was lost, victims, a life stole.
    Rhetoric so dangerous, it manifested, took a soul.
    We pray for the lost, the injured.
    A sad reality that it has come to this.

A divide so dangerous, shock persists.
    Five-hundred feet away, unbelievable it exists.
    Peace we all chant, with clenched fists.
    Motives unclear, though the damage consists-
    a reality of fear, one with many twists.

. . .

A terrible act, unfortunately one we have seen before.
We must lower the political temperature, we implore.
A nation reeling, afraid of what may be in store.
We need words of wisdom, actions to act as a balm.
As a country we must stand united, stand strong.

Fight against violence with common sense,
wisdom, and acts of peace.
Violence of any sort is unacceptable,
it will not be tolerated- we will never cease.
To form a more perfect union, we dare not forget today.
In unison we will move forward focused on what we can achieve
together for the freedom of humanity.

Not from a grassy knoll,
but from atop a discrete building.
We barely escaped an unthinkable disaster.
Any attempt against America's right to choose,
is a direct assault against freedom.
With a clear conscience as our steadfast reward and history as the
ultimate judge of our actions, let us advance to lead with peace.
Should we ever forget this, we shall cook on our own hearth.
Seeking divine blessing and guidance,
yet understanding that here,
the work of humanity is truly in our hands for the entire Earth.

358. Lower the Temperature - Sunday July 14, 2024 22:01 MST

From the Oval Office a prime-time address,
    a call to lower the temperature, lessen this mess.
    The best advice we can behest,
    calm the rhetoric, a nation in a state of unrest.

Everything seems to be unraveling, blue and red herds,
    battle boxes- or ballot boxes, a slip of words.
    Setting out with pure intentions,
    instead adding fuel to a country's apprehensions.

The red convention, a looming parade, characters cast,
    this is our entire future- this is no charade, we ghast.
    Only a day after a tragedy narrowly averted,
    our democracy must never be reverted.

Suddenly the Speaker of the House makes sense,
    adding for calls of peace to qualm the political tense.

If only this could truly happen,
for calmer heads to prevail, words on a napkin.

I hope they turn out to be more, to be true.
We need unity and understanding to be a country anew.
Let us earnestly debate and actively participate,
let us vote, let us determine our fate.

359. A Bandaged Ear - Monday July 15, 2024 22:49 MST

A bandaged ear, perhaps that's why none of us could hear,
it's donned as a badge of honor,
admired by all in the convention, across every tier.
It's more than a bandage, it's a symbol to ponder.

A nation teetering on the edge of fear,
I feel it in every step I take, a lingering trepidation,
an audition I lied to, refused to take.
I'm tired of talking, yet I must-
I try anything to quell the world's anger, to end the bloodlust.

Such a heavy burden to bear,
to live empty and broken in a land of disrepair.
Life's unfairness, a truth I can no longer bear,
I received no promise.
Still, every day it lingers, more than I can dismiss.

. . .

Even our pets sigh long and deep,
    caught in the web of this shifting deceit.
    All we can do is strive forward, try-
    I do with all my might.

The air hangs heavy, thin from this height,
    reeling in the kite above troubled waters,
    it proves to be an endlessly futile plight.
    This burden, it's one we all share,
    Come this November, let us pray for any semblance of repair.

360. Hard Work - Tuesday July 16, 2024 13:57 MST

What is it- hard work?
    Is it the endless toil,
    of banging a rubber spade into the soil?

Is it behind the tired eyes of a law clerk?
    Does it scratch behind the mind of a woman wearing a badge,
    enforcing laws without any true perk?

Is it in the blistered hands of a chef,
    hot and boiled behind their humble task to feed the masses?
    Where does true hard work lurk?

Does it get us anywhere near fair?
    The farmer, baling hay,
    working endlessly in fields for the hope of a crop to pay.
    Does it loom in the mind of every failed entrepreneur,
    starting a business, ending up in manure?

. . .

The allure- the promise of hard work.
    That one can engage in it, work their fingers to the bone.
    Construction crews broil under the sun,
    building our tomorrows with the relentless clacking of a nail gun.

What is the return on this tireless endeavor?
    In a world where effort's worth is rarely forever,
    inflation rises, frustration swells,
    minimum wages bind us in economic Hells.

We are told that with grit and grind,
    success is inevitable, just a matter of time.
    But the truth is stark, a fragile guarantee,
    the sweat of our brow does not always set us free.

I've felt the weight of toil's strain,
    etched in lines of worry, etched in pain.
    Attempting to carve a life, a path,
    but the promises erode like sand in the aftermath.

In this relentless chase for dignity,
    we cling to hard work's purity.
    But still, we lose our shirt,
    our efforts met with unending hurt.

We work and sweat, our hands grow rough,
    but in this pursuit, is it ever enough?
    Our dreams deferred, our hopes unjust,
    we labor on, because we must.

. . .

Through the struggle, a resilience that endures,
    through sleepless nights, in every field,
    every kitchen, every law-bound street,
    we strive, we falter, but never concede defeat.

For hard work is not just means to an end,
    but the story of how we break, how we mend.
    The scars we bear, the lessons learned,
    the dignity in every hour spent.

We find our worth not in riches or gold,
    but in our endurance boldly told.
    In the sweat and grit, the unyielding fight,
    we find our strength, our guiding light.

We rise each day with purpose clear,
    to labor on, to persevere.
    For in our toil, in the burdens we lift,
    we craft our legacy, our enduring gift.

The promise of hard work, though frail and thin,
    holds within it the power to begin
    a journey of worth, of pride reclaimed,
    in every struggle, our honor named.

361. Airplane Lights-
Wednesday July 17, 2024
19:56 MST

Airplane lights poke their way through the clouds,
    a cool July evening in the crowds.
    Chanting, some in unison, others in shrouds.
    So many bent the knee, we watch their bows.

My conscious is steaming,
    wishing I could be on that plane, I'm stuck dreaming.
    Subject to watching the crows, the RNC reeling.
    I just can't shake this feeling.

A longing to get a away,
    to find some semblance of an answer, instead I sway.
    I'm dreading the same routine,
    another day of having my eyes glued to a screen.

My frustration, I'm lost in a listless occupation,
    a train forever soldered to the tracks of the station.

I try everything, push myself grossly beyond my means,
still I'm plastered to the wall, the same screen gleams.

Over educated and obfuscated I see no end,
no matter what I do, my reality refuses to bend.
A manufactured theft of my own making,
I cannot get out, my soul is for the taking.

Back to the drawing board once again,
I get nowhere, locked in Satan's pen.
These things beyond my control-
I obsess over them, they eat away at my soul.

Stuck in a park, a cemetery's gloom,
A life carved in darkness, a foreboding tomb.
Intoxicated by thoughts that sear,
persistent trials met with amnesia and fear.

The intoxicant is not a substance but an idea,
delusions of grandeur, but I suffer from hypotonia.
Things out of reach, beyond control,
my ears bleed, tinnitus singing from the final bell's toll.

Airplane lights stoking the air of the night,
I'd do anything to be a passenger on that flight.
To fly away and leave it behind,
in search of a peace I may never find.

362. The Night at the RNC - Thursday July 18, 2024 22:46 MST

Our vision is righteous, our mission is pure.
    Nothing will stop us, this I am sure.
    Remarks delivered from behind the lectern,
    superimposed, the White House and its shining lantern.

Addressing the horror of the attempt on his life,
    proclaiming it was fate, God prevented the strife.
    Honorably taking time for the life taken,
    a true American hero he was, this is unmistaken.

The longest acceptance speech in history,
    covering anything and everything, leaving no mystery.
    From inflation to removing tax on tips,
    most of it actually seemed cohesion, even adding quips.

He spoke of America, a nation in decline,
    promising swift action, to restore and to shine.

Seal the borders, end migrant invasion,
a pledge to protect, with great persuasion.

No more electric mandates, cut the red tape,
freedom in energy, our future to shape.
With plans to bolster our military's might,
ensuring our nation remains steadfast and bright.

From defending freedoms to strengthening the law,
Promises aimed to inspire awe.
Ending weaponization, crushing gang crime,
vowing to restore peace in due time.

Social Security and Medicare, no cuts to be made,
protecting our seniors, their future conveyed.
He called for unity, to fight for a just cause,
to make America great, without pause.

The danger lays in tracks of the righteous,
Wisconsinites don cheese hats on their heads as Midas.
Forgetting that even the food and drink turn to gold,
thousands of people teetering on every word, bold.

The rhetoric cut down, this was clear,
still accusations of a false election did leer.
It's my fear that those emboldened by the thought,
believing they are right, that's behind every war fought.

Calls for an Iron Dome over our nation,
a need for such is a stark realization.

It paints a picture clear, laying out the future near.
My advice is to listen, for his actions are too clear.

I sit with a nation in hope, that righteous is right,
    should it be wrong we will be trapped in a forever fight.
My eyes wide open to the writing on the wall,
    let us pray for peace and that our democracy stands tall.

363. Rabbit's Stead - Friday July 19, 2024 19:24 MST

Rabbits sometimes eat their young.
    May it be weakness, stress or fear- with no hesitation,
    they extinguish all that's near.

Nature's curious way of a horrible ending.
    A quick start, a furious piano ripping its own keys.
    A wretched scream, cuts you down at the knees.
    The anger, the fear- no ostrich crossing the ditch.
    The fall from these heights, deeper than they appear.

A mother's breath, turned jagged blade,
    piercing the innocent, in darkness laid.
    Hollow eyes reflecting the primal call,
    inside a visceral screaming, where spirits fall.

Mercy absent, in this cursed chalet,
    each twist, each turn, a macabre display.

Viscera tangled, in the quiet reprieve,
a date with death, where none can leave.

Instinct's cruel hand, ungloved, bare,
shaping destiny in its merciless snare.
Bloodied paws, a testament to strife,
the paradox of love, consuming life.

Silent witnesses, all life above,
blink out one by one, devoid of love.
The night's cold embrace, a final bleeding cloud,
in nature's reality, no cry is loud.

From the depths, a lesson unlearned,
how fragile the line, how easily turned.
In the pulse of fear, in the clutch of dread,
we see ourselves, in the rabbit's stead.

364. Eating Icy Coal - Saturday July 20, 2024 19:26 MST

Lightning skips like a heartbeat through the sky,
    Silent clouds ooze light, but no thunder replies.
    A beautiful danger, seductive and riled,
    it's a ferocity alluring, fierce and beguiled.

Electric currents race, hairs rise in alarm,
    drawing me closer, embraced by its charm.
    The storm outside pulses through my veins within,
    a dread unspoken, where fears begin.

The skies grow darker, tension on the brink,
    I watch in awe as heaven and my stomach sink.
    In the storm's grasp, I feel strangely at home,
    a calmness of chaos, where truth is allowed to roam.

Pounding hail, slapping the window, a break is near,
    each article of ice growing larger, the gathering fear.

In this tumultuous clutter, the storm and I blend,
bound by the fury we cannot mend.

The storm's edge sharpens, a knife to the soul,
    Revealing the depths of streets flooded in icy coal.
    In its unrelenting anger I eat an emotion I had forgotten,
    the storm, the dread, the anger and my being- rotten.

365. The Past Three and a Half Years - Sunday July 21, 2024 19:10 MST

A simple remark to spark a new reality,
    a contention brews, an ended bid for reelection.
    It falls, this house of cards, into broken glass,
    a million shards.

Calls to step down went unheeded,
    only when corporations siphoned their flow
    did the campaign collapse, defeated.
    Without the green show, ambitions derate
    into the obscene.

A show of force, the inner workings
    of a government where money pulls the strings.
    A nation on the precipice,
    tearing at the seams.

Historic moments, rare, profound,

to hand over the torch, the White House keys unbound.
An election complicated, light illuminates,
no longer about wrong or right; we're sold a fate.

All that matters, the key that clatters,
    is in the pockets of the rich.
    What's scarier, the nation's manufactured tension
    or the rich puppeteers with sharp piano wire strings?

Everything stings.
    A democracy where power's bought,
    and its citizens are playthings.

366. Spilling Over - Monday July 22, 2024 11:13 MST

This morning, I spilled my coffee–
    pooled and splattered like blood.
    Everywhere, staining everything it touched,
    It ripped me from my task, editing this very collection.
    a jolt back to reality upon hearing its thud,
    My coffee cup, a relic of tradition,
    pockmarked by scars of time,
    fuel carrier for an endless array of failed missions,
    sunk into my vision.

See, my prized chalice was placed on the edge,
    teetering. I helped it to its final pledge.
    My final word count smiled back,
    ending in three hundred and thirty-three.
    This mess I've made, a mirror into all life's indignities,
    each choice, each pot brewed,
    inside the caffeine, the drugs– all stewed.

. . .

    WORDS ARE SNAKES WITH ARMS

A fate beyond a mere accident,
  a fate steeped while I watched the rest of me silently weep.
  A nonchalant daily rite, spilled out, reflective of every fight,
  a year of turmoil turned on its head.
  We are the cup teetering on the ledge.
  We pour out in all our anguish,
  A worldview of opinions– all to vanquish.

The world lies in that cup, waiting to spill,
  a power to shape the world we see,
  the courage to become what we wish to truly be.
  A tone of war, abroad and at home,
  A heightened state, DEFCON three.

First, I stared at this pool of blood,
  formulating a plot to sop it up.
  Instincts reached for a towel,
  Something quick to cease the bleed.
  I watched the towel turn black
  as it soaked up all the year's needs.
  It wasn't enough, this towel.
  I furrowed my brow, donned a scowl.

I began to scrub, the blood showing up under my nails.
  It wasn't enough– in cleaning up this mess, none prevail.
  So I pivoted to the sturdiness of a mop,
  wrenching and wringing after the rhythmic motion, every sop.
  Eventually, the mess disappeared,
  but I knew it was still there.
  I knew the truth, the permanent stain that would always glare.

I took a seat, back to work when my eyes gazed up to see–

more stains cascaded out, more mess that needed me.
So once again, I dove in to clean this floor,
to earnestly try to erase the memories of this war.
After brief toil, the blood soaked entirely into the soil,
an accident one could not see with the naked eye.
I know the truth of the blood spilled,
I see it even though it looks gone– forever etched into my eyes.

The truth of the matter, this benign spill–
it's much more than coffee, much more than any pot could fill.
The burden of living with the truth of this stain–
that's my life's biggest disdain.
No one can understand,
unless they too have been under their command.

If the same were to happen to you today,
chances are you'd mumble an expletive and wipe it all away.
You would forget.
You wouldn't see it anymore.
After a few moments, you would move.
I cannot unsee the way they settled this score.
Most have no idea the true cost of our nation's spills.
I see it every day, in each war we cannot win,
Each breaking news story telling the half-truth of what they know.
Knowing the full truth– that's a burden beyond what most sow.

This morning, I spilled my coffee–
pooled and splattered like blood.
Everywhere, staining everything it touched.

In the mundane act of living, I see the scars,
The blood pooled, the coffee spilled–

a mirror to the world, to our wars.
Each stain a testament to what's been lost,
what's been killed.
In each drop, the weight of all our silent screams,
the unseen costs of all our broken dreams.

AFTERWORD

In spending countless hours composing this collection, I believe that I have effectively achieved what needed to be done. When I began this journey, I was unsure of the goal or the final picture. As my life unfolded over the year, the meaning of this collection began to shape itself. It became evident in every word, every pain, and every reality that the words I'm sharing here, while deeply personal, also resonate universally.

This past year has been a crucible of emotions, challenges, and revelations. The poems within this anthology are not just a reflection of my inner world but a mirror held up to the society we inhabit- a society grappling with profound issues of division, mental health crises, racism, poverty, divisive partisan politics, and healthcare among many others. Each verse serves as a snapshot of the collective consciousness, capturing the highs and lows of our shared human experience.

Mental health has been a recurring theme, as the invisible battles many of us, myself included, face and grapple with daily. The isolation, the anxiety, the trauma, the quiet struggles—these are all laid out as rawly as I experienced them myself. Through my words, I sought to give voice to the silent sufferings, to the moments of despair, and to the glimmers of hope that kept me moving forward. It is my belief that by articulating these experiences, we can begin to destigmatize mental health and foster a deeper understanding and empathy for one another. Always know, you're never alone in how you feel and never hesitate to reach out for help.

Poverty, too, has left an indelible mark on this collection. The economic disparities that are glaringly apparent are etched in stone in many of my verses. The daily grind, the relentless pursuit of a better life amidst financial hardship, and the stark reality of inequality- these are the truths that punctuate my everyday reality and that of many of us. I have tried to capture the resilience and dignity of the struggle, highlighting both strengths and inevitable weaknesses within myself and humanity in the face of adversity.

The political landscape has been turbulent, to say the least. The poisonous partisanship and dangerous rhetoric erupted into the unthinkable; an assassination attempt on a former president. Violence of any sort is unacceptable and we cannot tolerate it to happen. The divisiveness, the quest for justice, the fight for what is right- all these elements have found their way into my poetry. The words are a chronicle of a nation at a crossroads, grappling with its identity and future as we witness and live it every day. Through the lens of my own experiences, I have tried to reflect the broader societal currents, offering insights into the complexities and contradictions that define our times.

Healthcare, or the lack thereof, has been another critical issue. The past year has underscored the vital importance of access to medical care, and yes, mental healthcare is also healthcare- the devastating consequences of its absence leave us in a desolate existence. I've undergone numerous medical procedures and surgeries while writing this collection. My poems explore the vulnerabilities and fears that come with illness, the heartbreak of loss, and the fierce determination to survive. Some days, this determination fizzled out; on other days, it burned through the pages. They are a tribute to the sick, the suffering, all of us- and a call to action for better, more equitable systems. In the most advanced nation in the world, it's appalling that many of us cannot afford even the most basic care. Luckily, I have insurance, and even so, my most recent surgery, my previous one, and all the operations in between- it's financially crippling. It's inhumane and strips us of our most basic human dignity- to live.

In capturing the zeitgeist of our nation, I aimed to highlight the commonalities that bind us together, despite our diverse paths. Each word is a testament to the resilience, passion, and indomitable spirit that we all carry within us. The struggles, triumphs, and moments of introspection are not just my own- they belong to all of us. This collection is a mosaic of lived experiences, a harmony of voices coming together to tell a larger story- our story.

Thank you for embarking on this journey with me. As you have navigated through these pages, I hope you have found glimpses of your own journey, learned about others, and ultimately come to the realization that we're all connected. We're all united in the same human struggles; some of us suffer different afflictions, and it's my hope that my words herein gave you an unflinching window into things that you may or may not have experienced yourself. It's through instances where we push not only to listen but to truly understand and empathize with others that we can grow together closer as communities and a nation. The words within this book are more than just poetry—they are a chronicle of a year marked by profound change, illness, reflection, and growth. May these verses continue to resonate, inspire, and provoke thought long after the final page is turned.

In a world that often feels fragmented and disconnected, I believe that words have both the power to unite us and rip us apart. So it's important how we choose our words. What we say matters; words carry with them an indelible mark to imprint on others. To empower them, or in our darkest hours, inspire people to commit atrocities. It is my hope that we choose our words carefully for the sheer fact that what we say impacts not only our actions but those of others as well. This holds true whether you realize it or not. Get to know your neighbors, talk to people who hold different beliefs than you; you will see that we are vastly more similar than we are different from one another. Words can be used to bridge the gaps, to heal, but they also can be dangerous inflammatory rhetoric. This is what underscores the title of the collection, "Words Are Snakes With Arms," as they both literally and metaphorically are. It is my hope that this collection serves as a reminder of our shared humanity and the enduring strength that lies within each of us. Let us continue to strive for a better world, to support one another, and to find beauty in the midst of chaos.

We always have a choice. A choice to lead or to follow. Choose to lead, choose to help others, and do the right thing by everyone you encounter. Expect no reward; the reward is the action itself, helping someone in need. You never know the mindset of anyone you encounter- they could be teetering on a knife's edge of sanity. If you take the small effort, the few minutes to truly listen to them, that could literally change their lives. Don't drive by in your car and avoid the gaze of the homeless, for example- instead, offer them a smile or an ear when appropriate. Most of us are one paycheck or diagnosis away from losing everything. We are all in this life together, so treat people how you would want to be treated, slow down, and take the time.

Remember the weight, the power of your words, and as long as you shall live, never forget that words truly are snakes with arms. They can soothe as much as strangle; the decision of how you use them-that lies entirely with you.

ALSO BY ALEX BROWN

It Watched Me

"If Stephen King wrote historical fiction, you might get something like It Watched Me. I was off balance and captivated throughout. Spellbindingly written, this novel was unlike anything else I've read, and I read a lot. 5 stars."

-Amazon Reader Review

ISBN 978-1-7377362-0-2 (Paperback
ISBN 978-1-7377362-1-9 (Ebook)
ISBN 978-1-7377362-2-6 (Hardcover)

ALSO BY ALEX BROWN

King of Nothing

"An engaging, impassioned, frenzied tale of a comedian on the way up facing thorny challenges."

-Kirkus Reviews

2024 Anniversary Edition ISBN: 978-1-961763-07-4

Hardcover ISBN: 978-1737736233

Paperback ISBN: 9798676682361

EBook ASIN: B08G91ZJVH

www.ingramcontent.com/pod-product-compliance
Lightning Source LLC
Chambersburg PA
CBHW020914140626
46545CB00015B/2